RIO: UNRAVELLING THE CONSEQUENCES

RIO

UNRAVELLING THE CONSEQUENCES

edited by

CAROLINE THOMAS

FRANK CASS

First published in 1994 in Great Britain by
FRANK CASS & CO. LTD.
Newbury House, 900 Eastern Avenue,
Ilford, Essex IG2 7HH, England

and in the United States of America by
FRANK CASS
c/o ISBS,
5804 N.E. Hassalo Street,
Portland, Oregon 97213-3644

Copyright © 1994 Frank Cass & Co. Ltd.
Reprinted 1996

British Library Cataloguing in Publication Data

Rio: Unravelling the Consequences –
(Special Issue of "Environmental
Politics", ISSN 0964-4016; Vol.2, No.4)
  I. Thomas, Caroline II. Series
  333.7

ISBN 0-7146-4110-3

Library of Congress Cataloging in Publication Data

Rio: unravelling the consequences / edited by Caroline Thomas,
    p. cm.
  "Special issue of the journal Environmental politics, vol. 2, no.
4, 1993."
  Includes index.
  ISBN 0-7146-4110-3 (pbk.)
  1. Environmental degradation. 2. Environmental policy. 3. United
Nations Conference on Environmental and Development (1992 : Rio de
Janeiro, Brazil) I. Thomas, Caroline. II. Environmental politics.
Vol. 2, no. 4 (Supplement)
GE140.R56   1994
363.705–dc20   93-50950
                                           CIP

This group of studies first appeared in a Special Issue: 'Rio:
Unravelling the Consequences' of Environmental Politics,
Vol.2, No.4, published by Frank Cass & Co. Ltd.

Typeset by Regent Typesetting, London
Printed and bound in Great Britain by
Antony Rowe Ltd, Chippenham

In loving memory of
Bernard Thomas
Rev Silvey
Ken Fowler
and
Carole Mears

Contents

Abbreviations

BATNEEC	best available technology not entailing excessive cost
BSCD	Business Council for Sustainable Development
CSD	Commission (of UN) on Sustainable Development
CCAMLR	Convention on the Conservation of Antarctic Marine Living Resources (Canberra Convention)
CCTMHWD	Convention on the Control of Transboundary Movements of Hazardous Wastes and their Disposal
CFC	chloro-fluorocarbons
CITES	Convention on International Trade in Endangered Species
CPWCNH	Convention for the Protection of the World Cultural and Natural Heritage (Paris Convention)
CSD	Commission on Sustainable Development (see UNCSD)
CWIIEWH	Convention on Wetlands of International Importance Especially as Waterfowl Habitat (Ransar Convention)
EAP	Environmental Action Programme (from Lucerne conference)
EBRD	European Bank for Reconstruction and Development
ECOSOC	Economic and Social Council (of UN)
EAC	environmental absorption capacity
EMC	emission reduction credits (USA)
EMINWA	environmentally sound management of inland waters
EPA	Environmental Protection Agency (USA)
FAO	Food and Agriculture Organisation
FBC	fluidised bed combustion
FGD	flue gas desulphurisation
GATT	General Agreement on Tariffs and Trade
GCM	general circulation models
GDP	gross domestic product
GEF	Global Environment Facility
GEMS	Global Environmental Monitoring System
GHG	greenhouse gases
HMIP	Her Majesty's Inspectorate of Pollution
IAP-WASAD	International Action Programme on Water and Sustainable Agricultural Development
IDO	Interim development order

IDWSSD	International Drinking Water Supply and Sanitation Decade
IGCC	integrated gasification combined cycle
IMF	International Monetary Fund
IGO	intergovernmental organisation
ILA	International Law Association
INF	intermediate nuclear forces
ICWE	International Conference on Water and the Environment (1992 Dublin)
MTO	multilateral trade organisation
NAFTA	North American Free Trade Agreement
NFFO	Non-fossil fuel obligation
NGO	non-governmental organisation
OECD	Organisation for Economic Cooperation and Development
SAP	Structural Adjustment Programme
UNCED	United Nations Conference on Environment and Development
UNCSD	United Nations Commission on Sustainable Development
UNCTAD	United Nations Conference on Trade and Development
UNCTC	United Nations Centre on Transnational Corporations
UNDP	United Nations Development Programme
UNEP	United National Environmental Programme
UNESCO	United Nations Educational, Scientific and Cultural Organisation
VIP	ventilated improved pit

Beyond UNCED: An Introduction

CAROLINE THOMAS

It is doubtful whether the United Nations Conference on Environment and Development (UNCED) and its output were appropriate for averting global environmental and developmental catastrophe. At the most fundamental level, the causes of environmental degradation have not been addressed, and without this, efforts to tackle the crisis are bound to fail. The crisis is rooted in the process of globalisation under way. Powerful entrenched interests impede progress in understanding the crisis and in addressing it. They marginalise rival interpretations of its origins and thereby block the discovery of possible ways forward. The intellectual debate inside and outside UNCED has been dominated by these entrenched interests. This monopoly on respectable knowledge determines the allocation of responsibility and consequent remedial action. The result is that the crisis is to be tackled by a continuation of the very policies that have largely caused it in the first place.

The interstate system is incapable of dealing with the crisis. The state itself is suffering from a crisis of legitimacy and a crisis of capacity. In some ways it is too small for dealing with the crisis, which has global aspects; in other ways it is too big, given the local aspects. These crises pose opportunities for, as well as obstacles to, the emergence from the outmoded structure of the interstate system of a global society based on fundamental human rights. The crisis of the state is stimulating discussion about political identity, human rights, democracy and accountability. It opens up space for real discussion of a new world order and the role of democratic participation below and between states, and on which the whole sustainability process ultimately depends.

Now that the dust has settled, it is vital to establish whether the United Nations Conference on Environment and Development (UNCED), held

Caroline Thomas is at the Department of Politics, University of Southampton. The author gratefully acknowledges the financial support of the ESRC's Global Environmental Change Programme, and helpful discussions with Tony Evans, Darryl Howlett, Melvyn Reader, Julian Saurin and Jeremy Smallwood during the compilation of this collection.

in Rio in June 1992, and its output, were appropriate for averting global environmental and developmental catastrophe. I have an uneasy feeling that they were not.

Since Rio, the predominant focus of mainstream academic scrutiny has been on the five official agreements signed there. Two of these were legally binding; none of them contained specific commitments [*Grubb et al., 1993*]. Such studies are helpful, because they offer detailed examinations of the process of politics at work. However, in terms of setting us on a path for global sustainability, attention must be focused on the underlying structure in which this process is played out.

At the most fundamental level, the causes of environmental degradation have not been addressed, and without this efforts to tackle the crisis are bound to fail. The state, rather than facilitating improvement, is often an obstacle. In many instances it is incapable of tackling the crisis which is rooted in the globalisation under way in the international system. Powerful entrenched political and economic interests, sometimes but not always state-based, impede progress in understanding and addressing the crisis. They marginalise rival interpretations of its origins and thereby block the discovery of possible ways forward. The intellectual debate inside and outside UNCED has been dominated by these entrenched interests, which is perhaps surprising when we consider the range of interests represented at the Preparatory Committees (Prepcoms) and UNCED through the community of non-governmental organisations (NGOs). The result is that, in very broad terms, the environmental crisis – which is of course a developmental crisis – is to be tackled by a continuation of the very practices and policies that have largely caused it in the first place, albeit perhaps in a slightly modified form. For example, environmental impact asssessments will do little to soften the destructiveness of IMF/World Bank structural adjustment policies which ravage societies and states across the world.

A fundamentally different approach is needed. At the heart of this lies empowerment of individuals and communities; democratisation not only within states but in international organisations such as the UN; and basic accountability and transparency in influential decision-making entities like the International Monetary Fund (IMF), World Bank, General Agreement on Tariffs and Trade (GATT) and the exclusive Group of Seven. The ultimate purpose of such bodies must be to promote the interests of the majority of global citizens, not of a small and privileged minority. Security is no longer (if it ever was) a simple matter of ensuring the survival of territorial borders against the encroachment of neighbouring states. Rather, it is a matter of acknowledging and facilitating the emergence from the outmoded structure of the interstate system of a global society based on fundamental human rights.

The International Political Agenda

Will environmental issues, and the associated notion of sustainable development, retain the central place they occupied in international relations in the run-up to Rio? Steve Smith's contribution to this collection cautions that there are powerful political reasons which may well keep these issues on the periphery both of the practice and of the academic study of international relations. He argues that both the states-system and the academic discipline are dominated by specific interests which feel threatened by proposals to take the environment seriously. He warns that both environmental issues, and those who research them, may be marginalised unless they address the fundamental relationship between knowledge and power. His words are not designed to diminish the status of such issues or the efforts of their exponent. Indeed he believes such issues should have a more central place along with other issues such as gender and identity. Rather, he is challenging those working in the area to step outside their theoretical framework and to confront the fundamental structures in which the environmental question is being played out. It is no use taking the agenda as given; the agenda itself has to be questioned.

The causes of environmental degradation are fundamentally rooted in the process of globalisation which has effectively rendered the territorial state incapable of fulfilling its traditional functions. Therefore our conceptualisation of the problem, and of possible ways forward, need to be located within our understanding of globalisation and its catalytic effect on re-articulating international political space [*Held and McGrew, 1993: 264*].

Giddens defines globalisation as 'the intensification of worldwide social relations which link distant localities in such a way that local happenings are shaped by events occurring many miles away and vice versa' [*Giddens, 1990: 64*]. Held and McGrew suggest that:

> Globalisation can be conceived as having two interrelated dimensions: scope (or 'stretching') and intensity (or 'deepening'). On the one hand, the concept of globalisation defines a universal process or set of processes which generate a multiplicity of linkages and interconnections which transcend the states and societies which make up the modern world system: the concept therefore has a

spatial connotation. Social, political and economic activities in one part of the world can come to have immediate significance for individuals and communities in quite distant parts of the global system. On the other hand, globalisation also implies an intensification in the levels of interaction, interconnectedness or interdependence between states and societies which constitute the modern world system [*Held and McGrew, 1993: 262*].

For Giddens, globalising tendencies are not driven by a single causal logic, but by a number of processes occurring within the political, industrial, military and capitalist institutions of modernity [*Giddens, 1990*]. Accepting this explanation, Held and McGrew refer to globalisation as 'a complex multidimensional process which operates simultaneously across several institutional domains' [*Held and McGrew, 1993: 264*]. An important consequence of globalisation for the environmental debate is that the site of degradation is often removed from the initial agent. Thus the relationship between cause and effect may not be obvious, and consequently attributing responsibility is not straightforward.

International political space is filled not simply by sovereign states with governments representing well-defined territorial boundaries, but increasingly by social forces below and above the state level which are necessitating a reassessment of the dominant notion of political community. To a very limited extent this was evident at UNCED, in that non-state actors such as NGOs played an important role, and the principles of democratisation and accountability in international organisations figured high, at least in the Prepcoms. Perhaps even more important was the recognition that implementation of Agenda 21 would require more the efforts of sub-national actors than of the state itself. (See, for example, John Gordon here on the role of local government, Yagya Karki for the critical role of NGOs in population programmes and Darryl Howlett for the critical role of women and local groups as water managers.) However even allowing for the increased role of NGOs, UNCED was most definitely a meeting of states, and the agreements that came out of it were interstate agreements. As such it failed people. Furthermore, other actors with entrenched interests and enormous power failed even to engage in a constructive debate about the fundamental causes of the crisis and possible solutions. The hierarchy of the Catholic Church would not entertain the demographic debate, and the Pope had a huge influence on limiting the agenda. Transnational corporations argued successfully for self-regulation, and had powerful allies in the richest states. Where was the challenge to these powerful actors? Even the NGO community has, to an important extent, been co-opted into the mainstream debate. While this may make for more comfortable relations with the IMF, World

Bank, and rich governments, and hence lend respectability and the appearance of being taken seriously, it is questionable whether it will achieve much for the disempowered or the environment. The total failure of UNCED to address fundamental causes of the crisis removed any possibility of meaningful effort to address the sustainability problem.

Julian Saurin's contribution to this collection represents an important attempt to understand the problem of environmental degradation within the framework of globalisation, and recognises the consequent implications for the re-articulation of international political space. He examines the relationship between the historically coincident processes of modernisation and global environmental degradation, the latter being understood as the rupture of eco-systemic tolerances in a systematic and reiterated fashion, due to persistent subordination of eco-systemic requirements to the logics of capital, bureaucracy, consumption and so on. Globalised modernity generates particular modes of knowledge, and simultaneously displaces, marginalises and then destroys others. Specific forms of large-scale environmental degradation occur as a routine consequence of modernity, not as an exception. He illustrates his argument with reference to agriculture and its attendant expert knowledge system. The distancing of the site of degradation from its original cause confuses the allocation of responsibility. In the post-Rio context, this poses enormous public policy problems regarding the level of appropriate legislation: local, national, international or transnational.

Paikiasothy Saravanamuttu's piece also engages with the question of the re-articulation of international political space. He is well aware that such thinking is subversive of the conventional wisdom of International Relations and also of state practice. Hence, knowledge about it is marginalised within the dominant paradigm of international relations. He argues that instead of thinking about environmental issues in isolation, we need to focus on the nexus between environment, development and security, and in this context we must redefine security and development. This will be difficult, for existing structures and institutions represent mobilisations of bias and values from a different era. They are bound to project these concerns onto any consideration of the environment, security and development linkage. He argues that this nexus 'militates towards a new culture of world politics which transforms attitudes consonant with meaningful interdependence'. The significance of non-state actors in world politics, and of the progressive democratisation of the activity itself, is central. Accordingly, it meets resistance from the powerful Northern states which see themselves as the chief architects of the New World Order. This is based, in theory at least, on respect for the traditional values of state sovereignty and non-intervention, and is tempered with humanitarian values under the rule of inter-national law. It meets resistance also from the Southern states where national sovereignty and state-centric realism exercise a compelling hold. However, Saravanamuttu comments that 'Citizens or persons are relegated to the periphery in the traditional paradigm of international relations, but have a habit of asserting themselves as instruments of change. They are indeed the catalysts for the new culture of world politics.'

The potential role for citizens' groups and individuals as catalysts for the new culture of world politics is clear in an examination of the elevation of environmental issues to the centre-stage of world politics in the late 1980s. Within states, key individuals and the movements with which they were associated, such as Chico Mendes and the rubber tappers in Brazil, or Sunderlal Bahuguna and the Chipko movement in India, have influenced national politics and captured the imaginations of people outside their borders. At the international level, NGOs and an individual with great vision, Mikhail Gorbachev, have had global appeal and were key agencies for effecting the change in status of environmental issues [*Thomas, 1992; Walker, 1993*]. Gorbachev in particular put forward a conception of security more in line with global social reality than with the artifical map of a world of theoretically sovereign states. It is instructive to see how this happened, and also how the effort was undermined.

While a gradual increase in public and government attention on environmental matters since the 1960s can be detected, it is only in the latter half of the 1980s that environmental issues emerged as central in the diplomatic arena. By that time it was widely believed that failure to act would be likely to result in irreparable harm to our planet. The scientific consensus on many issues such as ozone depletion and global warming was growing, but was far from watertight, and many uncertainties remained. Does the imperative of urgent action implicit in the knowledge of irreparable harm explain the centrality of environmental issues in international discourse in the late 1980s? The answer is no. After all, knowledge of the severity of other global threats, such as the nuclear arms race, has not resulted in immediate, meaningful global action. The sudden prominence of environmental issues had far less to do with the enormity of those problems themselves than with the coalescence of certain political developments.

The sudden high diplomatic profile of environmental issues in the run up to Rio derived largely from the activities of NGOs who took advantage of the political space provided by the fortuitous ending of the cold war. Indeed, the ending of the cold war provided a real window of opportunity without which the environmental cause could not have been promoted so successfully at the international level. This coincided with greater awareness on the part of intergovernmental organisations of environmental issues, something that had been building up since the Stockholm Conference of 1972. Partly as a result of NGO campaigning, international lenders like the World Bank and branches of the UN were taking on board the fact that links existed between economic development and environmental degradation. Previously the environment had not been an issue of concern to any part of the Bretton Woods system. However, by the early 1980s a consensus had emerged amongst NGOs that environment and development were inextricably linked, and this idea was given credibility by the Brundtland Commission which advocated further growth as a prerequisite of environmental protection and sustainable development.

The reduction in tension between the superpowers in the second half of the 1980s, the associated lessening of ideological conflict between the two blocs of developed states, and the conclusion and ongoing negotiation of practical arms reduction agreements between them, presented an opportunity for environmental concerns to attain high diplomatic profile. The passing of the cold war facilitated discussion of global problems that depend on international cooperation if they are to be addressed with any possibility of success. With the creation of this political space, the superpowers themselves were quick to seize the opportunity and express primary interest in environmental concerns which had been receiving increasing attention at the NGO and intergovernmental organisation (IGO) level for two decades.

The relationship between the superpowers in the mid-1980s was propitious. In 1985, Reagan entered his second, and necessarily his last term of office at the White House. In contrast to the 'evil empire' rhetoric of his first term, aspects of his foreign policy moderated, and his dealings with the USSR softened. This was aided by the arrival of Mikhail Gorbachev as CPSU leader in 1985, which brought a new era of openness at the Kremlin and major changes in Soviet domestic and foreign policy. The period 1985–87 saw a profound change in attitude at the Kremlin, accompanied by sweeping peace proposals. In the arms negotiations, the USSR suggested more far-reaching reforms than the West had hitherto put forward, such as in the field of on-site inspection. With remarkable speed, the superpowers signed the Intermediate Nuclear Forces (INF) Treaty in 1987. This represented a major step forward in international cooperation. For the first time, the superpowers agreed to the eradication of a complete weapons system, and to intrusive on-site inspection and verification procedures. Recognition of the interdependence of global security underlay the agreement.

Gorbachev played a key role in elevating the diplomatic profile of environmental issues by calling for international co-operation to tackle fundamental transnational problems, the resolution of which would form the basis of a more secure world. His international stance directly reflected his domestic position. He wanted to ensure that particularist interests in the USSR did not compromise the interests of the state as a whole, and similarly he wanted to ensure that the global interest was not sullied by particularist, self-seeking state interest. Within the USSR, the economy was in complete disarray and the cost of sustaining the military competition with the USA was a burden the USSR could not afford to carry. The policies of perestroika and glasnost went hand-in-hand with an international position supportive of peace and an enhanced role for the UN as the expression of the community of mankind. In his book *Perestroika*, published in 1988, Gorbachev called for a new international political thinking: 'We are all passengers aboard one ship, Earth, and we must not allow it to be wrecked. There will be no second Noah's Ark' [*Gorbachev, 1989: 12*]. Recognition of the appalling state of the Soviet domestic environment, its clear links with the internal domestic and political situation, and the psychological as well as physical effect of the Chernobyl accident, undoubtedly fuelled his awareness and conception of environmental issues, and probably also his attitude to standard-setting and verification. The help the USSR received after Chernobyl lent weight to Gorbachev's conversion to multilateralism. Economy, ecology and security were becoming increasingly interconnected in his thinking: 'International economic security is inconceivable unless related not only to disarmament but also to the elimination of the threat to the world's environment' [*1988b: 146*].

Gorbachev's position was reiterated and extended by Foreign Minister Shevardnadze at the forty-fourth session of the UN General Assembly. While emphasising the environmental threat which the world faced, he stressed that the greatest threat to the world still came from nuclear weapons. However, he put forward a holistic conception of security which he believed was necessary to tackle all the problems facing the international community:

> Before the eyes of just one generation the sphere of politics has linked up with environmental conservation to give mankind the science of political ecology. No one can master it alone, entangled in the fetters of narrow interests.
>
> Political ecology requires urgent planetary decisions at the highest political level and an internationalisation of national efforts through the UN ...

Defining for itself the main principles of the concept of ecological security, the USSR considers disarmament, the economy and ecology as part of an integrated whole [*Shevardnadze, 1989: 342*].

This represents a sea-change in the Soviet approach to international relations. Shevardnadze continued to expand on these ideas over the next few years. It is interesting to note that not only was he calling for a holistic conception of international security, but also that he used mechanisms from the old security to help inform the new. For example, he suggested machinery for reducing the military danger be used to prevent ecological disaster. He may have been thinking here both of the technology for information gathering, such as satellites, and also institutions such as verification procedures like those developed by the International Atomic Energy Authority. He suggested also that the 'open skies' concept, a confidence-building measure for the superpowers under which both military–political blocs would have access to the air space of the other bloc for observation purposes, be applied in the ecological area. This was supported by Gorbachev, who stated that: 'ecological confidence-building measures could be based on the methods, procedures and instruments similar to those used in arms control' [*Gorbachev, 1990*]. He advocated regular reporting by states on ecological accidents, the limiting of military activities on ecological grounds, and open inspection to ensure that technology was not misused.

The US response to Gorbachev's new vision was positive but cautious. It is important not to loose sight of the fact that the USA had exhibited a far stronger commitment to environmental protection at the domestic level than the former USSR. Also it had played an active role in international negotiations, such as the ozone question, and in bilateral negotiations such as those with Canada over acid rain. However, the new approach to security espoused by the USSR, based on the interdependence of actors in the world community and also the interdependence of economy, ecology and security, had not been taken up by policymakers or academics in the USA. Bush's vision of a New World Order had yet to be fully expounded. Indeed, there was never a significant statement from his administration suggesting the interdependence of concerns or the elevation of the environment into a primary security concern. Even the ecological devastation of the Gulf War did not prompt a change of emphasis.

The vision of Gorbachev has all but evaporated at the level of domestic and international politics. The idea of setting aside short-term national interest in favour of long-term global vision and a holistic international security based on the interrelationship between environment, development and security concerns, has fallen prey to the narrow concerns of national interest. Contradictory processes seem to be at work. In contemporary world politics, nationalism seems to have a growing appeal. It is both reinforcing and challenging the authority of the state as the institutional focus for political identity. We are witnessing the disintegration of multiethnic states into smaller, ethnically uniform states. While in a sense this process may be in line with greater decentralisation and the democratisation of politics, the manner in which it is occurring exhibits all the most unpleasant characterisics of the 'chauvinism of individual cultures' [*Jenkins, 1993: 14*]. Groups based on language, religion, ethnicity or culture are fighting in the former USSR, Eastern Europe, the Balkans, parts of Western Europe and much of the developing world to achieve nation-statehood, regarding self-government as the best vehicle for achieving material and physical well-being of their respective group. However, the fact of the matter is that the sovereign state itself is in crisis, and is unlikely to meet the aspirations of the groups who aspire to statehood. The state is suffering from two partly related crises: a legitimacy crisis, and a crisis of capacity. These crises pose formidable obstacles to the new concept of security, but potentially also an opportunity for its advancement.

International law confers external legitimacy on states through *de facto* recognition. However, domestic legitimacy depends on a consensus among a state's citizens to accept the authority of its institutions to make decisions on their collective behalf. Many contemporary states achieved independent statehood – that is, external legitimacy – either through armed struggle against a colonial power, or peacefully when international law established former colonial boundaries as the legitimate boundaries of new states. However, to varying degrees, domestic consensus is lacking throughout the world, the majority of states being weak and fragmented. Moreover, even the West European states, often regarded as the model for nation-statehood, are not entirely without legitimacy problems. We need look no further than Northern Ireland for substantiation.

The current legitimacy crisis is not entirely new. Research has shown that of the 216 wars occurring in the period 1945–86, 168 represented domestic conflicts – that is, challenges to the state's legitimacy. In 1993 there were an estimated 48 civil wars going on. The lack of legitimacy and associated instability of the state seems to be increasing. The riots in Los Angeles in 1992 represent a significant, albeit limited, challenge to the legitimacy of the US state. Some states, such as the USSR, Yugoslavia and Somalia, have essentially failed. Others are on the road to failure. Ethnic, religious and other particularist interests are becoming more politically significant, and the weakness of state institutions to cope with these centrifugal tendencies is all too obvious. This legitimacy crisis is hardly surprising, given that the majority of states exist as legal rather than social facts [*Jackson and Rosberg, 1982; Jackson, 1990; Thomas, 1990*].

The already formidable task of holding the state together not through force but through enhanced legitimacy is compounded by the capacity crisis of the state which is unable to control domestic economic and social developments. The capacity crisis arises directly out of the process of globalisation. As Held [*1993: 25*] remarks, 'The very process of governance can escape the reach of the nation-state.' For Rosenau, globalisation has affected states in a number of critical ways. It has narrowed their scope, reduced their autonomy, and constricted their capacity to adapt to change. [*Rosenau, 1990: 127*]. National economies are ravaged by unstable commodity prices and fluctuating interest rates on debt repayment resulting from political choices made in the North; societies are ravaged by the adverse effects of structural adjustment programmes drawn up by the IMF and World Bank; serious national economic planning is all but impossible. Externally formulated 'reforms' often benefit the ruling elite to the detriment of the general population, thereby further undermining the legitimacy of the state. There is a simplistic sense in which the state lacks capacity as it is too big for small issues, and too small for big issues.

The capacity crisis fuels the legitimacy crisis, particularly given the context of increasing populations and environmental problems, and exacerbates pre-existing social and political tensions within and between states. Clear links exist between economic viability, political stability and ultimately security [*Myers, 1989: 211*]. An example is instructive. How will Bangladesh, one of the poorest states in the world, cope with the predicted rise in sea level in the Bengal Delta of over two metres by 2050, resulting from a lethal combination of greenhouse-related rising seas and local subsidence due to the increase in number of wells dug to water a burgeoning population? The Woods Hole Institute estimates that 18 per cent of Bangladesh will be under water by 2050, and this will result in the dislocation of 40 million people [*Milliman et al., 1989*]. With nowhere else to go inside Bangladesh, millions of Bangladeshis will be forced to flee to India as the only alternative to death. This will not be the first time that large-scale population movements have taken place between these two countries: during the civil war in Pakistan in 1971–72, millions of refugees fled into India. This resulted in heightened political tension in India in the border region, as the regional labour market in India was undercut by the influx of refugees. India is therefore unlikely to welcome further influxes of these people; she will be suffering herself on account of climate change. Moreover, political difficulties between India and Bangladesh over migration have already resulted in the building of a wall to stop Bangladeshi migration into Assam [*Gordon, 1993*].

While the legitimacy and capacity crises of the state pose great obstacles in the short-term to the formulation and acceptance of a holistic conception of security based on a global society rather than a system of sovereign states, they also stimulate discussion about political identity, human rights, democracy and accountability. The state is not about to go away, so there are fundamental questions to be addressed regarding the appropriate scope and limits of its authority, and also of the authority of other institutional foci below and above the level of the state. Out of the current crisis there is an opportunity for what Held calls 'cosmopolitan democracy' and 'a new international democratic order' [*Held, 1993: 37–44*].

The International Economy

While the proximate cause of widespread environmental damage has been the premium placed on economic development defined in terms of industrialisation and the promotion of intensive agriculture, the future sustainability of such development (even assuming that it is desirable) is doubtful unless the environmental dimension is incorporated. The operation of the international economy has led to unsustainable production and consumption in the North, and the adoption of inappropriate, and similarly unsustainable development paths in the South. To illustrate this point here it is well worth quoting Held at length:

> The globalisation of economic life – broadly, the growth of complex economic interconnections among states and societies – has not by any means been a uniform process, affecting each country and region in a similar way. From the outset, this process has involved great costs for the autonomy and independence of many ... globalisation has been characterised both by 'hierarchy' and 'unevenness'. Hierarchy denotes the structure of economic globalisation: its domination by those constellations of economic power concentrated in the west and north ... it is likely that the economic summits of the leading industrial countries will supplant super-power summits as the primary arena within which to discern new contours of hierarchy and power ... The other side of hierarchy is unevenness. This refers to the asymmetrical effects of economic globalisation upon the life-chances and well-being of peoples, classes, ethnic groupings, movements and the sexes. The contours of these processes of unevenness are not difficult to discern ... They

are broadly correlated with geography, race and gender ... Un-
evenness is a phenomenon of both international and national
development. The categories of social and political stratification
must, therefore, be thought of as denoting systematic divisions
within and across territories [*Held, 1993: 30–31*].

With the passing of the cold war and the opening of the former Eastern
bloc to Western economic policy, the international economy has been
truly globalised. With the state being rolled back there and throughout
the world, the global homogeneity thus produced is lessening the options
for discussion of different economic philosophies, and largely determining that the debate remains within the context of tinkering with the
present liberal system (which has created the problem in the first place),
and of course built on all the injustices outlined above by Held, rather
than transforming it. It follows that the opportunities for environmental
improvements are being couched in terms of market instruments rather
than traditional standard setting or more radical transformation. These
are presented as the cheapest and most efficient way to address environmental decline. Yet several contributions to this collection indicate that
such market answers to environmental decline are both theoretically
contestable and operationally difficult.

At UNCED, despite the range of government and non-governmental
actors present, the importance placed on economic efficiency as a means
to environmental ends was clear. The contribution here by John Devlin
and Nonita Yap notes that the language of economic efficiency and
structural adjustment permeates UNCED documentation. Yet they are
particularly concerned because they believe the compatibility between
economic efficiency and environmental sustainability is highly contestable theoretically, and extremely complex operationally. Their chapter
explores the contradictions between economic efficiency and environmental sustainability with reference to the market-oriented structural
adjustment programmes (SAPs) that have been undertaken in low-
consumption countries in the 1980s. By referring to recent studies on the
environmental impacts of SAPs in Thailand, the Philippines, Côte
d'Ivoire and Malawi, they identify the operational complexity of the
market-environment linkages and challenge the idea that efficient economies are the most environmentally friendly ones. They conclude that the
SAP prescriptions of free trade, unrestrained markets and inactive states
are not consistent with sustainable development, understood as environmental sustainability coupled with relative equality between states,
poverty reduction and political stability.

This conclusion is worrying, given that the whole thrust of the IMF and
World Bank debt management strategy has been the application of

structural adjustment policies, and there seems little sign of a more imaginative policy on the horizon. Moreover, it has been argued convincingly elsewhere that structural adjustment policies increase environmental degradation [*Reid, 1992; George, 1992*]. At a basic level, the more land taken up to grow cash crops for export, the more landless peasants have to move onto unsuitable marginal land to eke out a subsistence. In the case of Brazil, for example, this accelerates Amazonian deforestation. One author has drawn tentative linkages between the major debtors, structural adjustment policies and deforestation rates [*George, 1992*]. The problem of debt is fundamental: the debtor states as a whole began the 1990s 61 per cent more in debt than in 1982. Sub-Saharan African debt grew by 113 per cent in the period 1982–90. Currently an annual $50 billion net flows from South to North, and this does not even take account of the money lost through falling commodity prices. Even where SAPs have succeeded in increasing exports, falling commodity prices have interfered with the potential gain for the developing countries.

At UNCED the importance already attached to international trade for environmental protection was reiterated. The forum where this will be addressed is GATT. Yet Marc Williams' piece here suggests that caution is necessary, for a clear division exists between advocates of free trade, who seem to have won the day, and environmentalists. The former, for example the World Bank, GATT and liberal economists, argue that environmental protection is better served by liberal trade policies which serve sustainable development by decreasing the barriers to trade. This results in optimal use of world resources. Liberal economists urge international co-operation to protect the environment, but they do not support trade bans or related measures. Nor do they support measures to harmonise environmental standards, arguing that countries differ in the amount of pollution or environmental degradation they are willing to bear. By contrast environmentalists argue that the current international trading system promotes environmental degradation, and hence they are opposed to further liberalisation. They have concentrated their efforts on GATT, campaigning against GATT rules which they feel undermine national efforts to protect the environment. Northern NGOs have campaigned to get governments to move unilaterally against foreign products which infringe environmental standards. Environmentalists are in favour of international co-operation, but feel that it must result in a harsher regime than existing national legislation. In other words, it must be built around the highest, rather than the lowest, common denominator, or it will undermine achievements in environmental protection.

Williams argues convincingly that neither the free trade nor the environmentalist model have all the answers for tackling the vast scope of problems of environmental degradation. The liberal position is deficient because it does not ask questions about the structural nature of power in the global economy, and simply assumes that all choice in the world economy is equally unconstrained. He illustrates his case by reference to the trade in hazardous wastes from North to South which results in the poisoning of Third World populations. To defend this by reference to economic efficiency and the cause of faster economic growth is, Williams argues, morally bankrupt. Yet at the same time as liberal theorists fail to confront the issue of power relations in the world economy, so the environmentalists ignore the centrality of power relations. To impose common standards on all countries irrespective of their ability to carry the cost of environmental protection is to disadvantage some over others. Moreover, the basic asymmetries of economic power in the current system mean that the adoption of unilateral trade measures by stronger countries reinforces existing forms of protection and is regarded as a form of eco-imperialism by many poorer states. Williams concludes that neither liberal theory nor environmentalism adequately deals with the myriad of issues raised around the whole area of international trade and the environment, and what is needed is not grand theory but even-handed, open-minded attention to individual cases which will require different answers.

Alan Ingham's contribution to this collection lends weight to the arguments already voiced here by John Devlin, Nonita Yap and Marc Williams. He tests whether the creation of markets in environmental goods, as opposed to traditional standards or command and control methods, will result in optimal levels of pollution at minimum cost. He is especially interested in the appropriateness of tradeable permits in the case of the environmental pollutant sulphur dioxide (SO_2) which is largely responsible for acid rain. He acknowledges that economists have long recognised that many environmental problems are due to the absence of property rights and markets. But until recently environmental policy was seen to be in the hands of scientists and engineers who favoured emissions level standards, rather than considering the costs and benefits. Now, economists are stressing the advantages of the market, and using simple models to support their preferred policies. However, Ingham argues that this carries with it the danger that the market approach is being oversold in comparison to what it can do in practice. As with Devlin and Yap, Ingham is concerned that operationally this policy may be inappropriate, as the assumptions of simplified models may not apply in practice.

An examination of the market in tradeable permits currently being developed in the USA to control SO_2 emissions at minimum cost leads Ingham to suggest that markets have not emerged where they might have been expected, and casts doubt on whether they will emerge to a significant extent in the future. On the basis of these conclusions, he questions whether the use of emission permits markets will work in the UK. It is clear that if markets can be established, they are a very attractive way of ensuring a given level of reduction in a least cost way, in both ensuring that polluters adopt the correct avoidance strategy, and in minimising regulatory and monitoring costs. However, severe problems arise where the number of polluting firms is small (as is the case in the UK where the trade in permits would be dominated by Powergen and National Power), and where these firms are regulated utilities. Ingham concludes that whether correctly functioning markets can be established in the UK remains open to question. He advocates that the system of control must be chosen in relation to the degree of competition that is likely to occur rather than that which is assumed in models designed to sell the tradeable permits package.

If we extend these words of caution to other pollutants and countries, then it is clear that market mechanisms must not be assumed to be the global panacea for attaining optimum levels of pollution at minimum cost. This brings to mind Williams' conclusions concerning international trade and its relationship to the environment: grand design answers are inappropriate, and what is needed is a flexible approach that can consider the requirements of individual situations.

One important question which must guide us in our assessment of the suitability of classical market policies for sustainability is: do those who preach the policy actually practise it? Chomsky argues forcefully that the answer is no, and therefore caution is required. He argues that while promoting free market policies in the rest of the world, the rich countries protect themselves. He is well worth quoting at length:

> ... the rich powers remain opposed to free trade as they virtually always have been, except when they feel they can prevail in competition. The World Bank reports that protectionist measures of the industrial countries reduce national income in the South by about twice the amount of official aid, itself largely export-promotion, most of it directed to richer sectors (less needy, but better consumers). *In the past decade, twenty of twenty-four countries belonging to the Organization for Economic Co-operation and Development (OECD) have increased protectionism*, Reaganites often leading the way in the crusade against economic liberalism. These practices, along with the programmes dictated by the Inter-

national Monetary Fund and the World Bank, have helped double the gap between rich and poor countries since 1960. In Latin America, the real minimum wage declined sharply from 1985–92 as neo-liberal 'structural adjustment' programmes were imposed, while the number of poor rose almost fifty per cent between 1986 and 1990 – 'economic miracles', in technical terminology, because real gross domestic product (GDP) rose (in parallel with external debt) while the wealthy and foreign investors were enriched. *In Africa, the impact was even more severe for the general population: a study by the IMF conceded that from 1973–88, 'the growth rate is significantly reduced in IMF programme countries relative to the change in non-programme countries', putting aside the consequences for the poor majority.* Resource transfers from South to North amount to 'a much understated $418 billion' from 1982–90, Susan George observes, the equivalent in today's dollars of some 'six Marshall Plans for the rich through debt service alone', while commercial banks were protected by transfer of their bad debts to the public sector – apart from Japan, the only OECD country, it seems, that accepts the capitalist principle that the taxpayer has no responsibility to pay for the mistakes of commercial banks. As in the case of the savings and loan institutions, and advanced industry generally, 'free market capitalism' is to be risk-free for the masters, as fully as can be achieved (emphasis added) [*Chomsky, 1993: 162*].

Moreover, Chomsky argues that the poorer countries have really not seen anything yet, compared to what is in store for them through current trade agreements and those under negotiation or discussion, such as the proposal for a Multilateral Trade Organisation (MTO), or GATT-II. Even Canada, belonging to the rich country grouping, is hurting under the North American Free Trade Agreement (NAFTA), owing for example to restrictions on the production of generic drugs. The US International Trade Commission has estimated that US companies stand to gain $61 billion a year from the Third World if that country's protectionist demands are satisfied at GATT – a figure that will dwarf the debt service flow of around $50 billion per annum [*Chomsky, 1993: 162*]. Chomsky accuses the USA, in particular, of trying to protect 'intellectual property', and is concerned that US-based corporations, through the control of biotechnology, will control 'the means of life generally, locking the poor majority into dependence and hopelessness'. It is arguable that appropriate protection of biodiversity rests in the knowledge and culture of local communities rather than in foreign investments [*Shiva, 1993: 3*]. This makes very worrying the contents of an interpretative statement

which Clinton is expected to annexe to the Biodiversity Convention when
he signs, for it shifts the focus of the Convention from protection of the
earth's living diversity to protection of corporate demands for monopoly
control of life forms. Also, Shiva argues that it goes against some of
the major objectives of the Convention, since it weakens, rather than
strengthens, the capacity of local communities and Third World countries
to protect biodiversity and to adopt development models that reward
biodiversity conservation rather than reward its destruction. Of great
concern to the Third World Network is the role played by some US
environmental NGOs. The World Wild Life Fund – US, the World
Resources Institute and the Environmental and Energy Study Institute,
in collaboration with three biotechnology companies (Merck, Shamam
and Genetech), have prepared a draft interpretative statement which has
been submitted to the US government. Shiva questions the role of these
NGOs which, she argues: 'should be playing a leadership role in resisting
the patenting of life (and) are instead facilitating a process that will
contribute to the violation of the rights of non-human species and non-
Western cultures' [Shiva, 1993: 2].

The issue of intellectual property rights has featured in the discussions
on the possible creation of an MTO. Whereas GATT deals with issues
relating to the trade in non-agricultural goods, the proposed MTO would
also have powers over agricultural goods, trade and investments in the
service sectors, foreign investments, and rights over technology, – that is,
intellectual property rights [Peng, 1993a: 20]. Peng argues that while
GATT's liberalisation principles would be applied not only to trade but to
services and investment, the developing countries would effectively be
denied access to technology by the new intellectual property rules. The
new GATT would be at least as powerful as the IMF and World Bank. A
broad range of economic areas would be at its command. However, it
would also have an integrated dispute settlement procedure, – that is,
non-compliance in one area, such as intellectual property rights (IPRs),
could be subject to retaliation in other areas, such as restriction of the
import of a country's main exports. Thus, as in the case of IMF and World
Bank policies, MTO policies will have potentially far-reaching consequences not only for economies but also for politics and society
everywhere, and especially in the poorer countries. National sovereignty
will be eroded further, as will the powers of civil society – for example
parliaments and local communities. It would erode the already limited
powers of UN agencies such as the Conference on Trade and Development (UNCTAD), the Economic and Social Council (ECOSOC) and the
newly created Commission on Sustainable Development (CSD) [Peng,
1993b: 23]. Thus, fundamental building blocks of sustainable develop-

ment as outlined in Agenda 21, in the form of participatory democracy and transparent institutional decision-making, will be undermined.

One area of the international economy that received little attention at UNCED was the role of business, in particular multinational corporations. This was a very serious omission, for as the largest users of raw materials globally they contribute to environmental problems and hence potentially to their solution. Their influence is clear when we consider that the largest 500 (which incidentally generate more than half the greenhouse gas emissions produced annually) control about 70 per cent of world trade, 80 per cent of foreign investment, and 30 per cent of world GDP (about US $300 billion per annum) [*Ling, 1993: 9*].

No code of conduct was forthcoming at UNCED; the idea was accepted that businesses would regulate themselves. Moreover, even references to transnational corporations were deleted from Agenda 21 during the fourth Prepcom [*Third World Network, 1992a: 11–12*]. Some commentators suggest that the Business Council for Sustainable Development (BCSD), comprising the chief executives of 48 multinationals, as the only independent sector grouping helping to foot the bill for UNCED, had an undue influence on Agenda 21. The question of corporate sponsorship of UNCED has caused much controversy, especially since some of the multinational sponsors not only had dubious environmental records but also had a record of heavy funding of anti-environmental lobby groups, for example, ICI and ARCO. A conflict of interest seems possible, in that the BCSD's public relations consultants were Burson-Marstellar, who also appear to have helped with UNCED public relations. That company: 'helped Exxon and Union Carbide present the best face possible after the disasters in Valdez and Bhopal and helped stem the negative publicity surrounding the Three Mile Island nuclear reactor failure. They also lobbied for the Mexican government on the environmentally-questionable Canada-Mexico-US free trade agreement' [*Third World Network, 1992b: 22*].

The only mention of corporations in Agenda 21 was to promote their role in sustainable development. The Secretary General of the UN's Centre on Transnational Corporations (UNCTC) (which was dissolved, and thus lost its mandate, shortly before the final UNCED negotiating session as part of Boutros Boutros-Ghali's UN reforms) had submitted a report to UNCED which enunciated proposals for greater accountability, harmonisation of company-level environmental accounting procedures and environmental pricing [*Grubb et al., 1993: 37–40*]. The Group of 77 and the Swedish government had endorsed the UNCTC's proposals for greater corporate accountability to be written into Agenda 21, but they were defeated by the rich governments in inter-government negotiation

[*Third World Network, 1992: 22*]. In the event, Agenda 21 reflected more the ideas of the BCSD than the UNCTC.

The idea that self-regulation of business can work is questionable, since even assuming good intentions, there are limits to how far it can go before it affects a company's competitive position in the domestic or global economy. Moreover, the record of the BCSD companies advocating self-regulation has not been encouraging: for example, Brazil's Aracruz Cellulose is the world's largest exporter of bleached eucalyptus pulp; the US's Dupont is the largest producer of ozone-destroying substances; and Japan's Mitsubishi is the leading destroyer of tropical forests [*Greenpeace, 1992*].

Demography and Consumption

The third major issue on the post UNCED agenda is the relationship between population, consumption and environmental degradation. Politicisation in the run-up to Rio meant that this was not adequately addressed there, although a chapter of Agenda 21 is devoted to population and a follow-up Conference on Population and Development is planned for 1994.

There is no doubt that environmental impact results from both population and consumption patterns; accordingly, action is required by the North and the South. Bush's comment before UNCED that the US lifestyle was non-negotiable placed a question mark over his commitment to international co-operation to deal with the environmental–developmental crisis [*Seabrook, 1992: 51*]. The richer Northern countries, housing only 20 per cent of the world's population, are responsible for 80 per cent of global consumption and 85 per cent of the world's gross national product. Those countries have per capita incomes 15 times higher than the Southern countries. The richer states must take the major share of responsibility for the global pollution that has occurred to date. It has been argued that 'mathematically speaking, if the rich reduce their wasteful consumption by 25 per cent, worldwide pollution will be reduced by 22.5 per cent. But if the poor 75 per cent reduce consumption totally and disappear from this earth altogether, the reduction in pollution will only be 10 per cent [*Mohamed, 1992: 28*].

While the figures themselves may be contestable, the political message is not. Similarly, it has been argued that 'if levels of consumption and waste do not change, the 57 million Northerners who will be born in the 1990s will pollute the Earth more than the extra 911 million Southerners' [*Bello, 1993: 11*]. Moreover Bello argues that beyond its impact on the global environment, overconsumption in the North directly degrades the environment in the South. He points to Japan's ecological relationship with South-east Asia as an example: 'Apart from devouring Southeast Asia's forests, the Japanese economic machine is now exporting industrial pollution on a massive scale to the region' [*Bello, 1993: 12*].

However, it cannot be denied that the *local* population–environmental resource balance deteriorates as the population grows. This is a major problem in many of the poorer parts of the world where the carrying capacity of the land is already overburdened. For the majority of inhabitants of our planet, this is important. Karki, for example, shows how rapid population growth in Nepal has accelerated the natural tendency to environmental degradation which characterises the Himalayas. The natural resource base, essential for the survival of the vast majority of Nepalese, is rapidly depleting. The cultivated person to land ratio has increased dramatically, agricultural farming has become less productive, and forests and common lands have been encroached upon beyond their limits for human habitation and cultivation. Often, government policy and external 'expert' advice has not helped. (This brings to mind Saurin's arguments relating to 'expert knowledge' in agriculture and the potential role of local knowledge, all too often marginalised.)

This situation is not uncommon in other parts of the world. However, the precise relationship between population increase and land degradation is not always easy to establish, for other factors intervene. For example, Bello points to recent research on famine in the Sahel, which has thrown some doubt on the idea that population pressure on the land was the principal cause of famine. He points instead to the 'complex interaction of several factors, including global climate change, the conversion of the Horn of Africa into an arena of superpower conflict, the rise of repressive regimes that perpetuated unequal socio-economic structures, the spread of export agriculture, and global financial and trading systems biased against Africa' [*Bello, 1993: 14*]. World population has quintupled since the early 1800s, and it is expected to grow from 5.4 billion in 1991 to 10 billion in 2050. Over 50 per cent of this increase is expected to occur in seven countries: Bangladesh, Brazil, China, India, Indonesia, Nigeria and Pakistan. Ninety-six per cent of the increase is taking place in developing countries. It is particularly worrying that over the last couple of years, the projections for population growth have had to be revised upwards due to a slowing down in the decline in fertility rates of certain countries, for example, China, India, Morocco, the Philippines and Colombia [*UNFPA/Myers, 1991: 11*]. Moreover, these revised projections may require further upward revision. If the slowing in the decline in fertility rates already mentioned is not arrested, population could increase fourfold to approximately 23 billion by the end of the twenty-first century, as opposed to the currently estimated 11.3 billion. Developments in the Middle East and Africa will be particularly important: fertility rates in sub-Saharan Africa have not changed in the last quarter of a century.

The relationship between population and environment was spelled out in an independent report *Our Health. Our Planet* sponsored by the World Health Organisation as part of its submission to UNCED [*1992*]. The report charged that overpopulation already resulted in environmental destruction which killed millions of people every year, largely owing to their own contamination of water, soil and air. The ill-effects are mostly experienced by inhabitants of the developing world, and it is there that the population challenge will have to be addressed. The problem will interact with, and compound, other problems such as rapid urbanisation, and the demands on the natural resource base will be magnified. The South Commission recognised that societies in the developing world 'must willingly accept a firm commitment to responsible parenthood and the small-family norm' [*South Commission, 1990: 282*].

The social and political repercussions of this situation are clear. In some parts of world, the resource issue itself will motivate political tensions within and between states. In others, it will exacerbate preexisting tensions and add to existing instability. The case of access to fresh water is instructive. Current demand for fresh water exceeds supply in various parts of the world: the Middle East, northern China, east Java (Indonesia) and parts of India. In 88 developing countries with 40 per cent of the world's population, water deficits already place 'a serious constraint on development' [*UNFPA/Myers, 1991: 39*]. Falkenmark has predicted that in sub-Saharan Africa, by the year 2000, 350 million people, or half the population, will live in water-stressed states, and another 150 million in states suffering from absolute scarcity. By 2025, Nigeria, Ethiopia, Somalia, Tanzania, Malawi, Lesotho and Zimbabwe are projected to suffer absolute water scarcity (cited in Ornas and Mohamed Salih [*1989: 216*]).

The security implications of resource issues like fresh water are becoming more obvious daily [*Thomas and Howlett: 1993*]. The most fundamental factor is that shortages and other problems such as pollution and floods will be played out on a political canvass characterised by the grave instability of states themselves, and instability in many interstate relations. The situation in the Middle East is already critical. In South Asia it is deteriorating rapidly. Housing one quarter of the world's population, the regional politics of South Asia are extremely volatile. States there are fraught with internal ethnic or religious differentiation, and these problems often cut across interstate boundaries. The larger the population, the more competition for water resources. Even within India this has already fuelled trouble between various states, for example the noteworthy tension between Tamil Nadu and Karnataka over the River Cauvery waters. The construction of dams by Karnataka, against the terms of existing agreements, means that only one rice crop, rather than two, can be grown in the delta in Tamil Nadu. Violence against Tamils in Bangalore, Karnataka, resulted in the destabilisation of the minority Congress government at a very delicate point in India's history following the assassination of Rajiv Gandhi. Already complex interstate relations will be exacerbated by water, which is already an issue in Indo-Pakistani, Indo-Bangladeshi and Indo-Nepalese relations. The resource-population relationship is so sensitive that the Pakistan census of 1991 was suppressed. The population is expected to be growing at 3.1 per cent per annum (thus 150 million by 2000, and 250 million by 2025), almost all dependent on the waters of the Indus system for food and water. The division of the waters of this system is currently subject to an agreeement with India, but is likely to be put under serious pressure [*Gordon, 1993*].

The population issue was raised in Principle 5 of the Rio Declaration, and in Chapter 5 of Agenda 21. The former urges states to reduce and eliminate unsustainable patterns of production and consumption and to promote appropriate demographic policies; the latter is devoted to 'Demographic Dynamics and Sustainability' and had three programme areas. The first addresses the links between demographic trends and sustainable development, and urges more research into their relationship. The second calls on governments and other actors to formulate integrated national policies for environment and development, taking demographic trends into account. The third calls on governments and local communities to implement these programmes. Population targets and terms such as contraception are not even referred to, due to opposition from Rome and the Philippines in particular. The omission of targets was probably wise, since hope of fulfilment is slight. More constructively, the emphasis was on social policies and priorities that would be helpful; in particular, the right of women to decide on the number and spacing of children, and their right to education and access to information.

Karki shows very clearly just how vital, and how difficult, implementation of Agenda 21 will be with regard to demography. Twenty-five years of family planning programmes in Nepal (and many other countries) have failed. The approach must be altered to tackle several problems simultaneously, rather than pushing a contraceptive delivery and sterilisation service in isolation. The reduction of infant and child mortality is essential for slowing the pace of demographic growth; parents will not avoid pregnancy unless they are sure their existing babies will survive to adulthood. Reduction of infant mortality correlates with the education, health, social status, housing and general well-being of mothers, and the general level of socio-economic development of a country. Hence the stress on the rights of women and on an integrated, multi-dimensional approach in Agenda 21 is the key to success. Yet there will be cultural obstacles to this in many parts of the world, not only Nepal where the dominant Hindu culture values sons more than daughters. Karki argues that implementation will require grassroots mobilisation and participation, and that NGOs, rather than government officials, can play a crucial role in facilitating this. He does not underestimate the scale of the challenge, and while stressing the key role of NGOs as facilitators, he identifies the essential role for governments in demonstrating their commitment by the provision of funding for purposes which do not show an immediate economic return; in other words, they must invest in human capital by welfare provision. Unfortunately, this goes against the grain of IMF and World Bank lending policies, and thus to a certain extent is beyond the reach of the majority of developing country governments even had they the political will to do so.

Conclusion

Even assuming that the majority of states want to co-operate to deal with environmental and developmental issues, unless the richest and strongest are among their number then little can be achieved. Moreover, environmental degradation involves many global processes and transnational actors which are beyond the reach of states, individually and sometimes even collectively. The power of organisations such as transnational corporations, the IMF and the Catholic Church is such as to place a question mark on the capacity of sovereign statehood. Furthermore, implementation of sustainability largely depends on sub-national groups. In this context, one of the most revealing features of the UNCED agreements is the glaring disjunction between the actors who signed them – states – and those on whom implementation largely depends – non-state actors, particularly sub-national groups.

The record of the Rio Summit in terms of rich country commitments is poor; consider the lack of specific policy commitments in all the UNCED agreements, the lack of new finance, the lack of far-reaching technology transfer, the lack of attention to fundamentals like debt repayment and terms of trade. The record of the Catholic Church hierarchy and transnational corporations is as poor, perhaps even poorer in some respects.

The post-Rio process to date does not appear promising, especially in terms of facilitating the work and acknowledging the role of the sub-national groups on whom the whole sustainability effort ultimately depends. A whole section (III) of Agenda 21 was devoted to strengthening the role of major groups. Its preamble talks of 'the global partnership for sustainable development' which needs the participation of all groups and organisations. In particular, it emphasises the active involvement of women, children and youth, indigenous people, non-governmental groups, local authorities, workers and trade unions, business and industry. Yet if we consider the CSD, charged with the tasks of UNCED follow-up, national reporting and aspects of UN system co-ordination, then the prospects seem mixed. While the CSD has adopted rules for NGO participation generous by UN standards, Gordon's contribution here points out that the CSD has so far made no effort to incorporate discussion of the local level, or to invite international local government bodies to be key participants in its future work programme. The CSD is not alone; Gordon comments that neither individual governments nor the Intergovernmental Negotiating Committee for a Framework Convention on Climate Change appear interested in discussing actions to limit greenhouse gas emissions at the sub-national level. Yet their participation is crucial. It is instructive that loans, grants and technical assistance from the World Bank, from the GEF and from the EBRD are reserved almost exclusively for national governments. In other words, 'nation states, despite Rio, still consider themselves as the only important actors on the stage ... unless (local government and local action) can be integrated fully into the international political process, prospects for success are small' (Gordon, this volume). And of course, any efforts to move towards greater democratisation and accountability through the CSD will potentially be swamped by the continued unfolding of the debt crisis and the potential implications of an MTO.

Indeed, it is not only the significance of the CSD that is so affected by the international economy; the whole UNCED process is affected. Matthew Paterson's piece here on the politics of climate change after UNCED argues that what matters most is not the Framework Convention signed at Rio, but the global economic environment. The recession is limiting the likelihood of abatement programmes in the North, and also the potential for technology transfer to limit the future growth of emissions in many developing countries.

It seems then, that there are two parallel processes at work: one seeking to promote fundamental human rights through the exercise of participatory democracy, the other seeking to promote the interests of a minority through limiting the scope for national choices and democratic participation. The words of Chomsky are appropriate here:

Within the culture of respectability, the traditional tasks remain: to reshape past and current history in the interests of power, to exalt the high principles to which we and our leaders are dedicated, and to file away the unfortunate flaws in the record as misguided good intentions, harsh choices for the properly educated. For those who are unwilling to accept this role, the traditional tasks also remain: to challenge and unmask illegitimate authority, and to work with others to undermine it and to extend the scope of freedom and justice. Both tendencies exist, as they almost always have. Which prevails will determine whether there will be a world in which a decent person would want to live [*Chomsky, 1993: 163*].

Those of us interested in environmental–development issues have to make our choice: to interpret them within the culture of respectability, with all the limitations we know that imposes on knowledge, allocation of responsibility and consequent action; or to interpret them within the bigger canvass of global politics. While the latter option presents the more difficult challenge academically and practically, it also presents a greater opportunity for the democratisation of politics on which sustainability largely depends.

REFERENCES

Bello, W. (1993), 'Population Control: The Real Culprits and Real Victims', *Third World Resurgence*, No.33. May.
Chomsky, N. (1993), 'World Order and its Rules: Variations on Some Themes', *Journal of Law and Society*, Vol.20, No.2, pp.145–63.
George, S. (1992), *The Debt Boomerang*, London: Pluto Press.
Giddens, A. (1990), *Consequences of Modernity*, Oxford: Polity Press.
Gorbachev, M. (1988a), *Perestroika*, London: Collins.
Gorbachev, M. (1988b), 'Address to the UN General Assembly', *Soviet News*, 14 Dec.
Gorbachev, M. (1990), 'Address to the Participants in the Global Forum on Environment and Development for Survival', *Soviet News*, 31 Jan.
Gordon, S. (1993), 'Resources and Instability in South Asia', *Survival*, Vol.35, No.2. pp.65–87.
Grubb, M. *et al.* (1993), *The Earth Summit Agreements*, London: Earthscan and RIIA.
Held, D. (1993), *Prospects for Democracy*, Oxford: Polity Press.
Held, D. and A. McGrew, (1993), 'Globalization and the Liberal Democratic State', *Government and Opposition*, Vol.28, No.2. pp.261–88.
Jackson, R. (1990), *Quasi-states: Sovereignty, International Relations and the Third World*, Cambridge: Cambridge University Press.
Jackson, R. and C. Rosberg, (1982), 'Why Africa's Weak States Persist: The Empirical and the Juridical in Statehood', *World Politics*, Vol.35, No.1, pp.1–24.
Jenkins, S. (1993), 'The Melting Pot Bubbles Over', *The Times*, 18 Aug., p.14.
Ling, C.Y. (1992), 'Unequal Negotiations in an Unequal World', *Third World Resurgence*, No. 24–25, Aug.–Sept., pp.7–10.
Milliman, J. *et al.* (1989), 'Environmental and Economic Implications of Rising Sea Levels and Subsiding Deltas: The Nile and Bengal Examples', *Ambio*, Vol.18, No.6.

Mohamed, M. (1992), 'Rich Must Change Lifestyle', *Third World Resurgence*, No.24/5, Aug./Sep.

Myers, N. (1989), 'Population Growth, Environmental Decline and Security Issues in Sub-Saharan Africa', in Ornas and Mohamed Salih (eds.) *[1989]*.

Ornas A.H. and M. Mohamed Salih (eds.) (1989), *Ecology and Politics: Environmental Stress and Security in Africa*, Uppsala: Scandinavian Institute of African Studies.

Peng, M.K.K. (1993d), 'A New Global Giant to Rule the South?' *Third World Resurgence*, No.29–30, Jan.-Feb.

Peng, M.K.K. (1993b), 'Nine Points against the MTO and the Uruguay Pact', *Third World Resurgence*, No.29–30, Jan-Feb.

Reid, D. (ed) (1992), *Structural Adjustment and the Environment*, London: Earthscan.

Roseanau, J. (1990), *Turbulence in World Politics*, Hernel Hempstead: Harvester Wheatsheaf

Seabrook, J. (1992), 'Negotiating the Western lifestyle', *Third World Resurgence*, No.24–5, Aug.-Sept.

Shevardnadze, E. (1989), 'Statement at the UN General Assembly', *Soviet News*, 4 Oct.

Shiva, V. (1993), 'Violating Peoples' Rights, Protecting Corporate Profits', *Third World Resurgence*, No.34, June.

South Commission (1990), *The Challenge to the South*. Oxford: Oxford University Press.

Third World Network (1992a), 'UNCED Ignores Ten Critical Issues', *Third World Resurgence*, No.24–5, Aug.-Sept.

Third World Network (1992b), 'The Sustainable Council for Business Development', *Third World Resurgence*, No. 24–25, Aug.–Sept., p.22.

Thomas, C. (1990), 'New Directions in Thinking About Security in the Third World', in K. Booth (ed.), *New Thinking about Strategy and Security*, London: HarperCollins.

Thomas, C. (1992), *The Environment in International Relations*, London: RIIA.

Thomas, C. and D. Howlett (eds.) (1993), *Resource Politics: Freshwater and Regional Relations*, Buckingham: Open University Press.

UNFPA/Myers (1991), *Population, Resources and the Environment*, London: Banson.

Walker, R. (1993), *Six Years that Shook the World*, Manchester: Manchester University Press.

WHO (1992), *Our Health, Our Planet*, Geneva: UN.

Environment on the Periphery of International Relations: An Explanation

STEVE SMITH

Media attention on Rio and its aftermath, coupled with growing academic interest among political scientists and international relations scholars in environmental issues, might suggest that the environment is now central to political activity within and between states. This seeming centrality of environmental concerns may be mistaken. Powerful reasons, essentially political in nature, may keep the environment on the periphery both within the practice of international relations, and within the academic subject of international relations. Academics studying the environment tend to work within a pluralist framework which assumes exactly what needs to be confronted. Both within the states-system and within the academic discipline of international relations, there is a dominance of specific interests, such that proposing that the environment needs to be taken seriously threatens the whole edifice. Environmental scholars, and environmental issues, may be marginalised unless the fundamental relationship between knowledge and power is addressed.

What does it mean to claim that the environment is on the periphery? How can such a politically significant movement, fresh from the media attention of the 1992 Rio Summit, be anything other than central to political activity within and between states? After all, if there is one political issue that seems on the rise throughout the world, then this must be the environment. Similarly, there has been a massive expansion of academic interest within the disciplines of political science and international relations in environmental politics. Not only are there mainstream accounts of environmental issues and green politics in the two

Steve Smith is Professor of International Politics at the University of Wales, Aberystwyth.

disciplines (see Dobson [1990], Goodin [1992], and Weale [1992] in political science; and Hurrell and Kingsbury [1992], Thomas [1992], and Young [1989] in international relations), but textbooks on both domestic and international politics now have sections dealing with the environment (see Dunleavy et al. [1990] for a British politics example, and Art and Jervis [1993], and Brown [1992] for examples from international relations). In this article I examine whether the seeming centrality of environmental concerns is not in fact mistaken by reference to two dimensions of the role of environmental politics: within international relations as practice, and within the academic subject of international relations. I argue that there are powerful reasons, essentially political, that may keep the environment on the periphery in each setting.

Such a view may well seem heretical to those who work within the environmental politics area. However, my overall claim is that too often practitioners and academics alike fall into the trap of being drawn by the ethical, moral or even common-sense logic of their argument or position without sufficient attention being paid to the 'realities' of political and economic power. As someone who works in probably the most conservative academic discipline, one which reifies the state as the centre-piece of political and economic analysis, I want to put forward a set of reasons why environmental politics may be destined to stay on the periphery of international relations (and of the discipline of international relations).

Perhaps an historical precedent is to be found in the politics and study of European integration. In the 1950s and early 1960s, the logic of integration as a practice and as an (often interrelated) academic field, forecast the end of the states-system. Whether by functional stealth or by neo-functional co-option the state was to be overtaken by other actors. Arguably a similar neglect of high politics is present in most contemporary environmental work as was present in the heady days of European integration. Moreover, the states-system has faced many challenges before, and since, that posed by European integration. Yet for all its faults, and crucially for all its constraining and silencing of alternative notions of political community, the states-system remains the dominant political structure of international relations.

My claim is not that environmental politics *should* remain on the periphery of either the practice or the study of international relations, nor that these two activities are in any sense separate. Indeed, I am particularly concerned to see such issues as the environment, ethnicity, gender, and culture move far more towards the centre of the practice and study of international relations. I write not from a realist position, but from one that does not underestimate the political and economic interests conjoined and entangled within *both* the modern state and the academic community. In short, my concern in writing this contribution is not to act as an academic de Gaulle, bringing back 'high' politics to derail the 'low' politics of environmental concerns, but as someone working within the academic discipline of international relations who sees much of the work in environmental politics as *underestimating* the fundamental barriers, both practical and academic, to the development of policies and approaches that place the environment at the centre of analysis. The world of power, social, political, economic and academic, is far less conducive to environmental concerns than the last decade's experience might suggest. In this sense the environment shares with gender and race the dubious privilege of being *an* issue in political and academic circles, but I wonder whether that means anything more than that it is impossible not to pay lip-service to it.

I will look at these barriers under two broad headings, political and academic. I have to admit that I am very unhappy about making this simple division, for the blindingly obvious reason that they are so clearly fundamentally interrelated. Yet I feel that this is the best way to get to grips with two somewhat distinct *logics* of the problem. That is to say that there are reasons why environmental issues may well be peripheralised in the world of international relations and a separate set of reasons why this will occur in the academic discipline. They illustrate two rather different aspects of how power operates.

I must hasten to add that the arguments that follow are certainly not omitted from much of the recent scholarship on the subject of environmental politics and international relations. Hurrell and Kingsbury [*1992*], for example, introduce their edited book with an excellent chapter looking at the difficulties facing international attempts to deal with environmental issues. Similarly, Albert Weale's recent account of the politics of pollution [*1992*] has a sophisticated discussion of the international dimension of pollution control. Oran Young's pioneering work on environmental regimes and co-operation (see Young [*1989; 1990*] as examples) has been focused on the processes by which the international states system can develop environmental regimes.

Each of these writers takes as his starting point the states-system and analyses how inter-state agreement and co-operation can be achieved *despite* it. These attempts place all these writers within the pluralist camp in international relations theory. This is only one of the alternatives within international relations theory, as each author well knows; yet each writes *from within* that theoretical perspective, and therefore overtheorises and overdetermines the range of outcomes. In essence, those writers who are concerned with environmental issues tend to sit within one theoretical perspective, and thereby assume exactly that which needs to be questioned. Again, note, this does not mean that these writers are in any sense unaware of the objections to their positions, – much the opposite – only that they, and their analyses, are located within a theoretical framework.

This framework is, like all such seemingly 'neutral' academic frameworks, ideological and normative, and thereby makes crucially important assumptions about the nature of political and economic processes and their interrelationship. As will become clear below, I am concerned that much of the academic work on environmental issues depends on the writers working within a set of essentially *un*contested concepts and assumptions, and that it is these which do much of the work in defining what is practical and even what is theoretically possible. As is the case in so many social sciences, the really interesting questions are found at the margins and on the peripheries where these assumptions and concepts clash and contradict each other.

I want to look first at the logic of the world of environmental practice in international relations to see whether there are grounds for claiming that it is, or will become, peripheral. I want to put forward ten reasons why the current focus on the environment may be a temporary one. I do not want to present what follows as an either/or alternative, but rather want to claim that to the extent that the following factors dominate international politics then the environment will be moved to the periphery.

The *first* argument is that it is not at all clear just what being concerned with the environment actually means. The phrase 'environmental issues' may well conjure up a specific set of arguments and images in contemporary Britain, but what does a concern with the environment actually mean in an international political sense? The obvious point to make is that the term has no one meaning, and that the various meanings depend upon one's cultural, economic, ethnic, gender and religious location. This is not to say that there are not pressing environmental problems, such as the greenhouse effect, depletion of the ozone layer, the transportation of hazardous wastes, marine pollution and acid rain. But such problems admit of many more than one interpretation. Within the richer economies, it is difficult to get political agreement as to what should be done even given considerable scientific consensus. When a wider set of cultural viewpoints is introduced, the problem becomes much more extreme. There is simply no one logic which follows from the identification of an environmental problem, let alone any one solution.

In this sense the environment is *an* issue in international politics, just like all the others, and it is optimistic indeed to think that it is so compelling that it can impose a logic or a set of solutions on politicians located in different political and economic settings. Of course this is recognised by the vast majority of environmental activists, but there is an important sense in which they often speak of the environment *as if* it was an overriding priority *with one logic*. Appealing to the needs of the environment may well be very similar to appealing to notions of justice, emancipation, equality or security; these terms are essentially contested and thereby represent yet another arena for political debate rather than a cause that transcends politics. To speak of the needs of 'mother' earth may well reflect *a* logic, but there are other interpretations of need with which that logic must compete.

In the academic world this problem is exactly the reason why the environment tends to be studied within a pluralist framework. The need for, and problems of, managing co-operation is the starting point for academic discussions of environmental politics, whereas in the political world the tendency is to see one version of environmental politics as being so compelling as to override national differences. This conflict becomes particularly problematic when the environment is an issue between less developed and richer states. In short, to speak of the environment and of the need to prevent its degradation is merely to specify yet another issue for the agenda of international politics, one which will not replace the existing mechanisms of inter-state relations, and not transcend the states-system by refocusing attention on an issue that is in some way 'beyond' or 'above' international politics. No such transcendental imperative follows from a concern with the environment, whatever the scientific consensus or environmental activists think. Maybe there should be, but that reflects a specific view of the salience of the environment in comparison to other issues and needs.

My *second* point builds on this argument and is that if the environment is just one issue amongst many others in international politics, then it will be subject to exactly the same structural influences and processes as apply in other areas. The fact that the issue concerns the environment will not alter the mechanisms of international politics, however much the need for new mechanisms might be obvious to activists and academics alike. The history of the states-system's ability to cope with other issues of world significance, notably nuclear and biological weapons, and famine, does not augur well. In short, maybe the environment is simply the latest in a series of issues, with no more likelihood of transcending the limitations of the states-system than its historical precedents. Of course, this does not mean that the environment must be peripheral *per se*, but it does mean that it would be wishful thinking indeed to assume that there is likely to be a progressive solution of environmental problems.

The reasons for this pessimistic view are well known, so only the headlines are necessary here. The central obstacles that the states-system produces are: first, the absence of world government, and a self-help system amongst states; second, the dominance of the state as actor and as reference point for the demands of publics and interest groups; third, the resultant centrality of state rivalry, crucially insofar as it becomes *relative* and not *absolute* gains and losses that matter to leaders; fourth, the fact that most environmental issues involve collective goods, thereby providing serious difficulties for creating and enforcing environmental regimes to deal with them; fifth, the possibilities for free-riding in issues dealing with the 'global commons'; sixth, the problems of defining the scope of regimes and the fundamental difficulty of deciding on a fair way of paying for environmental measures; seventh, the central role of the state as the site of entrenched economic power and as the guarantor of the economic interests of its populations, and, more saliently, of its corporations; and eighth, dominance of the concept of sovereignty, reflecting an unwillingness either to set precedents for future international activity or to see any external body have a say in matters of 'domestic' jurisdiction. Just because an issue concerns the environment, therefore, does not mean that it can overcome the ways in which states do business. Added together, the first two points indicate that the environment has all the potential for becoming yet another, maybe just another, set of issues on the international agenda, no more implying a need for solutions outside the framework of the states-system than other historically important issues. Yet, of course, it is exactly this kind of appeal that lies at the heart of much environmental activism.

A *third* factor is the tendency for states to adopt communitarian logic in their foreign policies, in sharp contrast to the cosmopolitan logic that informs nearly all environmental politics. Governments simply pay lip-service to cosmopolitan appeals, and rarely do anything to further them if doing so either runs against the interests of their dominant public groupings or if so doing costs their state more than it does other competitors. Thus signing declarations or making speeches can be easily undertaken because all too often these are self-implementing, and cost-less, activities. The whole history of agreeing reductions in CFCs and other greenhouse gasses shows how difficult it is not to put state interests (narrowly defined) first. Exactly the same points could be made about the unwillingness of European governments to do anything that involves costs in the face of the appalling events following the break-up of the state of Yugoslavia. Indeed, it was the same logic that caused so many problems during the Gulf War of 1990–91.

The *fourth* difficulty arises from the fact that appealing to the needs of the environment can be a very emotive and persuasive move in the language of political manoeuvre. Most of the issues are technically complex and give politicians considerable room for using the environment as a justification for whatever policy they want to impose. In the UK the clearest example is over energy policy, where proponents of nuclear power are now, rather perversely, pointing to the environmental damage caused by fossil fuels as a reason to continue to build nuclear power stations. The whole 'green' consumer bandwagon is a further case in point, especially when consumers seem willing to pay more for goods that 'protect the environment'. In addition, of course, there is the fact that what the phrase 'protecting the environment' means will differ according to political, religious, cultural and economic contexts. Thus politicians will use the environment much as they do such vacuous phrases as 'the national interest' and 'sovereignty'; in each case these are empty terms, meaning what politicians want them to mean. They enable the user to claim the moral high ground, especially when politicians can point to a mass of research undertaken by government scientists. That this information is often suspect, and is challenged by pressure groups and the media is not the point; the point is that governments tend to enjoy considerable advantages in any such exchanges, with, in the UK at least, a history of public deference towards government expertise.

This is exactly why the complexities of the issues are politically important; rare is the citizen who is really sure of the scientific evidence, and therefore much of the time it is impossible to act with certainty on any one issue. The environment seems to have been co-opted by politicians of all parties, so that each of them claims to act in a way that protects it, and all policies can be justified as environmentally conscious. The result is a kind of stasis whereby the environment is dragged in to justify each party's policies, with the real work in environmental policy going on behind the public gaze. If all parties are 'environmentally-conscious' then how can we choose between them? In the same way that no leader would say that he or she was proposing a policy that was *against* the national interest, so no politician will propose a policy that is *against* the environment; the term becomes virtually meaningless in political debate.

Far more serious, and controversial, is my *fifth* point, which, simply stated, is that environmental concerns are salient neither for governments nor for publics. This would doubtless enrage many activists who, whilst accepting that governments were decidedly slippery when it came to doing anything about the environment, would none the less claim that environmental concerns were important to increasing sections of the population. There is a real need to distinguish between statements supporting environmental issues and a willingness to suffer any loss of standard of living in order to do anything towards implementing those concerns. Opinion polls may well report that large percentages of the populations in developed countries are concerned about greenhouse gases or about acid rain, but these findings have to be treated with considerable care. After all, what might it say about you if you were not concerned about these issues? There is a high probability of bandwaggoning and fadism. Everyone feels that they should be worried about the environment and live a greener life, but how far will they go to translate that feeling into action?

More problematically, there is the worry that environmentalism is particularly related to social class. Green issues may well be central only to a small group of the middle class, and be seen as luxurious by those who do not have the money to buy even the necessities. If this is problematic within countries, think what it means in the international political system, where the spread of resources is very skewed.

Even within developed economies the crucial point is that very few voters actually exercise their votes according to environmental issues. This one fact is probably the main reason why the environment may well become increasingly peripheral within political systems. Of course, one reason why voters do not exercise their votes in accordance with environmental matters is that parties do not neatly divide on environmental lines. Skilful public relations can make each party have a 'credible' declaratory environmental policy, one that can safely be dropped or suffer implementation problems after an election. In this sense, voters do not have much of a choice since each alternative will say similar things about the need to protect the environment. Where there have been green parties, their record is rather poor. Even the German Greens suffered as the costs of reunification provided voters with another, more important, concern, and as electoral success forced the party to deal with the altogether more complex problem of what to do about the environment. The fact is that elections are not fought on single issues, and green parties run the risk of being single issue parties. Moreover, when individuals vote they tend to do so on the basis of primarily economic reasons. Not only may environmental issues be far less relevant than economic ones, but they could threaten individuals' economic interests.

In the early 1980s, the anti-nuclear movement in Western Europe and North America received considerable media attention. This was the period when some of the largest crowds ever demonstrated against Cruise and Pershing missile deployment in many European countries. Yet in the very year when the peace movements were at their most popular, conservative governments won large majorities in West Germany and in the UK – and in my judgement the peace movements were much more powerful a political force than have been any environmental groups. Elections will not be decided on environmental issues, and the result of this is that politicians will not feel that they have to do anything other than make the appropriate noises. The environment is rarely a vote winner. It will not therefore be an issue over which parties will differ enormously, since they need to do no more than to say enough of the right things to keep happy the small proportion of their voters who care about the environment. The sad fact is that economic indicators are still by far the best predictors of electoral fortunes. Environmental concerns are therefore peripheral to the bulk of the populations in developed economies; in less developed economies they are likely to be far less salient to populations, since their main worries are likely to be much more basic. Misuse of the environment may well contribute to hunger in the medium term but the immediate concern is likely to be how to meet today's food requirements rather than the long-term alteration of cultivation patterns. Thus within developing societies, the environment is nothing like as important as much European thinking suggests. The experience of the green movements in Europe in the last decade or so may be very unrepresentative of either the salience of environmental issues in that part of the world in the future or of their role in other parts of the world. To many in underdeveloped economies, a concern with the environment that goes beyond meeting immediate basic needs must look very luxurious, if not altogether perverse.

My *sixth* point concerns the nature of policy-making. In liberal democracies, let alone in authoritarian regimes, foreign, defence, scientific and technological policies are not made in democratic ways. This means that any public concern over the environment is likely to be less influential in the policy process than in other areas of policy-making. Thus, to the extent that governments are democratic or responsive to public opinion, they will be less so in the likely areas of environmental interest than in others. What this means is that policy-making in areas that deal with environmental interests will be influenced more by factors such as bureaucratic infighting and by corporatist pressure groups than by public opinion. Now, these kinds of influences are unlikely to press for treating environmental considerations as central. Indeed, it is precisely this form of decision-making that is most likely to see environmental issues pushed to the background. One paradox is that on environmental issues both trades unions and employers often share a common interest; for each it imposes costs, in the form of jobs for the former and profits or market-leading investment opportunities for the latter.

To the extent that governments have to justify their environmental policies to their populations and legislatures, they can fall back on the same excuses and explanations as they use in foreign and defence policy (see Smith [*1986*]). They can limit the discussion by the use of the secrecy card, and forestall criticism by the 'if you had access to the technical expertise that we have then you would agree with us' argument. They can also blame foreign governments for dragging their heels, or, in the UK case, point to the precedent that might be set by allowing the EC to have a say in setting environmental policy. Furthermore, when governments deal with areas such as the environment, they usually, with the exception of the USA, face a legislature with few investigative powers of its own and little in the way of staff expertise and resources to challenge the government line. Behind all of this lies the view of politicians that there are very few votes in issues concerning the environment.

In short, environmental policy, because it necessarily involves both international and technical matters, belongs to a class of policy-making that tends to be even less democratic than is the norm within political systems. Certainly, to the extent that environmental policy involves international co-operation, then it falls into the category of policy-making where there is least democratic influence. Those forces that shape policy in these kinds of issue-areas tend to be precisely the kind of forces that will peripheralise environmental concerns.

My *seventh* claim is that there is a great danger of falling into the trap of the technical fallacy in looking at the international politics of the environment. There are two aspects of this. First, there is the danger of assuming that there are technical solutions to environmental problems; this of course takes us back to the problems that functionalist writers had in forecasting the end of the nation-state. The distinction between on the one hand technical expertise, which is the realm of the specialist, and on the other political judgement, which is the concern of the politician, is not tenable. In this sense all technical judgements have a political dimension; there is no rarefied discourse free from normative considerations. Moreover, the assumption is that the technical case will be so overwhelming as to mean that all scientists or experts will see the same solutions as being necessary. Unfortunately, this looks like a very Western view of the problem, and certainly those environmental specialists who write from non-European or non-American perspectives tend to call for very different types of solutions to problems. Thus the degree of technical agreement may well be overstated. There is no one technical logic at work.

The second aspect of this problem is that those who speak of the need to create 'epistemic communities' are well aware of the limitations of these groupings [*Haas, 1990a; 1990b; 1992*]. Haas documents the critically important role that the epistemic community played in achieving the Montreal Protocol on CFCs, but goes on to note that there is nothing like that consensus in the area of global warming [*1990b: 359*]. Importantly, he points out that this is due to the fact that the costs of acting over global warming are so large, especially when the socio-economic consequences of that action would be considerable and by no means equally shared. The worry persists that epistemic communities are possible in only a small number of uncontroversial cases, so that their central role in the Montreal Protocol is not a guide to the future. Epistemic communities may be the exception that proves the rule. Thus the future may see far less technical agreement than the recent past, thereby reducing the importance of the claim that 'the scientific community' is united on the need to do something about the environment.

The *eighth* point is that the centrality of environmental issues may depend on the nature of wider political and economic developments. Put crudely, the environment may matter more during periods of little international tension, but matter much less if the old 'high politics' agenda reasserts itself. The fate of environmental concerns during the 1990–91 Gulf War is a case in point; when war is involved, environmental concerns do not take centre-stage. Of course, writers such as Mathews [*1989*] and Buzan [*1991*] have tried to widen the concept of security, so as to move away from the old definition of it as equalling the high politics of war/peace, but the worry is that environmental aspects of security will be seen by politicians as qualitatively different from the old war/peace agenda. Environmental threats to security may well be much more pressing than politicians accept at the moment, but these threats are long-term, whereas politicians are seldom interested in longer than the horizon of the next election. They are also by definition cross-national problems, thereby opening up the very political issues of who pays and who should do what; the old problems of collective goods and free-riding raise their heads. Finally, they are so completely tied into socio-economic matters that politicians see only costs in acting, whereas the costs of inaction will become apparent only in the very long run. Thus, not only are environmental threats to security unlikely to be taken seriously by any one actor, but they are also likely to be seen as far less important than immediate, or even potential, military or even economic threats. The international political system is not constructed in such a way as to make it in anyone's interest to act for the planet.

The *ninth* factor to be taken into account is that putting environmental issues at the centre of international political debate in the developed economies would mean facing up to the trade-offs required between environmental protection and growth or standard of living. This seems to me to be a very real problem for those who wish to see the environment treated more seriously. On the one hand there are obvious trade-offs *between* countries insofar as environmental measures require different responses from different states. This is where relative not absolute costs and opportunity costs become paramount. Given the centrality of economic growth to governments, especially in terms of how much its economy is growing in comparison to its competitors' economies, environmental regulation will always be seen as a potential complicating factor, both relatively and absolutely.

Within states, the very sad fact is that populations are rarely willing to sacrifice growth in income to accommodate environmental protection. Certainly, a policy of increasing taxation to protect the environment will be defeated by a rival party's (fallacious) claim that they can achieve the same result without the need for increased taxation. Whatever the strength of the argument that the environment needs to be taken more seriously, governments, and especially industry, are unwilling to agree if the consequence might be less growth, and, as Habermas noted in 1976, the central task of modern capitalist governments is to achieve economic growth. This is a very considerable barrier to environmental issues being more central in the future.

Finally, if the trade-off between environmental concerns and growth is important in the case of discussions within the developed economies, it is far more problematic when it comes to the case of relations between the developed and less-developed economies. The central problem here is widely known and so can be simply stated: those in less-developed economies see environmental questions in a very different light from those in richer economies. There are four main differences. First, those in poorer economies may see a concern for the environment manifesting itself in calls for all states to make sacrifices as reflecting a desire by the leaders of richer economies to slow down competition from poorer economies, since their industries tend to be less environmentally friendly. Second, this raises the question of who pays for environmental protection; after all, the richer economies have become richer in periods when the environment was not a constraint on growth and development. Why should poorer economies pay to protect a precarious environmental balance created by the richer economies? Third, there is the seriously problematic issue of *which* social, economic environmental problems need attention first when resources are very limited.

Finally, there is the danger that a concern with the environment is the latest form of imperialism, applying Western standards to the entire world, especially when the West has come to dominate without showing any such concern for the environment, and moreover ruining it in the process. Of these problems, the one concerning who pays is particularly serious when it comes to creating either epistemic communities or international regimes to deal with environmental problems. If rich countries are concerned about the environment and about the damage to it being done by inefficient and environmentally unsound industries in poorer economies, then why should they not foot the bill? Why should poorer countries pay to make their industry fit Western environmental standards when doing so makes their products far less competitive? In short, the environment is not some kind of neutral issue between economies and societies at very different levels of development.

Together, these ten factors mean that there are fundamental obstacles to environmental issues playing a more central role in international politics. In many ways this problem has been faced by academics who write on environmental issues. Hurrell and Kingsbury say on the very first page of the introduction to their edited book that a central question is: 'Can a fragmented and often highly conflictual political system made up of over 170 sovereign states and numerous other actors achieve the high (and historically unprecedented) levels of co-operation and policy co-ordination needed to manage environmental problems on a global scale?' [*Hurrell and Kingsbury, 1992: 1*]. No one could accuse them, or any other of the writers mentioned above, of being unaware of these difficulties. Yet I want to claim that each of these writers works within a specific theoretical framework, the effect of which is to cause them to see the problem in a specific, and contestable, way. As stated above, writers who are concerned with environmental issues tend to see international relations from a pluralist viewpoint. I will now turn to look at the problems of this viewpoint.

There are five points to note. The *first* is that those from within international relations who write on environmental issues tend to be a very closed group, nearly all of whom share the same theoretical assumptions. In this sense they are insiders, who work within a theoretical tradition, rather than questioning the boundaries and assumptions of that tradition. This means that they, just like most academic sub-groups (and here think of the power of the shared assumptions at work in the area of strategic studies as an example), build up an academic identity. This identity works just as Thomas Kuhn claimed scientific paradigms worked; that is to say it defines the relevant problems, gives clear theoretical guidelines as to how to address these problems, and defines what count as answers. The work on environmental regimes or epistemic communities (see the special issue of *International Organization* [*Haas, 1992*] as a classic example of this tendency) proceeds by accepting certain theoretical assumptions and then looking at the empirical domain from behind these lenses. Note that I am not singling out environmental work in international relations for this criticism; it applies to a vast range of approaches and perspectives. But, in each case the result is to limit enquiry and to discipline debate. As in all the social sciences, the really tough questions tend to be where paradigms clash, not where they rule unchallenged.

This leads me to a *second* point, which is that environmental issues will not be central to international relations as a discipline because the dominant theoretical tradition in the subject, realism, does not see such 'low politics' issues as central. For the realism that is taught on the majority of university courses, the environment is no more than either a setting in which state actions take place or a relatively minor set of issues that should not be allowed to detract from the 'real' agenda of the subject. Not only does realism treat environmental issues as peripheral, but, far more importantly, it gives the student a set of very powerful reasons to distrust those who claim that they are or should be. These people are wishful dreamers who do not understand the way that the world *really* is; moreover there have been important predecessors to the modern environmental specialists, in the form of the inter-war idealists, and realists claim that these people did enormous damage by concentrating on what should be rather than what was.

For realists, then, international relations is all about states maximising power and the central concerns are focused on war and the threat of the use of force. To these specialists it is not simply irrelevant to stress the environment as an issue, it is downright dangerous. In essence, the subject of international relations has been so dominated by realism that other approaches are always struggling to challenge its claims. Of course, this is made all the worse by the connection between the realist study of the subject and the practice of international relations. Each reinforces the other, with the result that Realists claim to be telling it as it is, in contrast to the dreamers who worry about issues that are never going to be central to the leaders of states.

Given the troubles of the world since the cold war, it is easy to see how generations of students can be lulled into the belief that Yugoslavia or the Gulf are central issues in a way that the ozone layer or global warming are not. In addition, the continuation of conflicts only goes to show how marked are the continuities that exist in the states-system. Is the current world really that different to that which Thucydides wrote about two and a half thousand years ago? For realists the answers are clear. Accordingly, environmental issues are merely the latest in a long line of issues that forecast the end of the state and the transcendence of international politics. The current interest in them reflects nothing more than a concern that is easy to have at the end of the cold war, an interest that will soon give way as more traditional 'high politics' re-assert themselves.

Having said which, realists have it both ways by then claiming that their theoretical perspective can deal with environmental issues. In this sense, the environment may well be an issue but, crucially, one that will be dealt with in exactly the same ways and by the same actors (predominantly states) as all other issues. Hence the resort to regime theory by many environment specialists is a bit of a risk, since this is an approach that can be claimed as much by the realists as by the pluralists. Indeed, the more that relative gains and losses seem to matter in environmental regimes, and the more that states are central to decision-making, the more that Realists can co-opt the environment as fitting within their purview. Either way the environment gets peripheralised. The dominance of realist theoretical assumptions, whatever the issue being dealt with and whatever the methodology being used, remains the dominant feature of the discipline of international relations, and this poses a very deep challenge to those who see the environment as central.

A *third* factor is that there is another approach to international relations that has a lot to say about environmental issues, yet which is itself very marginalised in the discipline. This is the structuralist or globalist approach, influenced much by Marxist political economy. According to this approach, the central feature of international relations is that it takes place in a capitalist system. Thus, the main feature of environmental issues is what they reveal about the development of the world capitalist system. This fits in with a point made previously about the imperialist overtones of some environmental writings. The main point at issue here is that environmental issues do not fit automatically into one theoretical lens, despite the fact that nearly all writing is contained within the pluralist framework. The very same issues can be seen in very different ways from the Structuralist perspective. Again, to speak of the international politics of the environment begs the question of what exactly is the view of international politics involved.

Fourth, it should be noted that whatever the theoretical viewpoint involved, there are many other contenders for the most important issue of the subject of international relations. The discipline has traditionally treated war as the central issue, and this automatically privileges realism. But there are many other possible focal points. Human rights, gender issues, poverty and disease are just some, and these seem so important to many of those academics who do not buy into the Realist presentation of the world as a 'given' as to challenge seriously the centrality of environmental issues. In fact, this one point seems to be the main reason why the environment may become far less important as an issue than it is at present. This is not to say that it will not be part of an alternative agenda for the subject of international relations, only that there are many 'mainstream' issues and 'alternative' issues to challenge it.

One does not have to be a realist to think that there are many issues other than the environment which deserve to be treated as far more central than they are. It comes down to values, of course, which are the very thing that realists say they leave behind in their search for the 'realities' of the discipline. Yet there are many value systems other than realism which would place environmental issues below others in any hierarchy of importance. It would be wrong to imply some kind of strict alternative set of choices; indeed many environmental specialists would both define that term very widely and would see other issues as equally important; yet this should not hide the extent to which a concern with the environment reflects a specific set of concerns and interests and these are by no means universal in their application. And, importantly, the worry persists that conflict and war will easily push aside environmental concerns, especially if they affect the richer states. Therefore, both the developing set of 'alternative' concerns of international relations and the traditional theoretical framework of the discipline have reasons to treat the environment as less central than is assumed, or suggested, by those who write on it.

Finally, because the discipline of international relations is so obsessed with the state, then just as the state can treat environmental issues as of relatively minor importance, in deeds if not in words, so must the mainstream of the subject keep to 'where the action is'. Redefining security, in the Buzan [*1991*] sense, is very contradictory here. On the one hand, Buzan wants to broaden security to include environmental security: yet, on the other, he still locates his discussion at the state level. For Buzan, it is the state that is the primary referent of security studies, and not, for example, the individual or the society. Thus even if security is broadened in the way Buzan wants, it will still focus on the concerns of states. Since states will not be very much concerned with environmental issues because these are not electorally important, then even a broader security studies will have little role for environmental concerns. To take the environment seriously requires shifting the level of analysis away from the state to the society or the individual.

In conclusion, I have attempted to point out that environmental issues are likely to be less central than either practitioners in the environmental movement or academics who write on the subject suggest. To repeat a point made above, this is not to say that this is what I want to be the case; it is simply that much of the work on environmental politics overestimates the importance of the environment as a domestic political or an international political issue. My concern has been to show how there is a powerful set of economic and political interests that treat other issues as far more important than environmental concerns. Publics may well profess concern over the environment but this rarely translates into a political force, the recent advances of West European green parties notwithstanding. Internationally, the environment is of real concern to few leaders, and relative not absolute costs and gains of action or inaction are of most importance to them. The environment is simply not important enough to transcend that logic.

My contention is that environmental specialists should never underestimate how much entrenched power is behind the organs of state power that they are implicitly or explicitly attacking. The academic community of environmental scholars is very aware of this situation, as Hurrell and Kingsbury make clear, but even then there is a tendency to work within a pluralist framework which, as noted above, assumes exactly what needs to be confronted. Of course the regime literature provides a framework for analysing environmental issues, but what if that framework is itself undermined by rival accounts? Too much of the work of writers such as Oran Young and Peter Haas *proposes* regimes or epistemic communities as ways of dealing with the problems of the environment, whereas these approaches themselves need to be analysed and critiqued. In short, there is little in the way of critical analysis in the environmental literature. As a result optimism and suggesting solutions dominates the writing. My worry is that this will make it easy for environmental work to be marginalised.

In summary, my overall claim is that the environment is not a central political issue, and that it will not become one. Those environmental issues that leaders do deal with at an international level are not so pressing as to result in a transcendence of the states-system, and thereby fall into the same processes and procedures as all other issues. Within international politics there are many other issues that vie with the environment and for most of the world's population these are far more important.

Crucially, it is the inter-relationship between practice and theory that explains why environmental issues are in danger of being marginalised in the academic world as well as in the world of practitioners. Both in the states-system and in the academic study of international relations there is a dominance of specific interests, such that proposing that the environment needs to be taken seriously threatens the whole edifice just as would a proposal to take women's lives and opportunities seriously. Neither can be fitted in easily since to do so would undermine the cosy relationship between knowledge and power. That is what is at stake in any attempt to make environmental concerns more central, and that is why they may well stay on the periphery.

REFERENCES

Art, Robert and Robert Jervis (1993), *International Politics: Enduring Concepts and Contemporary Issues*, 3rd edn., New York: HarperCollins.

Brown, Seyom (1992), *International Relations in a Changing Global System: Towards a Theory of the World Polity*, Boulder, CO: Westview.

Buzan, Barry (1991), *People, States and Fear: An Agenda for International Security Studies in the Post-Cold War Era*, 2nd edn., Hemel Hempstead: Harvester Wheatsheaf.

Dobson, Andrew (1990), *Green Political Thought*, London: Unwin Hyman.

Dunleavy, Patrick, Gamble, Andrew and Gillian Peele (eds.) (1990), *Developments in British Politics 3*, Basingstoke: Macmillan.

Goodin, Robert (1992), *Green Political Theory*, Cambridge: Polity Press.

Haas, Peter (1990a), *Saving the Mediterranean: The Politics of International Environmental Cooperation*, New York: Columbia University Press.

Haas, Peter (1990b), 'Obtaining International Environmental Protection through Epistemic Consensus', *Millennium: Journal of International Studies*, Vol.19, No.3, pp.347–63.

Haas, Peter (ed.) (1992), 'Knowledge, Power, and International Policy Coordination', a special issue of *International Organization*, Vol.46, No.1.

Habermas, Jurgen (1976), *Legitimation Crisis*, London: Heinemann.

Hurrel, Andrew and Benedict Kingsbury (eds.) (1992), *The International Politics of the Environment*, Oxford: Oxford University Press.

Mathews, Jessica Tuchman (1989), 'Redefining Security', *Foreign Affairs*, Vol.68, No.2, pp.162–77.

Smith, Steve (1986), 'Reasons of State', in David Held and Christopher Pollitt (eds.), *New Forms of Democracy*, London: Sage Publications, pp.192–217.

Thomas, Caroline (1992), *The Environment in International Relations*, London: RIIA.

Weale, Albert (1992), *The New Politics of Pollution*, Manchester: Manchester University Press.

Young, Oran (1989), *International Cooperation: Building Regimes for Natural Resources and the Environment*, Ithaca, NY: Cornell University Press.

Young, Oran (1990), 'Global Environmental Change and International Governance', *Millennium: Journal of International Studies*, Vol.19, No.3, pp.337–46.

Global Environmental Degradation, Modernity and Environmental Knowledge

JULIAN SAURIN

Modernisation and global environmental degradation have coincided historically. When the relationship between the two is examined, globalised modernity can be seen to generate particular modes of knowledge, and simultaneously to displace, marginalise and then destroy others. Specific forms of large-scale environmental degradation occur as a routine consequence of modernity as is well illustrated by the example of agriculture and its attendant expert knowledge system. The distancing of the site of degradation from its original cause confuses the allocation of responsibility. In the post-Rio context, this poses enormous public policy problems regarding the level of legislation – local, national, international or transnational.

The Forms of Modernity

Without rehearsing the vast and continuing debates surrounding modernisation[1] and modernity, key elements are selected here for explanation: the processes of distanciation and the mediation of action; the salient characteristics of modernity such as technical-rationalism and bureaucracy; and the modes of knowledge generated and marginalised by modernity, specifically *episteme* and *techne*.

The core claim about modernity is that large-scale and systematic degradation occurs from its ordinary and standard practices. Degrada-

Julian Saurin is a Lecturer in International Relations in the School of African and Asian Studies, Sussex University. Acknowledgement is due to students and faculty staff of the International Relations Group at Sussex University, especially Dr Jan Aarte Scholte, Dr Marc Williams, Margaret Felton, Pam Shaw, Stephanie Lay and Yoshiko Ishiga, as well a to Caroline Thomas and Amanda Saurin, in the preparation of this contribution. The usual author's disclaimers apply.

tion here refers to anthropogenic environmental degradation, understood principally as the breaching or rupture of eco-systemic tolerances in
a systematic and reiterated fashion, a process derived out of the persistent
subordination of eco-systemic requirements to the logics of capital,
bureaucracy, consumption and so on. However, the processes of distanciation and mediation of action mean that the normality of degradation
inhibits countervailing actions. It is therefore not carelessness nor even a
lack of an awareness of degradation that constitutes the major barrier to
ecological sensitivity and propriety, but the inability to contain the
diffused manufacture of degradation. In this respect, there are strong
resonances and analytical inspiration in Bauman's [*1989*] analysis of
modernity and the Holocaust, and Sen's [*1982*] analysis of modern
commodity markets and famine. For Bauman it was the *mundane* operation of a bureaucratised and highly rationalised order that were precondi-
tions for the Holocaust to take place. For Sen it is the *normal* operation of
the markets that leads to famine. In both cases, it is not the exceptional
and unique that fundamentally informs such cruelties and degradations;
indeed as Rubinstein [*1978*] eloquently contested: 'It is an error to
imagine that civilisation and savage cruelties are antitheses ... In our
times the cruelties, like most other aspects of our world, have become far
more effectively administered than ever before' (quoted in Bauman
[*1989: 195*]). What distinguishes Bauman from Sen is that in the former
the conditions of modernity are necessary but not sufficient for the
Holocaust to have occurred – the forms of modernity had to be mobilised
for a specific purpose through the political project of Nazism – whereas in
the latter the characteristics of modern commodity markets are both
necessary and sufficient in themselves to generate famine. It is in the
differences between intended consequences, unintended consequences
and unintended but foreseeable consequences that the problem of global
environmental degradation needs to be interpreted.[2]

It is in the question of administrative form and organisational order
(and the type of knowledge generated therein) that modernity and
environmental degradation are most closely bound, alongside what
Giddens terms time–space distanciation and disembedding.[3] Principally
through technological change, industrialisation and commodification,
including the massive diffusion of symbolic tokens (such as money) space,
place and time become ruptured and distanced. Not only are production
processes and cycles extended over longer and longer time horizons, but
their spatial location becomes increasingly organised globally. Giddens
[*1990: 19*] argues that 'the advent of modernity increasingly tears space
away from place by fostering relations between absent others, location-
ally distant from any given situation of face-to-face interaction'. Moder-

nisation entails a fundamental severance between production and consumption: increasingly we produce what we do not consume, and we consume what we do not produce. The separation of material production and consumption also involves the removal and abstraction of knowledge about that self-same relationship. Thus, neither a perfunctory knowledge of the technical procedures of production nor the environmental circumstances and costs of production are visible to the distanced consumer. Furthermore, according to Giddens:

> In conditions of modernity, place becomes increasingly phantasmagoric: that is to say, locales are thoroughly penetrated by and shaped in terms of social influences quite distant from them. What structures the locale is not simply that which is present on the scene; the 'visible form' of the locale conceals the distanciated relations which determine its nature [Giddens, 1990: 19].

The effect of time–space distanciation is to render opaque – through the mediation of action – the relationship between intention, action and outcome, thereby confusing our comprehension of causality. Thus a crucial aspect of modernity is the exponential increase in the mediation of action which Bauman [1989: 24] defines as being 'the phenomenon of one's action being performed for one by someone else, by an intermediate person who stands between me and my action, making it impossible for me to experience it directly'. Thus, when we ask the question who or what causes deforestation or global warming it is immensely difficult to attribute responsibility from a simple depiction of agency. Held and Thompson argue that through time-space distanciation;

> Social systems [become] increasingly 'stretched' across time and space, [and] the link between social activity and spatial location becomes ever more tenuous, and space itself becomes commodified and constructed ... At the same time the traditions and routines which provided the individuals with a sense of 'ontological security' – that is, with a sense of confidence or trust that the world is as it appears to be – are transformed, and to some extent undermined, by the rapidly changing character of modern societies [1989: 8].

Distanciation is both constitutive of, and constituted by, the process of disembedding and re-embedding. By disembedding Giddens means 'the "lifting out" of social relations from local contexts of interaction and their restructuring across indefinite spans of time-space' [1990: 21]. Both the industrialisation and globalisation of agriculture and food systems confirms this process perhaps most clearly through the reconstitution of time-space when, as Goodman and Redclift argue:

> With [the] simultaneous access to geographically separate production zones, the formation of the world market freed industrial capitals from the seasonality of individual national agricultures, approximating the continuous production process characteristic of industry [*1991: 96*].

To the extent that mass markets required furnishing, so local ecological tolerances, in part shaped by growing seasons and other ecological cycles, become subordinated to the demands of a market-led logic.

It is in this regard that the application of techniques, methods and, hence, institutions which evolved in one socio-historical context to a distinct socio-historical setting are central to the globalised forms of degradation. For example, the monocultural agricultural techniques developed in the temperate zone of north-west Europe (with relatively restricted bio-diversity) from which 'Fordist' methods more easily arise, are transferred to tropical or sub-tropical zones containing great bio-diversity.[4] The environmental, financial and social costs of such a transfer are substantial, but have been socially and historically obfuscated. Once again, as Giddens contends, the significance of distanciated relations is that '[d]isembedded institutions greatly extend the scope of time–space distanciation ... This phenomenon serves to open up manifold possibilities of change by breaking free from the restraints of local habits and practices' [*1990: 20*]. However, to have this 'breaking free' effect, coordination across space and time is vital. It is precisely the development of such coordination that characterises the modernisation project.[5] Thus, modernisation simultaneously entails both a breaking free from 'traditional' constraints and restrictions, and intervention in and fragmentation of new social and spatial territory and their incorporation into modernity. The features of distanciation, mediation of action, disembedding and re-embedding inform the particular processes of modernisation, especially industrialisation, urbanisation, technological transformation of agriculture, rationalisation of authority, rationalising bureaucracy, the weakening of ascriptive ties and the rise of achievement, 'disenchantment' and the growth of science and secularisation [*Marglin, 1990; Banuri, 1990a*]. Also of critical importance is the reflexivity of knowledge – that is to say, the manner by which development is measured and assessed.

Turning to the quintessential characteristic of modernity, technical rationalism – and its attendant consequences of bureaucracy, specialisation of function, and expert knowledge – Giddens argues that the expert systems sponsored by bureaucracy are disembedding mechanisms because 'they remove social relations from the immediacies of context' [*1990: 28*]. More specifically

> an expert system disembeds in the same way as symbolic tokens [for example money], by providing guarantees of expectations across distanciated time-space. This 'stretching' of social systems is achieved via the impersonal tests applied to evaluate technical knowledge [*1990: 28*].

It is in the impersonality test and the associated claim to the universalisable quality of expert knowledge and expert systems that the transference of inappropriate, indeed fundamentally degrading institutions and practices occur. Tariq Banuri [*1990a: 87*] usefully specifies the metacultural forms of modernity which have been globalised, and which imply a coherent epistemology. These can be portrayed as the legitimisation of modern values which would encompass:

(a) Exchange theory   – impersonal relations, buyer–seller.
(b) Production theory– impersonal relations, employer– employee.
(c) Jurisprudence   – blind justice, universal, impersonal.
(d) Education theory – universal content (for example the National Curriculum, contrasting with Freire and Illich).
(e) Political science – bureaucratised efficiency, impersonal, rational, universalisable.
(f) Technology   – objective, expert, partitioning of knowledge.
(g) Moral philosophy– abstract principles.
(h) Communication   – impersonal, impartial.

Although Zygmunt Bauman uses the terms 'civilising process' for what I refer to as modernising development, his analysis of the redeployment of impersonal social power through bureaucratisation and technical rationalism in such processes is apposite. He writes:

> The increase in the physical and or psychic distance between the act and its consequences achieves more than the suspension of moral inhibition; it quashes the moral significance of the act and thereby preempts all conflict between personal standard of moral decency and immorality of the social consequences of the act. With most of the socially significant actions mediated by a long chain of complex causal and functional dependencies, moral dilemmas recede from sight, while the occasions for more scrutiny and conscious moral choice become increasingly rare [*1989: 25*].

Out of Bauman's observation about action, consequences and responsibility, I want to highlight the dimension of knowledge as being critical to empowerment in so far as self-determination presupposes appreciation of alternative possibilities. Within the rational-bureaucratic order, in which functional specialisation or division of labour entails the segmentation and fragmentation of knowledge, actions are confirmed as appropriate to the extent to which they fulfil readily identifiable functional requirements. No extra-functional considerations are necessary, still less desirable. Returning to Bauman again, and anticipating Shiva's depiction below of Western science as being violent, he comments that 'the civilising process is, among other things, a process of divesting the use and deployment of violence from moral calculus, and of emancipating the desiderata of rationality from interference of ethical, norms or moral inhibitions' [*Bauman, 1989: 28*].

If modernising development can be portrayed generally as the emancipation of rationality from ethics, norms and moral inhibitions, then an enclosure can be seen as critical to this differentiation. Enclosure as an aspect of modernity has not been generally identified, at least not formally, except in terms of the process of privatisation of property. The movement from commons to enclosure has formed a central dimension of the ecological critique of modernity, and it is especially revealing to consider the relationship between the sociology of the commons and the sociological consequences of enclosure particularly in respect to environmental understanding and knowledge.

Enclosure is both a physically delimiting process (of land, forests, villages) and also a social process of defining boundaries and social relationships (division of labour, property ownership). Correspondingly, it is also a process in which knowledge is re-constituted and reformed. The salient feature of modernisation as enclosure can be identified as the tragedy of the commons wherein the tragedy of enclosure is one of privatisation and commodification [*The Ecologist, 1992: 123–55*]. As such, enclosure 'cordons off those aspects of the environment that are deemed "useful" to the encloser ... and defines them, and them alone, as valuable'. In so far as property becomes privately enclosed, so it becomes commodified and thereby tradeable.[6] The redeployment of socio-economic power concomitant with enclosure 'redefines how the environment is managed, by whom and for whose benefits' (in the language of neo-classical economics this would centrally include the externalisation of all possible costs, or the internalisation of the least cost). In this respect 'enclosure not only redefines the forum in which decisions are made but also redefines whose voice counts in that forum'. The notion of 'voice' itself is construed as one in which particular forms of knowledge are recognised and others are not; thus, 'enclosure opens the way for the bureaucratisation and enclosure of knowledge itself' in which, 'all conflict is settled by criteria determined by the enclosers'. Finally, the enclosure of knowledge entails the replacement of discussion with measurement as the basis of decision-making.

Turning now to a detailed examination of knowledge and environmental knowledge in particular I wish, first, to identify the principal distinctions between Western-modern and non-modern science, and then turn secondly to the differentiation of modes of knowledge. The dominating status of post-Enlightenment science (what could be called in shorthand 'Western science') has been achieved through a readily identifiable social and economic development strategy, which itself has generated a particular relationship with Nature [*Merchant, 1980*], and which increasingly sought to equate science with knowledge *per se*. Western science therefore laid claims to the monopoly possession not only of knowledge, but also of what constituted knowledge, not least because of the tremendously strong teleological characteristic of Western science which judged other epistemologies in terms of their contribution to the fulfilment of, or deflection from, this *telos*.

One of the most powerful critiques of dominant scientific rationalism and its social and environmental impact is that put forward by Vandana Shiva. Her broad criticism of scientific rationalism rests upon the 'violence of reductionist science' upon socio-economic practices. She contends [*1987*] that modern science is 'violent even in peaceful domains' such as in medicine (radical surgery, chemo-therapies) or in agriculture (genetic engineering, pesticide use). This claim rests upon four propositions identified as follows.

First, there is

> violence against the subject of knowledge. It is perpetrated socially
> through the sharp divide between the expert and non-expert – a
> divide which converts the majority of non-experts into non-knowers
> even in those areas of life in which the responsibility of practice and
> action rests with them [*Shiva, 1987: 243–4*].[7]

Second, there is 'the violence against the object of knowledge' [*Shiva, 1987: 244*]. This is particularly the case in the biological sciences (vivisection, genetic engineering) and in agricultural sciences (mono-cropping, 'mining' forests) but also in the social sciences such as economics (human beings become 'factors of production' through the commodification of labour), and overall violence against the object of knowledge is clear when the 'innate integrity of nature' is destroyed.

Third, there is the 'violence against the beneficiary of knowledge.

Contrary to the claim of modern science that the people are ultimately the beneficiaries of scientific knowledge, the people – particularly the poor – are its worst victims' [*Shiva 1987: 244*]. This comes about in large part through the 'objectification' and 'abstraction' of people as 'consumers', 'producers', 'units' and so on.

Fourth, there is 'violence against knowledge' [*Shiva, 1987: 244*]. Other modes of knowledge which do not fall within, and cannot be confirmed by, the scientific rationalist mode are dismissed or ignored.

The identification of Western science as reductionist has been based on at least five assumptions. Vandana Shiva has identified these assumptions;

(a) that a system is reducible to its parts; (b) that all systems are made up of the same basic constituents which are discrete and atomistic; (c) that all systems have the same basic processes which are mechanical; (d) that knowledge of the parts of a system gives the knowledge of the whole system; and (e) that 'experts' and 'specialists' are the only legitimate knowledge-seekers and knowledge-justifiers [*Shiva, 1987: 245*].

Contrasting Western reductionist science with an as yet unspecified 'non-Western', 'non-modern' knowledge, Tariq Banuri develops what he labels the *impersonality postulate of modernity*, in which he suggests that 'impersonal relations are [seen in Western rationality] as inherently superior to personal relations [*1990a: 79*]. The impersonality postulate is built upon three key elements which Banuri claims inform all cultural maps – namely, the theories of self (ontology), the theories of knowledge (epistemology) and the theories of the universe (cosmology). Claiming that 'these cultural maps are both constituted by human agency and yet at the same time they are the medium of such constitution' [*1990: 81*] a matrix can be abstracted from Banuri's contrasting of the (superior) impersonal with the (inferior) personal;

	Impersonal	Personal
Ontology	Individualism	Holism
Epistemology	Positivism/literalism	Communication/ hermeneutics/semiotics
Cosmology	Instrumental	Relational

Banuri correctly claims that the impersonality postulate is 'pervasive as the foundational element of various Western theories', and that this is the case because the personal map is context-specific while the impersonal map is universal, and, so it is claimed, universalisable [*1990a: 82–3*]. The strength of this claim is most powerfully confirmed in the universality and impersonality of the natural sciences, but in the social sciences Banuri convincingly claims that it is most evident in 'neo-classical economic theory, which clearly defines the self as separate from the environment by treating preferences and attributes as metaphysical entities and the environment as an external datum' [*1990: 84*]. It would be perhaps useful to draw the empirical and historical implications of these claims, and this can be done through two examples. First, take the infamous article by Garrett Hardin [*1968*] in *Science* titled 'The Tragedy of the Commons'. Following the description of the herdsmen [*sic*] overusing the common pasture he writes:

> At this point the inherent logic of the commons remorselessly generates tragedy ... Adding together the component partial utilities the rational herdsman concludes that the only sensible course for him to pursue is to add another animal to his herd. And another; and another ... But this is the conclusion reached by each and every rational herdsman sharing commons. Therein is the tragedy.

Here is the application of 'superior' impersonal analysis and depiction of the community in question – rational, individualist, instrumentalist and positivist. I want to leave this example with the precise and biting criticism of Vandana Shiva who is worth quoting at length:

> Hardin chooses not to disclose the assumptions underlying this perverse logic (which is Hardin's but which, by an act of trans-ference, he foists on the poor unprotesting herdsman). These assumptions are: (a) that each herdsman sees himself as an atomised individual who is pitted against the rest of the community in a deadly competition for grabbing as much of the common goods as he can; (b) that in all societies production is not for satisfaction of needs, but for exchange in a monetised market with a view to making immediate profit; and (c) that every herdsman is so short sighted ('rational' in Hardin's vocabulary) as to sacrifice his future survival on the altar of immediate gain [*Shiva, 1987: 249*].

The second example comes from irrigation systems. In scientific irriga-tion the principles of distribution are assumed to be impersonal, universal and not context-specific. Irrigation supply is determined in terms of units, inputs, outputs and effective demands (notice how human beings do not appear in this list). Carl Widstrand notes in reference to the Gezira scheme (World Bank funded) that

> the 'average' farmer gets an 'average' amount of water for an 'average' crop over the year. Everyone gets water over the year but not necessarily at the precise or necessary moments. This concept is closely related to the idea of 'normal rainfall' and other peculiarities of the 'folklore of the normal' that simplifies administrative thought [*1988: 142*].

The 'normal', 'average' and abstracted 'unit' is distinctly impersonal, but equally available and amenable to rational and scientific ordering. Examples of the impersonality postulate as constituting the guide of knowledge and practice are legion. The special issue of *The Ecologist*, 'Whose Common Future?' [*1992*] is replete with them, but one could similarly turn to detailed studies such as those by Ramachandra Guha [*1990*] on scientific forestry and community knowledge in the foothills of the Himalayas or Vandana Shiva's *The Violence of the Green Revolution* [*1990*]. The central point to note here is that 'far from being a "free-for-all", use of the commons is closely regulated through communal rules and practices' [*The Ecologist, 1992: 127*].

Unlike scientific and industrialised agriculture organised on the principles of 'economically competitive food production' in which 'Fordist' production methods dominate over ecological sensitivity,

> each commons regime may be as different culturally from the next as all are from, say, a factory. But it is not only their cultural diversity that makes such regimes difficult to 'capture' in technical or universal terms. Ivan Illich makes this point when he says that the 'law establishing the commons was unwritten ... because what it protected was a reality much too complex to fit into paragraphs ... what makes the commons work cannot easily be encoded in written or fixed or "replicable" forms'. In other words no fixed essence, no 'average unit' nor hypothesised norm can be extracted, quantified and universalised into an impersonal rational-legal code, the consequence of which would otherwise be to 'transfer local power outside the community' [*The Ecologist, 1992: 126*].

Stephen Marglin, using the binary opposition of Banuri's impersonality postulate (personal/impersonal) has sought to distinguish types of knowledge further. First of all, borrowing terms from Keynes, he identifies two forms of truth. He uses the term 'organic' for 'propositions the truth of which depends on the beliefs of agents', and the term 'atomic' for 'propositions the truth of which is independent of these beliefs'

[*Marglin, 1990: 15*]. Clearly, organic truth is associated with the personal in so far as it is context-specific, whilst the atomic truth is impersonal, universal and context-free. Secondly, Marglin seeks to distinguish modes of knowledge further into two types, the *episteme* and the *techne*. I want to quote Marglin at length here:

> In the West, the knowledge system of management, particularly scientific management, is characterised not only by impersonality, by its insistence on logical deduction from self-evident axioms as the only basis for knowledge, but also by its emphasis on analysis, its claim that knowledge must be articulate in order to exist, its pretence to universality, its cerebral nature, its orientation to theory and empirical verification of theory, and its odd mixture of egalitarianism within the knowledge community and hierarchical superiority *vis-à-vis* outsiders. This system is called *episteme*.

Against this atomic system of knowledge Marglin poses an organic system of knowledge:

> By contrast, labour's knowledge – called techne – is not only personal, it differs from episteme in other fundamental ways ... it defies the analytic decomposability of episteme; it is often implicit rather than articulate; recognising the limits of context, it makes no claim to universality; it is tactile and emotional where episteme is cerebral; it is practical rather than theoretical, and geared towards discovery rather than to verification; finally, techne reverses the power relations of episteme: it is hierarchical internally but pluralistic externally [*Marglin, 1990: 58*].

Based on the working assumption that agriculture has become industrialised if 'industrialism presupposes the regularised social organisation of production' [*Giddens, 1990: 58*], then the techniques and methods of its regulation requires the constant supply of uniform and standardised information about production.

Globalisation and Modernity

The structures of modernity, including knowledge, identified above are not spatially restricted to the territory of the modern state; rather, structures have become globalised. Fundamentally structures should not be understood as rigidly determining and immutable frameworks, but as 'rules and resources' which at once enable and constrain social action. As such, this duality of structures identifies 'both the medium and outcome of the practices which constitute social systems'. Following Giddens, Sewell reiterates that social systems

> have no existence apart from the practices that constitute them, and these practices are reproduced by the 'recursive' (i.e, repeated) enactments of structures. Structures are not the patterned social practices that make up social systems, *but the principles that pattern those practices* [emphasis added] [*Sewell, 1992: 6*].

Substituting the term 'rule' for schema, both of which have virtual existence instanciated in action (that is, put into practice), Sewell argues that schemas are virtual to the extent that 'they cannot be reduced to their existence in any particular practice or any particular location in space and time: they can be actualised in a potentially broad and unpredetermined range of institutions' [*1992: 8*]. Thus, adopting Sewell's amendment one can examine how it is not the actual social practices – be this particular bureaucratic practices, particular production practices, for example – that are spread globally, but the schemas themselves. The transposable nature of schemas means that 'they can be applied to a wide and not fully predictable range of cases outside the context in which they are initially learned' [*1992: 17*]. If this analytical claim is pursued, then actual and specific forms of environmentally degrading practice do not need to be globalised for the structuring of global environmental degradation to occur. Instead, the schemas – or to use another synonym, organising principles – require transportation and diffusion.

The study of global environmental change has most usually inherited the analytical categories of either the natural sciences or of the geographical sciences. Thus, for example, Turner *et al.* [*1990: 14–22*], identify two overlapping types of global environmental change: systemic change and cumulative change. Global systemic change is defined as such if 'its attributes at any locale can potentially affect its attributes anywhere else, or even alter the global state of the system'. Thus, 'globally systemic changes need not be caused by global-scale activity; only the physical impacts of the activity need be global in scale' [*1990: 15*]. Turner *et al.* define global cumulative change as such if 'it occurs on a worldwide scale, or represents a significant fraction of the total environmental phenomenon or global resource'. Thus 'changes of this type include those that are local in domain but which are widely replicated, and which in sum constitute change in the whole human environment' [*1990: 16*]. Whilst these understandings are useful, they evade the critical social quality of global change, not least in respect of crucial local environmental degradation which occurs as a consequence of deeply distanciated and disembedded relations. Such local degradation may not merit being characterised as systemic or cumulative yet nevertheless their social, economic and political causes may be global in extent.

Rather than employing such restrictive categories, a different conception of the 'global' in relation to 'globalisation' needs to be developed. Following Robertson [*1992: 51*], globalisation can 'best [be] understood as indicating the problem of the form in terms of which the world becomes "united"' [*1992: 51*]. Robertson's central criticism of Giddens (which I reject if one accepts Sewell's critical amendments) is that he conflates modernity with globality. The transposable quality of schemas of modernity – notably commodification, technical rationalism through expert systems, bureaucratisation and industrialisation – are precisely the means by which 'globalisation as a concept comes to refer both to the compression of the world and the intensification of consciousness of the world as a whole' [*1992: 8*]. Robertson is nevertheless correct in identifying the inability to explain globalisation as arising from sociology's engagement in comparative methodologies of societies and international relations' examination of the interactions between states: in both cases an intellectual nationalism fundamentally inhibits the study of globalisation as the process of ordering *across* societies [*Scholte, 1993a; 1993b*]. Rather than system integration – for which the term internationalisation may apply – the process of globalisation entails 'normatively binding relationships among people across the world' [*Robertson, 1992: 7*]. These binding relationships are organised around the schemas identified above: it is through a 'bundle' of such schema that we can identify modernity.

What I have in mind here as the representation of globalisation, is the transposition and reproduction of 'bundles of schema', or, what has been termed *metaculture*. What is meant by metaculture? Robertson suggests the following:

> Metacultures (or cultural codes) constrain conceptions of culture, mainly in terms of deep rooted, implicit assumptions concerning relationships between wholes and parts, individuals and societies, in-groups and out-groups, and societies and the world as a whole [*1992: 41*].

Tying this to Robertson's specific conception of globalisation noted above, I want to argue that the concrete structuration of the world is founded upon the ordering principles of modernity identified earlier, and that these in turn both constitute and are constitutive of a metaculture of enclosed and enclosing scientific rationality.

Under such conceptions of modernity and globalisation the possibility and capacity of state agencies to mediate or temper the effects of

distanciated relations and thereby offset global environmental degradation appears severely limited. Such a possibility would entail the wilful
engagement of the state and modernity against itself: it would require the
intentional re-articulation of alternative schema. Having said this, the
globalisation of technical rationalism, expert systems and so on should
not be understood to mean the complete supplanting of non-modern
schema, but hegemony over them.[8]

Finally, I want to apply these ideas to a specific area of global
environmental degradation; the schema of commodification upon agriculture and biodiversity.

Agricultural Modernisation and Environmental Degradation

It is particularly revealing to examine the relationship between the
modernisation of agriculture and global environmental degradation for
three chief reasons: first, the clear manner in which agriculture has
become commodified; second, the manner in which agriculture became
transformed through its industrialisation (thereby disclosing elements of
other industrialisation processes); and third, the manner in which commodification and industrialisation both engender and require technically
rationalist organisational and epistemological modes.

Through both the use of instrumental power and the exploitation of
structural power the UK and then the USA were able, from the middle of
the nineteenth century, to establish an international food regime which
gradually, but definitively, eroded the local and national basis of agriculture.[9] The extension of the agricultural base beyond state boundaries
was achieved through several transformations which were distinctly
modern in character.

First, the widespread commodification and hence commercialisation of
agriculture enabled trade in agricultural produce to be spread over
greater distances thereby transcending dietary, ecological and productive
methods which were previously geographically and socially discrete.
Thus, whereas socio-economic development had been largely informed
by the local or national agricultural, investment and ritual cycles which
were mutually embedded in one another, commodified and commer-
cialised agriculture entailed the subordination of local calendars – which
would determine what was eaten, when it was eaten, in what quantities,
in what social context and so on – to the exigencies of globalised
agriculture following its own multiple logics and rhythms [*Marglin, 1990:
19; Goodman and Redclift, 1991*]. Whatever the specific quality of these
logics and rhythms, what became clear is that they were radically disembedded from the locale. As Marglin [*1990: 25*] argues: 'it is precisely the

intrusion of disembedded knowledge in the form of an agronomic episteme [for example the impersonality of commodification] that undermines the core values of sociality as commerciality displaces subsistence'.

The global transposition of commodification has the consequence that epistemic systems rooted in diverse eco-systems and the concomitant diverse cultural systems become weakened through the subordination to and agricultural episteme which is based on monocultures and mass production. As distanciation deepens, so knowledge regarding production and consumption recedes. The central consideration in this regard is made by Friedmann when she says:

> We do not know the social cost of the food we eat because it is not included in the price. This is true even for domestic food such as wheat whose true cost will be known only when the effects of unsustainable agricultural practices on natural resources and human health begins to be counted as part of the food system [*1990: 27*].

That we cannot know the social cost arises out of the distanciation of social relations, the extended mediation of action, and the increasing abstraction of knowledge.

Second, agriculture became progressively subjected to industrial processes and considerations which diminished the visibility of ecological constraints to new production methods. Commodification and then industrialisation resulted in agricultural modernisation being informed by standardisation, uniformity and predictability – Fordism as applied to agriculture.[10] In order, for example, to facilitate mechanisation of harvest and post-harvest processing crops became increasingly standardised. Thus, Vellve notes that in the EC:

> To figure on an official list and be legally marketable, a variety must be proved to be *distinct*, or distinguishable from others; *uniform*, that is all the individuals of the variety must be the same; and it has to be *stable* passing on its salient traits from one generation to the next [*1992: 68*].

Since commercial agriculture has become mechanised it has become vital to its operation that ripening of crops, especially fruit crops, is synchronised. Synchronicity - a distinctly modern concept and bureaucratic practice - can be most easily achieved through genetic engineering, which at one and the same time relies on expert knowledge systems, the separation of seed knowledge from farming knowledge, and the erosion of genetic diversity.[11] One major consequence of the disaggregation and specialisation of farming knowledge, in combination with the commercialisation of agriculture, has been that agriculturalists have become locked into agro-industrial capitals [*Goodman and Redclift, 1991: 104*] as 'crop management' has become increasingly reliant upon technically specialist knowledge – for example, agro-chemists, geneticists, agricultural engineers, agricultural economists.

Third, the gradual shift to mass production (Fordism), and trade in a narrow range of grains in particular, aided – indeed were fundamental to – the provision of rapidly growing urban populations (in part itself a consequence of the enclosure of agricultural modernisation). The bimodal structure of development [*Eicher and Staatz, 1990; Barraclough, 1991*] based on the notion of the secular decline of the significance of agriculture to growth, and the parallel increased significance of industry, derived out of the North-West European experience and applied to most of the rest of the world, contributed to the radical urban bias in global development. Solon Barraclough contends that 'the dynamics of modernisation and economic growth processes in societies with bi-modal agrarian structures usually generates poverty and malnutrition among large sections of the rural population' [*1991: 24*].

In addition, bi-modal development generates mass urban poverty which, in the matter of nutrition, demands the provision of cheap food. Wheat, in particular, constituted the main vehicle of proletarianisation both in the North and, after the Second World War, in the South as well. One can clearly see here how the structuration of urbanisation, commercialisation, industrialisation and commodification are mutually informing. Friedmann observes that 'As people in the underdeveloped parts of the world become dependent on commodified food their diets are ruptured from local ecology and tradition and restructured through international food markets' [*1990: 26*]. In each case, the transport of schemas, torn out of their original context, places production and organisational demands on localities which are evidently unsustainable.

Fourth, the development of food aid, again especially after the Second World War by the USA, constituted a powerful instrument for the shaping of global food markets and agricultural development, and in the integration of global capitalism in general. It is clear, from the work of Harriet Friedmann [*1990, 1982*] that 'US food aid conditionality took the lead by restructuring fundamental elements of food and agricultural policy' [*Crow, 1990: 40*] in Europe and in the South. In short, food aid, whilst being utilised to ensure political stability during the geo-politics of the cold war, rested upon a fundamental modernisation of agricultural production. The development of 'strawberry imperialism' and attached development aid for the provision of core markets, at once supplants local agricultural methods and local agricultural knowledge. Furthermore, the international politics of competitive dumping and agricultural subsidies are basic to the logic of the industrialisation of agriculture.

Conclusion

The intention in pursuing such enquiries in global agricultural modernisation is not to assert the superiority of what may have been euphemistically called 'local' knowledge nor indeed the superiority of *techne* over *episteme*. Instead such enquiries are informed by the requirement to understand how particular forms of environmental degradation occur as a consequence of structured social behaviour on a global scale. If repeated actions can be identified, it is necessary to ask how these can be accounted for; whether they are intended or unintended; and whether all consequences are intended or unintended. To begin to answer these questions will guide us in developing a theory of structure and environmental degradation. The transposition of schemas across the world, combined with the differential manners in which they become instanciated, seems to provide an initially revealing entry into the globalisation of degradation of modernity. It is the manner in which human beings interpret, unconsciously or otherwise, these schemas that their understanding of the world will be instanciated. As Michael Redclift acutely observes: 'It is their *knowledgeability as agents* which is of key importance in determining their behaviour towards the environment. Their consciousness of the likely effect of their behaviour affects behaviour itself' (emphasis in original) [*1992: 39*].

This study has sought to begin the identification of the relationships between modernisation, knowledge and globalisation in order to reveal modes of knowledge, both generated by and reinforcing of, particular types of socio-economic practice. Central to the critique is that global environmental degradation arises out of the *normal and mundane practices of modernity* and not from the accidental or abnormal. Knowledge of degradation is severely restricted and substantially mediated, itself a consequence of modernity. Thus, the structures of modernity not only create mass environmental degradation, but simultaneously mask its origins and formation. It is this tension that needs to be thoroughly addressed before appropriate legislative or regulatory instruments, either at the state or global level, can be instituted.

NOTES

1. See as examples of reviews of modernisation/development Eisenstadt [*1970*], Harrison [*1988*], Mouzelis [*1988*], Redclift [*1987*], and Scholte [*1993b*].

2. For a compelling analysis of structure, intention and violence see Galtung [1990].
3. I shall not discuss the third feature of modernity, reflexivity, identified by Giddens, but it is of great relevance to the questions of knowledge and techne considered below.
4. For different treatments of environmental and agricultural transfer see Crosby [1986], and Eicher and Staatz (eds.) [1990].
5. Giddens' commentary and analysis of surveillance are apposite in this respect.
6. The twin of the enclosure of land is dispossession and the generation of 'surplus labour' wherein labour, too, becomes commodified.
7. The origins in enclosure and bureaucracy outlined above is clear. Similarly, the implication for mediation of action is evident.
8. A concept of counter-hegemony and counter-culture is necessary here to give account of resistance to hegemonic schemas. However, reasons of space prevent this elaboration here.
9. Note that this transformation, while critically mediated through the state, has been increasingly conducted through the trans-national practices of agro-industrial capitals. See Sklair [1991]; Goodman, Sorj and Wilkinson [1987]; and Goodman and Redclift [1981].
10. Goodman and Redclift [1991] note important qualifications to this notion of Fordist agriculture (as opposed to Fordism in post-harvest processing) because the biological production-consumption cycle constitutes resistances to 'direct and unified transformation of industrial capitals, leading to partial and historically discontinuous appropriations of rural production activities' [1991: 91].
11. See the important work of Genetic Resources Action International (GRAIN) in Cooper, Vellve and Hobbelink (eds.) [1992].

REFERENCES

Banuri, T. (1990a), 'Development and the Politics of Knowledge: A Critical Interpretation of the Social Role of Modernisation Theories in the Development of the Third World', in Marglin and Marglin (eds.) [1990].
Banuri, T. (1990b), 'Modernisation and its Discontents: A Cultural Perspective on Theories of Development', in Marglin and Marglin (eds.) [1990].
Barraclough, S. (1991), An End to Hunger: The Social Origins of Food Strategies, London: Zed Books.
Bauman, Z. (1989), Modernity and the Holocaust, Oxford: Polity Press.
Cooper, D., Vellve, R. and H. Hobbelink (eds.) (1992), Growing Diversity: Genetic Resources and Local Food Security, London: Intermediate Technology Publications.
Crosby, A. (1986), Ecological Imperialism, Cambridge: Cambridge University Press.
Crow, B. (1990), 'Moving the Lever: A New Food Aid Imperialism', in H. Bernstein, B. Crow, M. Mackintosh and C. Martin (eds.), The Food Question: Profits versus People London: Earthscan.
The Ecologist (1992), 'Whose Common Future?', Special Issue, Vol.22, No.4.
Eicher, C. and J. Staatz (eds.) (1990), Agricultural Development in the Third World, 2nd edn., London: Johns Hopkins University Press.
Eisenstadt, S. (ed.) (1970), Readings in Social Evolution and Development, Oxford: Pergamon.
Friedmann, H. (1982), 'The Political Economy of Food: The Rise and Fall of the Postwar International Food Order', American Journal of Sociology, Vol.88.
Friedmann, H. (1990), 'The Origins of Third World Food Dependence', in H. Bernstein, B. Crow, M. Mackintosh and C. Martin (eds.), The Food Question: Profits versus People, London: Earthscan.
Galtung, J. (1990), 'Cultural Violence', Journal of Peace Research, Vol.27, Pt.3, pp.291–305.

Giddens, A. (1984), *The Constitution of Society: Outline of a Theory of Structuration*, Oxford: Polity Press.

Giddens, A. (1985), *The Nation-State and Violence: A Contemporary Critique of Historical Materialism, Vol.2*, Oxford: Polity Press.

Giddens, A. (1990), *The Consequences of Modernity*, Oxford: Polity Press.

Goodman, D. and M. Redclift (1981), *From Peasant to Proletarian: Capitalist Development and Agrarian Transitions*, Oxford: Blackwell.

Goodman, D. and M. Redclift (1991), *Refashioning Nature: Food, Ecology and Culture*, London: Routledge.

Goodman, D., Sorj, B. and J. Wilkinson (1987), *From Farming to Biotechnology: a Theory of Agro-industrial Development*, Oxford: Blackwell.

Guha, R. (1990), *The Unquiet Woods*, New Delhi: Oxford University Press.

Hardin, G. (1968), 'The Tragedy of the Commons', *Science*, Vol. 162.

Harrison, D. (1988), *The Sociology of Modernisation and Development*, London: Macmillan.

Held, D. and J. Thompson (eds.) (1989), *Social Theory of Modern Society: Giddens and his Critics*, Cambridge: Cambridge University Press.

Marglin, S.A. (1990), 'Towards a Decolonisation of the Mind', in Marglin and Marglin (eds.) [*1990*].

Marglin, F.A. and S.A Marglin (eds.) (1990), *Dominating Knowledge: Development, Culture and Resistance*, Oxford: Clarendon Press.

Merchant, C. (1980), *The Death of Nature: Women, Ecology and the Scientific Revolution*, New York: Harper & Row.

Mouzelis, N. (1988), 'Sociology of Development: Reflections on the Present Crisis, *Sociology*, Vol.22. pp. 23–44.

Redclift, M. (1987), *Sustainable Development: Exploring the Contradictions*, London: Methuen.

Redclift, M. (1992), 'Sustainable Development and Global Environmental Change: Implications of a Changing Agenda', *Global Environmental Change*, March.

Robertson, R. (1992), *Globalisation: Social Theory and Global Culture*, London: Sage.

Rubinstein, R. (1978), *The Cunning of History*, New York: Harper & Row.

Scholte, J.A. (1993a), 'From Power Politics to Social Change: Alternative Focus for International Studies', *Review of International Studies*, Vol.19, No.1.

Scholte, J.A. (1993b), *The International Relations of Social Change*, Milton Keynes: Open University Press.

Sen, A. (1982), *Poverty and Famines: An Essay on Entitlement and Deprivation*, Oxford: Oxford University Press.

Sewell, W. (1992), 'A Theory of Structure: Duality, Agency and Transformation', *American Journal of Sociology*, Vol.98, No.1.

Shiva, V. (1987), 'The Violence of Reductionist Science', *Alternatives*, Vol.12, pp.243–4.

Shiva, V. (1990), *The Violence of the Green Revolution*, London: Zed Books.

Sklair, L. (1991), *The Sociology of the Global System*, London: Harvester-Wheatsheaf.

Turner, B., Kasperson, R., Meyer, W. *et al.* (1990), 'Two Types of Global Environmental Change: Definitional and Spatial-Scale Issues in their Human Dimensions', *Global Environmental Change*, Dec., pp.14–22.

Vellve, R. (1992), 'The Decline of Diversity in European Agriculture', *The Ecologist*, Vol.23, No.2, pp.64–9.

Widstrand, C. (1988), 'Conflicts over Water', in C. Widstrand (ed.), *Water Conflicts and Research Priorities*, Oxford: Pergamon.

Structural Adjustment Programmes and the UNCED Agenda: Explaining the Contradictions

JOHN F. DEVLIN and NONITA T. YAP

One of the striking areas of agreement at the 1992 United Nations Conference in Environment and Development (UNCED) was over the importance of economic efficiency as a means to environmental ends. The language of economic efficiency and structural adjustment permeates UNCED documentation. The contradictions between economic efficiency and environmental sustainability can be illustrated by examining the market-oriented structural adjustment programmes (SAPs) that have been undertaken in low-consumption countries during the 1980s. Recent studies on the environmental impacts of SAPs in Thailand, Philippines, Côte d'Ivoire and Malawi show the operational complexity of the market-environment linkages and challenge the notion that 'efficient economies are the most environmentally friendly economies'. It can be concluded that sustainable development understood as environmental sustainability, relative equality between high-consumption and low-consumption countries, moderated levels of poverty and political stability is not consistent with SAP prescriptions of free trade, unrestrained markets and inactive states. Economic development and sound environmental management are complementary aspects of the same agenda. Without adequate environmental protection, development will be undermined; without development, environmental protection will fail [*World Bank, 1992: 25*].

The government leaders, lending institutions, and non-governmental organisations that met at the United Nations Conference on Environment and Development (UNCED) held in June 1992, were concerned with four distinct dimensions of the problem of sustainable development.

John Devlin is Vice-President of YESA, Guelph, Ontario; Nonita Yap is Associate Professor, University School of Rural Planning and Development, University of Guelph, Guelph, Ontario, Canada.

For environmentalists the principal focus was environmental sustainability and the concern was to agree upon strategies that would secure the
biophysical base of the planet. For populists the principal focus was
participation and the concern was to design strategies of policy formation
and implementation that were broadly democratic and inclusive. For
state leaders the principal focus was sustained economic growth. For the
leaders of low-consumption countries this required the renewal of efforts
to create a new international economic order in which national economic
development would be served by altered international institutional
arrangements. For the high-consumption countries the concern was to
hold on to current levels of consumption and technology while conceding
as little as necessary to environmentalists, populists, and the institutional
restructuring demands of the low-consumption countries. Finally, for
market theorists, the focus was economic efficiency and the concern was
to ensure that both environmental sustainability and economic development be pursued through market rational strategies.

These interests were not compatible, yet the elasticity of the notion of
sustainable development gave sufficient space for negotiation and agreement.[1] One of the most striking examples was the apparent consensus
over the importance of improved economic efficiency as a means to
environmental ends. The language of economic efficiency and structural
adjustment was woven throughout the UNCED documentation.[2] But the
compatibility between economic efficiency and environmental sustainability remains highly contestable theoretically and extremely complex operationally.

This contribution explores the contradictions between economic
efficiency and environmental sustainability with particular reference to
the market-oriented structural adjustment programmes (SAPs) that have
been undertaken in low-consumption countries during the 1980s. It
reviews the basic principles of SAPs, investigates their environmental
impacts through several brief country studies, considers some of the more
specific sectoral tensions and analyses some of the major theoretical
problems that stand in the way of any simple merging of SAP and
environmental objectives.

Structural Adjustment

Structural adjustment refers to a set of economic policy changes that are
intended to bring domestic economies into harmony with what are
perceived to be changing global economic tendencies. These global
tendencies include higher petroleum prices, reduced credit flows from
high- to low-consumption countries, and globalisation of production,

trade, transport and communication systems. Failure to adjust to these new global conditions has led, it is argued, to chronic balance of payments problems, debt crisis, inflation, government deficits, and slow growth. Structural adjustment programmes include exchange rate devaluations, restraints on government spending, controls on wage increases to public and private sector workers, improved regulatory environments for private-sector economic actors, liberalisation of trade, and encouragement for export-oriented economic activity. SAPs are also directed at reducing state economic regulation, constraining the size of the civil service and privatising public corporations.

That such programmes have exacerbated poverty problems has been widely noted [*Cornia, Jolly and Stewart, 1987; Nelson, 1989*]. SAPs have also generated problems of political instability [*Waterbury, 1989*]. The usual argument presented in the face of such problems is that the SAP policies are unpalatable but economically necessary responses to difficult circumstances. The concerns of governments are seen as legitimate but ones that have to be balanced against the hard facts of economic necessity.

SAPs are not designed to achieve environmental objectives. However, it is argued that SAPs are indirectly necessary to environmental sustainability because healthy economies are a necessary condition for effective environmental protection. The notion that 'efficient economies are the most environmentally friendly economies' [*Strong, 1993*] has gained wide acceptance. But if living standards and political stability are readily sacrificed to market necessities, it is to be expected that environmental concerns too will be traded-off against economic necessities.

Country Experiences

There is enough anecdotal evidence to suggest that SAPs cannot be assumed to be environmentally neutral.

Thailand

Thailand began a domestically initiated structural adjustment programme in 1981. It then requested World Bank structural adjustment loans in 1982 and 1983. The government also negotiated a two-year IMF standby agreement for the period 1981–83 [*Sahasakul, Thongpakde and Kraisoraphong, 1991*].

The Thai SAP included reduction of export taxes on rice and rubber, lifting of export quotas on cassava and maize and lifting the export ban on sugar.[3]

The reduction of the export taxes encouraged greater cultivation of cassava and rubber. Virgin forests were cleared to make way for rubber even though world rubber prices were declining in the early 1980s. Rubber plantations also started encroaching on steeper and more marginal lands. The catastrophic landslides and floods in southern Thailand in 1988 occurred mostly in upland young rubber plantations [*Reed, 1992*].

During the SAP period Thailand's forest cover continued to decline. Between 1985 and 1988 annual deforestation rate was estimated at 2,400 km² [*World Bank 1992: Table 33*] driven by commercial logging and clearing for agriculture.[4] Over 30 years 15.6 million hectares of forest land were cleared, reducing the forest cover from over 50 per cent of total land area to 20 per cent.

Industrial restructuring and export-based development in Thailand has effectively promoted more environmentally intensive industries [*Reed, 1992: 113*]. There has also been a shift in the type of industrial pollutants, from biodegradable residuals such as BOD and suspended solids to more complex and hazardous pollutants such as heavy metals, organic solvents, and oils. The link to export promotion is direct. The proportion of hazardous-waste generating industries approved by the Board of Investments (BOI) increased from 25 per cent in 1987 to 55 per cent in 1989. Such industries produce 90 per cent of the hazardous wastes generated in the country [*Phantunvanit and Panayotou, 1990*].

Despite the establishment of the National Energy Conservation Centre as part of the SAP, energy development in Thailand continues. Even with the devaluation of the Baht by 25 per cent between 1980 and 1989 the growth rate of oil imports rose in step with GDP suggesting that petroleum demand is very price inelastic and that conservation measures have been at best marginally effective.[5]

One of the alternative domestic energy sources being seriously developed in Thailand is lignite, perhaps the most heavily polluting of all energy sources. The Electricity Generating Authority of Thailand is projecting that by the year 2006 lignite will provide 32 per cent of energy demand in Thailand [*Phantumvanit and Panayotou, 1990*].

Another alternative source being developed is hydropower. Two hydroelectric projects totalling nearly 2000 megawatts are being planned.[6] The Seventh Economic and Social Development Plan (1992–96) recommends 'speeding up the negotiations' for the development of hydroelectric sources with Burma and Laos, exploration and development of petroleum with Burma, Malaysia, Vietnam and Cambodia.

Thus in Thailand the period of SAP implementation is correlated with increased deforestation, increased industrial pollution, increased petroleum consumption and planned increases in the use of lignite and hydroelectric power. Similar trends are apparent in other countries.

Philippines

In the Philippines, structural adjustment lending began in 1980 and has included two structural enlistment loans (SALS), one economic recovery loan and repeated IMF standby arrangements. Between 1980 and 1985 some 2.5 million new migrants (14.5 per cent of upland population) moved into upland areas putting increased pressure on upland soils. There was also increased entry into and further over-exploitation of coastal fisheries [*Cruz and Repetto, 1992*].

The Philippines has also accepted the relocation of dirty industries such as the Kawasaki Steel sintering plant established overseas in response to the environmental resistance in Japan [*Kitazawa, 1990*].

Increased petroleum prices under SAP have intensified domestic energy exploration and development, including dirtier sources and ecologically sensitive sites. The National Power Corporation's ten-year plan envisions the installation of at least 15 coal-fired plants throughout the country by 2005. Phase II of the coal-fired power plant in Batangas appears certain in spite of strong community opposition. The Plan also includes the construction and operation of two geothermal plants in Mount Apo, a dormant volcano and one of only two heritage sites in the Philippines. It is home to 84 mostly endemic wildlife species, including the endangered Philippine bald eagle [*Gamalinda, 1991*]. Even the mothballed Bataan nuclear plant is under reconsideration.

Assessment of the economic and environmental impacts of Philippine industrial policy reforms under SAP using a computable general equilibrium model suggests that the reforms were 'ineffective at best, and counterproductive at worst' [*Cruz and Repetto, 1992: 60*]. But the simulation shows that had the reforms been successfully implemented, resource-based exports and environmentally damaging production sectors would have expanded. Consequently soil erosion, deforestation, overfishing, mineral depletion, industrial pollution and energy use would have all increased.

Côte d'Ivoire

During the first 15 years after independence the Côte d'Ivoire was one of the outstanding economic successes in sub-Saharan Africa. The country enjoyed an average real GDP growth rate of seven per cent from 1960 to 1975, based largely on exports of primary products, especially coffee, cocoa, timber and seafood.

Following balance of payments problems in the late 1970s, four sequential SAL's were obtained from the World Bank from 1981–90 and complemented by adjustment loans from bilateral agencies.

In 1940 forests covered 90 per cent of the total land area of Côte d'Ivoire. However the booming cash crop economy combined with policies linking land ownership to active land use contributed to deforestation rates averaging about five per cent per annum immediately following independence.[7] Between 1966 and 1985 approximately six million hectares were logged with only 59,000 hectares replanted. Most logged-over areas were converted into farms. Under the SAP rates of deforestation remained high [*Reed, 1992*].[8] By 1990 more than three quarters of original forests were gone.

In Malawi tea and tobacco accounted for 54 per cent of export earnings in 1979. Falling tea and tobacco prices, higher interest rates, the drought in 1979–80 and influx of war refugees from Mozambique were among the shocks that led to balance of payments problem. Malawi received three consecutive SALs over the 1981–86 period. The government also secured a two-to-five-year IMF stand-by agreement.

SAL I identified declining stock of fuelwood as a problem. Fuelwood constitutes 80 per cent of energy consumption [*Harrigan, 1991*], not surprisingly, since both tea and tobacco require huge amounts of fuelwood for curing.[9]

Between 1983–84 and 1987–88 the average price of fertiliser increased by 87 per cent. For the 30 per cent of smallholder farmers who had been using fertilisers, the combination of land scarcity and removal of fertiliser subsidy left two options: first, more intensive farming without the use of fertilisers or, secondly, shifting to crops that were less fertiliser-intensive. Smallholder fertiliser use did decline in 1985–86. Farmers shifted from high-yield maize to groundnuts which were less fertiliser intensive. Maize supply declined, prices rose and maize imports became necessary [*Harrigan, 1991*].

Sectoral Linkages

SAPs change the relative prices of inputs through the elimination of subsidies, changed import tariffs and export taxes. They influence the input choices of producers, and the selections made by consumers. They can influence the adoption of particular production techniques, and a shift from one energy source to another. They thereby affect the ways in which resources are used.

By influencing such decisions, SAPs will have at least an indirect impact on the environment [*Mearns, 1991*]. But actual environmental impacts are in all cases unpredictable. In addition, because SAPs are introduced in economies that already are suffering severe balance of payments problems, it is never possible to link behavioural responses unambiguously to SAP policy changes. SAPs tend to accelerate or decelerate existing processes rather than to generate completely new types of behaviour.

However it is possible to suggest some of the structural linkages between price changes and environmental outcomes in environmentally-sensitive sectors.

SAPs and Agriculture

Most countries subsidise agricultural chemicals, fertilisers, pesticides, herbicides, which have negative environmental effects through groundwater pollution, salinisation and soil degradation. SAPs encourage the removal of such subsidies and for this reason alone it may appear that SAPs are environmentally friendly because the effect of the increased prices will be to discourage the usage of such inputs. But reduced use of agricultural chemicals will not always generate the most beneficial environmental outcome. It depends on how farmers react to these price changes. Will they continue producing the same crops at lower levels of productivity? Will they shift production to less chemically intensive crops? Will they alter their land use practices?

If open access resources exist farmers may simply clear more forests. The environmental cost is thus shifted from chemical contamination of ground and surface water to reduction of forest cover. If farmers cannot open new land they may intensify the use of the same land with fewer inputs, thus mining the topsoil. The environmental cost is thus shifted from chemical contamination to soil degradation. Actual environmental impacts thus depend on the type of crop, the cropping system, the quality of the soil, the topography of farm land, and alternative land use options. Thus, while all other things being equal a reduction of chemicals is an environmental benefit, in the absence of a careful modelling of alternative forms of economic behaviour and their environmental consequences, the assumption that rising input prices are unambiguously environmentally beneficial is not justified.

With respect to increasing producer's prices for agricultural exports, such increases may lead to efforts to increase output with increased use of agricultural chemicals (despite the higher prices) and possibly also the opening up of new land. Thus, rising commodity prices may also result in further environmental degradation.

SAPs and Deforestation

Deforestation has become a central focus of environmental concern. Locally it is associated with microclimate disruption, increased soil erosion, siltation and flash flooding. At the international level the concern is over the destruction of wildlife habitat and loss of biodiversity as well as the reduction of the global carbon sink with its implication for global climate change. Country-specific studies indicate that the roots of deforestation are a complex combination of cultural, social, political and economic factors. Demand for cut logs is the most proximate cause of deforestation. Forest clearing rates are primarily influenced by commercial logging practices but also by land tenure security, relative poverty and access to alternative economic opportunities for the rural poor. The actual permutation varies not only from country to country but even from region to region (See literature review by Kummer [*1991*]). Once forests are logged over intense land use conflicts can arise between reforestation and agricultural exploitation.

Some sectoral SAPs have encouraged higher concession and stumpage fees to capture some of the high rents for state budgets and such increased fees may in some cases reduce cutting. However, the rates of deforestation in several SAP countries suggest that SAPs are ineffective in slowing down the exploitation of forest resources. Given the pressure on balance of payments, high international prices for cut logs and forest products are difficult to resist.[10] Governments will be under pressure to maintain cutting and lumber exports so long as an international demand exists.[11] Cutting will respond to the spread between prices and fees not the fees in isolation. Hence a quota system rooted in long-term environmental management strategy is what is required to control forest cover losses.

SAPs and Industrialisation

SAPs encourage the establishment of labour-intensive industries many of which are also waste-intensive and therefore potentially pollution-intensive. These need not be dirty industries purposely located in 'underpolluted' areas. It is enough that SAPs encourage countries to fall back on resource exports and resource-intensive processing. Since resource extraction and preliminary processing are among the most environmentally destructive phases of production, SAPs in effect encourage low-consumption countries to specialise in environmentally intensive economic activity.

SAPs and Energy

Under SAPs energy conservation is stimulated by the desire to reduce energy imports, reduce energy subsidies, and reduce capital expenditures on energy projects. However, none of these objectives precludes the resort to cheaper energy sources. SAPs encourage the removal of subsidies on domestic petroleum and other energy prices. This might be expected to have a positive environmental impact since with rising petroleum prices petroleum use should decline and greenhouse gas emissions and air pollution should be reduced. However, if energy demand is inelastic other energy supplies will be sought – fuelwood, lignite, hydroelectric, or nuclear power. Each energy source poses its own set of environmental problems – deforestation, increased air pollution, widespread flooding, or the risk of nuclear accidents. Thus reduced petroleum use may simply change the type of environmental degradation rather than reduce it.

The environmental impacts of energy pricing policies must be judged with all energy alternatives in mind. Current development trajectories demand increasing supplies of energy and SAPs have not promoted alternative energy technologies that might reverse these long-run trends.[12]

SAPs and Poverty

Although SAPs are intended to put economies back on a growth trajectory, they do intensify poverty problems at least in the short run. Poverty has its own environmental impacts. It leads to intensified exploitation of available common property resources, including fragile or already threatened ecosystems.

Thus environment-market linkages are 'wicked' problems [*Mearns, 1991*] where neither behavioural nor environmental outcomes can be anticipated with any confidence. The guiding principle of SAPs – getting the prices right, both domestically and globally – cannot be assumed to create environmentally friendly or even environmentally neutral outcomes.

Theoretical Presuppositions

Trade

SAPs encourage movement toward international market prices and encourage increases in exports based on the principles of comparative advantage. But the logic of comparative advantage breaks down once capital is mobile [*Daly, 1992*]. Freed from regulatory constraints, capital will seek out locations that offer maximum levels of profitability within a global division of labour. Competition between countries will inevitably encourage competition over the least stringent environmental standards just as there has been competition over the lowest wage rates, the least organized labour forces and competition over the least onerous taxation levels. Enforcement of environmental standards under a free trade regime will require stronger regulatory and enforcement capacity. Yet SAPs encourage state downsizing and deregulation.

The repeated calls in multilateral forums, including UNCED, to avoid using environmental criteria as a basis for trade discrimination is a telling example of confusion. If states forego the right to refuse to consume environmentally degrading products there will be no national level enforcement mechanisms to back up international protocols.[13] It is unlikely that international financial agencies would suggest that states should continue to trade with countries that refuse to pay their bills, repay their loans, or guarantee fair market practices. But this same right of refusal is denied in cases where countries devastate their environments at the cost not only of their own citizens but of the global community. Why should environmentally destructive harvesting and production practices be treated with less resolve than failure to pay one's bills? Clearly an ideological adherence to the principles of free trade is being placed well above the concern for environmentally responsible economic development.

The effort to increase exports may generate perverse outcomes. The global market in every product category is finite and the greater the number of producers the lower prices will trend. Global competition will continue to bid down resource rents, thus increased exports of resource-intensive products may increase environmental degradation but not achieve significant increases in foreign currency earnings.

The logic of structural adjustment suggests that successful adjustment for low-consumption countries requires the willingness of developed countries to open up their markets. However, while the Bank and the Fund can force low-consumption countries to liberalise they have very little leverage over high-consumption countries. As a result the conditions necessary to the success of the global liberalisation strategy have not been met. Developing countries are being forced to open their economies without reciprocation from the developed world [*World Bank, 1987: 21*].

Getting the Prices Right?

There are inherent market failures in the natural resource sector. Many environmental benefits have public good characteristics. They cannot be turned into marketables nor can access to them be easily prevented. Thus, environmental policy management, even in a market framework, requires an active state role to adjust private to social costs and benefits [*Reed, 1992*]. Macro-level SAPs are systematically unconcerned with environmental externalities even though some sectoral SAPs have begun to address these issues.

Ultimately, environmental stability and economic efficiency can be mutually reinforcing goals. However, the environmental economics debate has indicated that the pursuit of economic efficiency in the absence of a prior definition of environmental values will lead to environmental degradation. The assumption of a wide range of 'win–win' situations in which SAPs promote environmental sustainability is not justified. Economic development, which has been pursued primarily in a manner consistent with market conditions over the past two centuries, has carried unquantifiable environmental costs. Further economic development will increase those costs whether it is pursued in a market efficient manner or not.

Environmental effectiveness requires the setting by public authorities of acceptable environmental limits (see, for example, Kneese [1977], Nijkamp [1980], and Schultze [1977]). Economic efficiency in general and SAPs in particular must be subordinated to environmental objectives. Once the acceptable environmental framework is set, market efficiency can be pursued. But the problem to be solved is how to determine environmental boundaries. World prices are clearly not the 'right' environmental prices.

Structural adjustment programmes attempt to subordinate issues of collective welfare to issues of market efficiency. In the process they de-link economies from many difficult questions of social choice by setting economic adjustment as the overwhelming priority. Market-oriented approaches suggest that efficient outcomes will protect environmental values if all environmental externalities are internalised. But the conceptual, technical, and moral issues involved in assigning economic values to environmental functions and effects are profoundly contestable. Complex valuations are required, but the setting of environmentally rational prices for forest cover, soil fertility or sustainable yield of biophysical systems require assumptions over discount rates, inter-generational equity, future markets and costs. Such valuations are partially choices of collective social values and partly processes of assuming risks under conditions of ignorance.

SAPs and Collective Problem Solving

Thus environmental sustainability is full of conceptual difficulties and unavoidable and inherently contestable collective choice problems. In the face of any change in policy regime, the bearers of costs and the recipients of benefits are seldom the same individuals or countries. Hence there must be political conflict and adjudication, bargaining and trade-offs. These difficulties are significantly increased when the relevant decision space is expanded from the national to the global level.

The global management of global environmental resources requires that market principles must be subordinated to globally defined environmental targets. How responsibility for meeting these targets will be distributed will inevitably be outcomes of bargaining processes. Effective environmental policy will require policy formation and enforcement mechanisms established at the global level [*Culpepper, 1991*]. Such processes would tend to override sovereignty and thus constitute an exceedingly difficult problem in international institution building. Conventions remain voluntary agreements in which the familiar benefits of free-riding apply. Defection from such agreements brings greater benefits the more rigorously the agreement is followed by the majority.

Conclusion

The consensus over economic efficiency as a means to environmental ends has been reached too hastily. Ultimately, sustainable development understood as environmental sustainability, relative equality between high-consumption countries and low-consumption countries, moderated levels of poverty in all countries, and political stability in all countries, is not consistent with free trade, unrestrained markets, and inactive states.

Neo-classical market theory, by concentrating on marginal change, characteristically accepts existing distributions of assets as given. In the case of environmental assets, the living standards in the high-consumption countries have been achieved at the cost of deforestation, soil erosion, air, water, and land pollution, global warming, and ozone depletion. The developmental history of the high-consumption countries is one of continuous consumption and destruction of environmental assets. It is thus not surprising that low-consumption countries question the validity of existing distributions of economic development. SAPs, by individualising problems of economic stabilisation ignore historical conditions and encourage low-consumption countries to pursue the same path of national self-interest that high-consumption countries pursued in earlier years. However such a strategy is not sustainable. What is required is a collective pursuit of environmental sustainability within a redistributive framework, precisely the sort of collective approach that UNCED promised to create.

At UNCED the market-oriented defenders of structural adjustment represent a single faction, but a faction that has enjoyed a remarkable and still growing influence. It is to be hoped that UNCED has launched a process that will eventually lead to a reduction of this influence.

The institutions of sustainable development must be sculpted in the resistant medium of international consensus. The tools of bargaining and diplomacy may not appear equal to the task but they are infinitely superior to the competitive logic of the market. As C.S. Holling so aptly puts it

Sustaining the biosphere is not an ecological problem, nor a social problem nor an economic problem. It is an integrated combination of all three. Effective investments in a sustainable biosphere are therefore ones that simultaneously retain and encourage ... renewal in society, economies and ecosystems. For nature it is biosphere structure, for businesses and people it is usable knowledge and for society as a whole it is trust [*1992: 1*].

NOTES

1. As Lele [*1991*] puts it:

   SD [sustainable development] has become a bundle of neat fixes: technological changes that make industrial production processes less polluting and less resource intensive and yet more productive and profitable, economic policy changes that incorporate environmental considerations and yet achieve greater economic growth, procedural changes that use local non-governmental organisations (NGOs) so as to ensure grassroots participation, agriculture that is less harmful, less resource intensive and yet more productive, and so on. In short SD is a 'metafix' that will unite everybody from the profit-minded industrialist and risk-minimising subsistence farmer to the equity-seeking social worker, the pollution-concerned or wildlife-loving First Worlder, the growth-maximising policy maker, the goal-oriented bureaucrat, and therefore, the vote-counting politician [*1991: 613*].

2. For example Agenda 21, one of the major outputs of UNCED, and described by the UN as 'a programme of cooperative action to ensure the security of the resources and life-sustaining systems of the earth and progress and well-being of all its peoples in the twenty-first century' has the following sections:

   In a number of countries, policies are necessary to correct misdirected public spending, large budget deficits and other macroeconomic imbalances, restrictive policies and distortions in the areas of exchange rates, investment and finance, and obstacles to entrepreneurship (Agenda 21. Ch.2. Sect.2.32).

   The international economy should provide a supportive international climate for achieving environment and development goals by (a) promoting sustainable development through trade liberalisation; (b) making trade and environment mutually supportive (Agenda 21. Ch.2. Para. 2.3).

   The removal of existing distortions in international trade is essential ... in agriculture, industry and other sectors, there is scope for initiatives aimed at trade liberalisation and at policies to make production more responsive to environment and development needs. Trade liberalisation should therefore be pursued on a global basis across economic sectors so as to contribute to sustainable development (Agenda 21. Ch.2. Para 2.7).

3. The increase by over 100 per cent of the acreage planted to cassava over a seven year period has been attributed to this differential export tax combined with a loophole in EC policy [*Reed, 1992*].

4. It is estimated that annual forest loss in Thailand would be cut in half by raising rural incomes by 50 per cent [*Reed, 1992*].
5. Total imports for crude oil and finished oil products grew 9.9 per cent by volume during the first four months of 1992 compared to the same period in 1991. This is considered an underestimate because one-half of the oil, primarily diesel, consumed in southern Thailand reportedly comes from smuggled supplies (*Bangkok Post Economic Review 1992, p.35*).
6. 'EGAT Rate Rise will Add 5% to User's Power Bill' (*The Nation*, 30 July 1992, B.12).
7. Use of fertilisers is reported at 11 tons per hectare, low compared to the average of 39 tons/ha for all low-income countries [*World Bank, 1992: Table A.7*].
8. Until 1990, the concession and stumpage fees in the Côte d'Ivoire together amounted to less than a quarter of one per cent of the average freight on board value of exported timber. Under a forestry sector adjustment program concession fees will increase 250–1000 per cent and stumpage fees by 300–1000 per cent between 1990 and 1995. There will also be increases in export duties and changes in concession policy. These are expected to lead to increased revenues for the government but these increases are still considered 'far too low to have any significant impact on concession management practices' [*Reed, 1992: 68*].
9. Timberlake [*1988*] observes that 'typically the annual yield of one hectare of tobacco requires all the trees on a hectare of open woodland' [*1988: 94*].
10. The price index for sawn wood doubled between 1986 and 1990.
11. Even where governments attempt to reduce cutting rates, illegal logging will be a major problem. The Philippines, already one of the most severely deforested countries in the tropics, has attempted to discourage log exports beginning in the late 1970s but illegal logging and exports have continued [*Porter and Ganapin, 1988*].
12. 'Third World "under pressure to burn fossil fuel"', *New Scientist*, 5 Sept. 1992, p.11.
13. Efforts to encourage the introduction of global management institutions have met with only partial success. Some conventions appear to be making progress in ratification and compliance, the ivory ban, and the Ozone Protocol. But even here there are continuing tensions. In other areas protocols are under stress. The Basel Convention on hazardous waste cannot achieve agreement on the banning of the hazardous waste trade. The worldwide moratorium on whaling is being seriously challenged by the whaling nations of Japan, Norway and Iceland.

REFERENCES

Cornia, Giovanni Andrea, Jolly, Richard and Frances Stewart (eds.) (1987), *Adjustment with a Human Face: Protecting the Vulnerable and Promoting Growth, Vol.I*, Oxford: Clarendon Press for the United Nations Childrens Fund.
Cruz, W. and R. Repetto (1992), *The Environmental Effects of Stabilization and Structural Adjustment Programs: The Philippines Case*, Washington, DC: World Resources Institute, Sept.
Culpepper, R. (1991), 'Managing the Global Commons: The Economic Setting and Financial Options', a discussion paper prepared for the National Round Table on the Environment and the Economy, Ottawa, Sept.
Daly, Herman E. (1992), 'Free Trade, Sustainable Development and Growth: Some Serious Contradictions', *Network '92*, Special Supplement, Reviews of Agenda 21, No.1, Geneva: The Centre For Our Common Future.
Gamalinda, E. (ed.) (1991), *Saving the Earth: The Philippine Experience*, Manila: Philippine Centre for Investigative Journalism.
Guerrero, E. (1993), 'A Comparative Analysis of the Prescription and Implementation of Environmental Impact Assessment in the Philippines', unpublished manuscript.
Harrigan, Jane (1991), 'Malawi', in Mosley, Harrigan and Toye (eds.) [*1991: Ch.15, 201–69*].

Holling, C.S. (1992), 'New Science and New Investments for a Sustainable Biosphere', a paper prepared for the Biodiversity Project, International Institute of Ecological Economics and the Conference on Investing in Natural Capital – a Prerequisite for Sustainability, 2 July.

Kitazawa, Yoko (1990), 'The Japanese Economy and South-East Asia: The Examples of the Asahan Aluminium And Kawasaki Steel Projects', in Lim Teck Ghee and Mark J. Valencia, *Conflict over Natural Resources in South-East Asia and the Pacific* (Singapore: United Nations University Press), Ch.3, pp.51–93.

Kneese, A.V. (1977), *Economics and the Environment*, Harmondsworth: Penguin.

Kummer, D.M. (1991), *Deforestation in the Postwar Philippines*, Chicago, IL: University of Chicago Press.

Lele, Sharachchandra M. (1991), 'Sustainable Development: A Critical Review', *World Development*, Vol.19, No.6, pp.607–21.

Mearns, R. (1991), *Environmental Implications of Structural Adjustment: Reflections on Scientific Method*, Sussex: IDS Papers, Feb.

Mosley, P., Harrigan, J. and J. Toye (eds.) (1991), *Aid and Power: The World Bank and Policy-based Lending*, London: Routledge.

National Economic and Social Development Board (1992), *The Seventh National Economic and Social Development Plan (1992–1996)*, Bangkok: Office of the Prime Minister.

Nelson, Joan (ed.) (1989), *Fragile Coalitions: The Politics of Economic Adjustment*, New Brunswick, NJ: Transaction Books.

Nijkamp, P. (1980), *Environmental Policy Analysis*, New York: John Wiley & Sons.

Phantumvanit, D. and T. Panayotou (1990), 'Industrialization and Environmental Quality: Paying the Price', Synthesis Paper No.3, presented at the 1990 TDRI Year-End Conference, Chonburi, Thailand, 8–9 Dec.

Porter, G. and D. Ganapin (1988), *Resources, Population and the Philippines' Future*, Washington, DC: World Resources Institute.

Reed, D. (ed.) (1992), *Structural Adjustment and the Environment*, Boulder, CD: Westview Press.

Sahasakul, C., Thongpakde N., and K. Kraisoraphong (1991), 'Thailand', in P. Mosley, J. Harrigan, and J. Toye (eds.), *Aid and Power: The World Bank and Policy-based Lending* (London: Routledge), Ch.13, pp.72–149.

Schultze, C.L. (1977), *The Public Pursuit of Private Interest*, Washington, DC: The Brookings Institution.

Strong, Maurice (1993), O.D. Skelton Memorial Lecture, Vancouver, Canada, 10 Nov. 1992, Ottawa: External Affairs, Canada.

Timberlake, L. (1988), *Africa in Crisis*, London: Earthscan Publications.

UNICEF (1988, 1989), *Report on the State of the World's Children*, New York: UNICEF.

Waterbury, John (1989), 'The Political Management of Economic Adjustment and Reform', in Joan Nelson (ed.), *Fragile Coalitions: The Politics of Economic Adjustment* (New Brunswick, NJ: Transaction Books), Ch.1, pp.39–56.

World Bank (1987), *Annual Report*, Washington, DC: World Bank.

World Bank (1992), *Development and the Environment*, World Development Report 1992, Washington, DC: World Bank.

International Trade and the Environment: Issues, Perspectives and Challenges

MARC WILLIAMS

Since the Rio Summit, increasing attention is being given to the role of trade and trade policies in promoting or hindering moves to protect the environment. The links between trade and the environment have led to a debate in which a polarisation has taken place between free trade theorists and environmental activists and which calls for explanation. Considerations of equity and efficiency should not lead to a simple dichotomy between protectionism or liberal trade.

International trade is one of the main mechanisms of interdependence, and a constitutive feature of globalisation. The importance of trade in linking national societies, therefore, makes it imperative that discussions of global environmental problems focus on the interdependencies between international trade and environmental degradation. The network of international trade is not only one of the main channels through which environmental problems are created and maintained. It also provides possibilities for confronting these problems.

In the first place, trade can be responsible for damage to the environment in a number of ways, for example, through the transport of hazardous wastes, trade in endangered species, the international exchange of pesticides, and deforestation. But trade's impact cannot be restricted to the point of transmission. It is also directly related to a system of accumulation, production, distribution and exchange. The search for economic growth, the pursuit of free trade policies, or the effects of protectionist measures may generate policies which in environmental terms are sub-optimal. Secondly, trade policy can be a vehicle through which threats to the natural environment can be curbed. Solutions to environmental problems may require international agreement covering trade in certain goods. Moreover, the need to harmonise

Marc Williams, School of African and Asian Studies, University of Sussex.

national regulations ensures that a potential role exists for trade policies in respect of global environmental problems such as ozone layer depletion, and greenhouse gas abatement.

The perspective taken on the impact of trade on the environment will determine the policy position articulated in the environmental debate. Two broad positions have been adopted with respect to the interrelationship between trade and the environment. Liberal economists tend to argue that no inherent incompatibility exists between trade and concern for the environment. These analysts attempt to show how concern for the environment can be accommodated within the basic paradigm of free trade. Environmental activists, on the other hand, contend that a fundamental conflict exists between the demands of environmental protection and a liberal international trade regime.

This study will begin with an examination of the linkages between trade and the environment. It will show that these linkages are complex, and that the current state of knowledge is tentative rather than conclusive. The second part focuses on the competing perspectives on the interrelationship between trade and the environment. Debates on policy are informed by the perspective held and this section will attempt to show that a fundamental conflict exists between proponents of free trade and supporters of environmental protection. The final section takes the argument a stage further by considering the links between ecology and the international trading system. It stresses the importance of power in the global political economy and the different interests of developed and developing countries.

Linking Trade and the Environment

Trade and the environment are connected in three ways [*Anderson and Blackhurst, 1992: 5*]. First, environmental degradation can be the result of trade and trade policies. Changing international specialisation and the consequent movement of production from one location to another, coupled with changing consumption patterns, affect the management of natural resources and the environment. The environmental impact of trade liberalisation is debated between environmentalists and liberal economists. The environmental lobby stresses the potentially damaging effects of a liberal trade regime on the environment, while economists insist that trade can be a positive force in curbing environmentally damaging policies. Secondly, the comparative advantage and hence international competitive position of a state may be affected by the environmental policies pursued by another state or group of states. When countries enforce environmental protection standards domestically, these measures may change international competitiveness. Environmental activists have supported moves to strengthen domestic environmental standards and to apply these to foreign trade. In contrast, economists tend to view such devices as unwarranted protectionism. Thirdly, trade policies can be used as bargaining counters in the search for international environmental agreements. In the search for solutions to global environmental problems, trade policies can play a role in enforcing and implementing multilateral agreements. Whereas environmentalists highlight the possibilities of using trade policy to provide incentives for multilateral co-operation, liberal economists are more sceptical of the benefits of such an approach.

Trade Policies and the Environment

Economists have only recently started investigating the impact of trade on the environment. The impact of liberal trade policies on environmental degradation can be approached in a number of ways. In this section the different ways (direct or indirect) in which trade can have either a negative or a positive effect on the environment will be examined.

International trade can have a negative impact on the environment through production, distribution or consumption and its impact on overall economic growth. These effects can be direct or indirect. First, the positive impact of trade on national income and the possibilities of expanding production can lead to a worsening of environmental quality. A key assumption behind free trade doctrines is that trade increases economic growth. Trade will tend to lead to increased economic activity and this can have adverse environmental consequences in so far as this results in increased energy consumption. Moreover, increased trade could lead to the intensification in the use of non-renewable raw materials [*World Commission on Environment and Development, 1987: 79*]. Access to foreign markets and the drive to take advantage of economies of scale is likely to lead to the concentration and centralisation of capital. This could lead to the use of increased fertilisers, chemicals and pesticides in agriculture and the move to larger, more pollution-intensive industrial plants.

Secondly, international trade neglects the environment because the goods produced are assumed to have a neutral environmental impact and no account is taken of the difference between producing for the home market and producing for foreign consumption. In contradistinction to these assumptions, Ekins [*1989: 186*] argues that goods produced for export will have different environmental impacts from goods produced for domestic consumption. This can be seen in the link between beef production for hamburgers and the destruction of rainforest.

Thirdly, international trade may have a negative impact on the environment because of the extended distribution networks. Given that domestic markets externalise environmental costs, international trade, in extending the distribution chain, will result in greater market failure and increased environmental costs [Ekins, 1989: 186].

Fourthly, international trade results in the reinforcement of certain patterns of consumption and taste transfer, both of which may increase pollution and environmental costs. Traded products may themselves have high pollution contents or through their consumption increase pollution and environmental degradation. The trade in pesticides, fertilisers, and chemicals, for example, can lead to environmental deterioration in the importing country. If different environmental standards are applied in the production and use of some products, for example motor vehicles, trade could result in deteriorating standards in importing countries.

On the other hand, it is possible to point to ways in which international trade can improve environmental quality and lessen environmental costs. First, trade that is not subject to protectionist barriers will increase international specialisation. If trade results in a shift in production from countries with low environmental absorption capacities (EACs) to those with high EACs then world welfare will improve.

Furthermore, as Anderson demonstrates, trade in goods that are relatively pollution-intensive can have a beneficial impact on the environment and welfare of a small country. If production is the source of pollution, the country will benefit through import of the good. If, on the other hand, pollution arises from consumption, the country will benefit if it exports the product [1992: 27–35].

Moreover, Walter has pointed out that the demand for environmental quality is a function of income. That is, the demand for environmental quality rises with incomes [1974b: 483]. Therefore, if as liberal economists argue, trade results in increased incomes, this will lead to a higher demand for environmental goods which may be met by governmental action to raise environmental standards [Pearce, 1991: 6].

Environmental Regulation and Trade

The impact of environmental regulation on trade patterns, the gains from trade, and international competitiveness are a major concern of policy-makers in developed and developing countries, and to environmental activists, business people and academic economists. Government officials and business representatives in developed countries fear that increased environmental control costs will lead to a loss of market share in international trade. If a country unilaterally imposes stricter environmental controls on its producers, and competitor nations do not follow suit or subsidise their producers, the competitive position of the former is likely to be eroded. Furthermore, the existence of widely differing environmental standards and a non-uniform policy on subsidies creates the possibility for increased trade conflict.

Policy-makers and producers in developing countries are afraid that environmental protection in developed countries will adversely affect their export prospects. Stricter environmental controls can become a disguised form of protectionism. This form of environmental protectionism is likely to be especially prevalent in agriculture, where health and safety requirements can form effective non-tariff barriers.

Environmental activists in the developed world are concerned that the ideology of free trade will be used to stifle attempts at environmental protection. Environmentalists campaign for more extensive environmental controls and are concerned that attempts to harmonise international standards may lead to the dilution of environmental controls in certain countries since they suspect that lowest-common-denominator modes of settlement will prevail in bargaining processes.

It seems plausible, a priori, that differences in environmental control costs will affect international trade and that countries with more stringent environmental regulations will suffer a loss of competitiveness. The impact of environmental control costs on trade patterns can be looked at from the perspective of the imposing country or from that of other countries. Trade responds to changes in relative prices and therefore a shift in prices resulting from environmental regulation will affect patterns of international trade. A number of studies suggest that environmental control costs account for a small proportion of total costs to industry, on average, [Dean, 1991] and find little evidence that they leads to significant reductions in output.

In an early study, Magee and Ford [1972] used partial equilibrium models to assess the possible theoretical effects of pollution abatement on the terms of trade and balance of payments of the United States. They concluded that the impact depended on the sectoral location of the pollution (export or import-competing), and the type of pollution (production or consumption). They argue that for import-consumption pollution and export-production pollution, abatement will result in an increase in US terms of trade and welfare. Conversely, the opposite occurs for import-production and export-consumption pollution – that is, the US experiences a deterioration in its terms of trade and welfare. A number of subsequent studies using a variety of methodologies have attempted to estimate the impact of environmental control costs on the pattern of trade. James Tobey [1990] argues that the imposition of environmental regulation has had a limited impact on international trade. His findings are consistent with that of other studies which provide no empirical support for the proposition that the imposition of environmental control costs causes trade patterns to deviate [*Dean, 1991: 6–10*]. These studies show that although the imposition of environmental policy will have an impact on the pattern of trade, in some industries this impact will be small and overall control costs do not affect export competitiveness.

Students of the relationship between the world economy and environmental policy have proposed two hypotheses to explain relocation of industrial production. It is widely believed that the imposition of strict environmental regulation in developed countries will cause so-called 'dirty industries' to flee to countries with less stringent environmental standards [*El-Hinnawi and Hashmi, 1982: 10–11*]. This industrial-flight hypothesis accounts for the push factor and the pollution haven provides the rationale for the pull factor. The pollution haven hypothesis predicts that the location of industrial production will be to the developing countries, since developed countries have roughly similar environmental protection standards and developing countries may purposefully eschew environmental protection in order to attract foreign capital. It has been argued that 'such relocations are desirable from a global efficiency viewpoint, since comparative advantage and differences in preferences are reflected . . .' [*d'Arge and Kneese, 1972: 270*]. For others, the possible economic benefits are likely to be outweighed by excessive pollution and environmental damage in the host country [*El-Hinnawi and Hashmi, 1982: 11*].

Evidence shows that neither the industrial flight hypothesis nor the pollution haven hypothesis can be substantiated [*Dean, 1991: 10–12*]. Direct foreign investment is influenced by a range of factors, and the share of environmental costs in output value is too small to be an important component in firms' decision-making. In other words, the savings to be made from relocation are insignificant. One source suggests that far from transnational corporations seeking pollution havens, their activities in developing countries can improve environmental quality. The *World Development Report 1992* argues that 'because it is cheaper for multinational corporations to use the same technologies as they do in industrial countries, these firms can be a potent source of environmental improvement' [*World Bank, 1992: 67*].

So far this examination of the impact of environmental regulation on trade has concentrated on trade in industrial products. An equally important sector of world trade in its potential effect on environmental quality is agriculture. James Tobey, in a survey of the potential effects of environmental protection in agriculture, concluded that 'it is unlikely that domestic environmental policies directed towards agriculture will have noticeable effects on patterns of international trade' [*1991: 94*]. His conclusions were based on a study of US trade performance in ten primary commodities. The two-tier structure of environmental regulation which exists at the global level with stricter regulatory regimes in the developed world and weak or non-existent controls in developing countries [*Runge and Nolan, 1990: 5*] creates the potential for trade loss by the industrial nations. But the limited market share held by developing countries limits the trade diversion effect of stricter environmental regulation in developed countries [*Tobey, 1991: 93*].

This brief discussion of the evidence on the impact of environmental regulation on trade patterns suggests that the effects are minimal. No evidence was found to support the claim that environmental control costs have a damaging impact on terms of trade and the balance of payments. But before leaving this issue it is necessary to point to some of the limitations of the various studies conducted to date. First, no agreement exists on the measurement of environmental control costs and apart from the different approaches taken in the various studies, it is possible that the estimates of costs arising from environmental regulation have been underestimated. Secondly, although such control costs may be low at this point, there is no guarantee that the costs of regulation will not increase in the future. The level at which they become significant has not been determined. Thirdly, discovering the trade effects of environmental control costs is difficult in the absence of a methodology that can isolate these impacts from other factors which influence the pattern of trade.

Trade Policy and International Environmental Agreements

Trade policies can be used to enforce or implement international environmental agreements in three ways. First, trade policy *is* environmental policy. In other words, the international environmental regime is constituted through regulations governing trade in a particular product. The Convention on International Trade in Endangered Species (CITES), the Convention on the Control of Transboundary Movements of Hazardous Wastes and their Disposal (the Basel Convention), and the moratorium on commercial whaling are examples of the direct use of trade measures to achieve environmental goals.

Secondly, the threat of the imposition of trade sanctions could be used to try to ensure compliance with an international treaty. No international environmental treaty includes provision for the imposition of economic sanctions in the event of non-compliance by any signatory. This exclusion is not too surprising given the problem of organising sanctions in a decentralised international legal system [*Chayes and Chayes, 1991: 289*]. And one survey asserts that the prevalent view in the literature on international co-operation is that sanctions are an ineffective way to promote multilateral co-operation [*Blackhurst and Subramanian, 1992: 261*].

Trade sanctions in this context refer to the disruption in trade of products not covered by the multilateral treaty. This is not to be confused with the trade provisions of a number of environmental agreements where the measures are directly related to trade in products covered by the agreement (For example, under the Montreal Protocol on Substances that Deplete the Ozone Layer the Parties agreed to restrict trade in CFCs and CFC-containing products with non-parties to the agreement). The main aim of such provisions is to ensure the effectiveness of the agreement through policing the activities of non-signatories. Blackhurst and Subramaniam [*1992: 262*] state that not only do the trade provisions of such an agreement create an incentive to join, but they also penalise non-signatories who can find themselves worse off than parties to the agreement, and worse off than in the pre-agreement position.

A third way in which trade could be used as a device to enhance compliance with environmental agreements is through the provision of positive incentives. Sand [*1991: 242–4*] lists four selective incentives used in international environmental negotiations: access to funding; access to resources; access to markets; and access to technology. Illustrations of the use of selective incentives in environmental agreements include the Paris Convention for the Protection of the World Cultural and Natural Heritage, which provides funds to assist members in preserving and conserving historical national sites; the Canberra Convention on the Conservation of Antarctic Marine Living Resources provides access to the use of natural resources as an incentive for states to join the regime; one incentive for joining CITES is its provision for market access; and technology transfer to developing countries is one of the provisions of the Montreal Protocol on the ozone layer.

The Political Economy of Trade and the Environment: Competing Perspectives

The relationship between trade and the environment is a contested one. A review of the literature suggests that the conflicting theoretical positions, diverse methodologies, and opposed conclusions can be divided into two broad perspectives. A perspective connotes a set of values, beliefs and assumptions. It is an intellectual framework rather than a specific theory and the adherents of a perspective are linked by a common set of assumptions concerning the objects of study and the methods to be employed in seeking answers to the intellectual puzzles generated by the perspective. I have termed these perspectives, 'liberal' and 'environmental'. Attitudes to the interactions between trade and the environment arise from conflicting perceptions of the benefits of free trade, the potential of market-based solutions to environmental degradation, the current workings of the global economy, and the desirability of continued economic growth. These differences give rise to conflicting policy proposals.

The Liberal Perspective

The liberal approach to environmental economics is enmeshed within a wider liberal economic paradigm. Particular assumptions concerning the nature of economic activity and the correct approach to economic theory; attitudes to nature and the pricing of the environment; and views concerning the merits of free trade and protectionism form the core of the liberal perspective.

The liberal approach to economic theorising is characterised by methodological individualism. This approach views the social whole as merely the sum of its parts. Liberal theories assume that all economic resources (covering production, distribution and consumption) are owned by individuals, and believe that in a perfectly competitive market no individual is able to influence the prices, or quantities of goods produced and consumed. Markets are seen as the sum of the buying and selling activities of discrete individuals. Moreover, liberal theorists assume that the free market economy is responsible for an optimal and efficient allocation of resources.

Liberal theory in the social sciences has rejected a unified political economy and created and maintained a separation of economics and politics. The dominant liberal approach to the study of economics assumes that it is an objective value-free, scientific discourse. The economic system, it is argued, operates under natural laws and it is the task of economic theory to discover these laws. Economic activity, it is argued, is socially and politically neutral, but liberal theorists recognise that in the real world political considerations do impinge on the workings of markets. But, on the whole, liberal theorists believe that governmental intervention in economic activity should be kept to a minimum.

The liberal perspective on nature is embedded within the discourse of Western science and technology [*Shiva, 1991*]. In this perspective nature is seen as a passive good which exists to be exploited for the benefit of humans. Nature is dead, inert material capable of being rearranged, and controlled by mankind. In other words, nature is externalised. The problem of environmental degradation arises because the unsustainable exploitation inherent in treating nature like a free resource was hidden in the centuries of capitalist accumulation [*Merchant, 1992: 41–58*]. Because nature is regarded as a commodity which can be subject to property rights, liberal theorists propose solutions that attach a price to nature. It is only through the pricing mechanism that natural resource costs will be internalised. For liberal economists, perhaps the most important market failure in the environmental and natural resource issue area arises from the absence of property rights over a wide range of goods and services [*Pearce et al., 1989: 5–7*] The negative impacts of pollution and environmentally harmful production and consumption are not automatically reflected in the market price of polluting industries or environmentally harmful economic activities. The broad objective of liberal theories in analyses of international trade is to find the optimal trade-off between trade and the environment. Liberal theorists see the improvement of the environment as arising from the correct pricing of environmental inputs. In this way economics can contribute to the improvement of the environment and the conservation of natural resources.

Liberal economic theory emphasises the dangers of protectionism. This is due to the assumed superiority of free trade and the belief that naturally functioning markets are better than those structured by government intervention. From the liberal viewpoint support for free trade is an objective and not an ideological stance. Liberal economists tend to argue that opponents of free trade are motivated by sectional interests, and that their activities sacrifice the national and international interests since a liberal trading system is in the interests of both the state and the world economy. Liberal economists argue that if the international economy operated according to the dictates of comparative advantage, global welfare would improve.

From the preceding discussion it is clear that in the context of the debate on optimal trade policies to follow in order to enhance environmental quality, the preferences of liberal economists are for trade liberalisation and against protectionism. Liberal theorists emphasise the benefits of free trade and highlight the dangers of 'old-fashioned' protectionism masquerading as environmental concern.

The case for trade liberalisation has been forcefully made by the World Bank. In the *World Development Report 1992*, the Bank argues that

> ... using trade restrictions to address environmental problems is inefficient and usually ineffective. Liberalised trade fosters greater efficiency and higher productivity and may actually reduce pollution by encouraging the growth of less-polluting industries and the adoption and diffusion of cleaner technologies [*1992: 67*].

From the liberal perspective, trade liberalisation is not the primary cause of environmental degradation. This arises from market failure and the inability of governments to engage in adequate environmental pricing. The fear that the influence of environmental groups on public policy will lead to increased protectionism [*Hillman and Ursprung: 1992*] is a constant concern of liberal theorists. Liberal economic analysis demonstrates that given the existence of different environmental assimilative capacities and preferences, protection of domestic industries cannot be justified on economic grounds [*Walter, 1974a: 112*]. As d'Arge and Kneese argue [*1972: 293*], the resort to protectionist devices against foreign producers 'cannot be substantiated on the basis of either long-term comparative advantage and efficiency òr on likely short-term impacts on the balance of payments and domestic incomes of selected countries'.

A key site of dispute between free trade theorists and environmentalists concerns the current and future role of GATT in promoting environmental objectives. GATT, the principal international organisation concerned with international trade, is based on liberal economic principles and concerned to maintain an open and rule-based international trading system [*Pearce, 1991*]. Consistent with the arguments outlined above, liberal economists reject the view that GATT's activities undermine environmental protection. They support the current efforts in the Uruguay Round to liberalise trade in agricultural commodities. The agricultural protectionist policies followed by the major developed countries distort world markets and enhance unsustainable practices. A move to a liberal regime in agricultural trade would benefit developed and developing countries and lead to more environmentally sound policies [*Runge: 1991*].

The Environmental Perspective

It is only recently that a powerful counter approach to the liberal perspective has developed. Although it forms a less coherent and consistent body of thought, and it is possible to distinguish between variety of ecological perspectives, I think that it is not unwarranted to identify certain shared assumptions which help to define a distinctive viewpoint on the nexus between trade and the environment. This environmentalist paradigm differs from the liberal perspective in a number of ways.

Environmentalists are more concerned with the protection of the environment than the promotion of economic growth. Environmentalists reject the separation of politics and economics and propose an approach to the economy which recognises its inherently social character. Environmentalists contest the the assumption that economics is a value free science, and argue that this view is ideological since it masks the real relations of power in the world economy. One summary of environmentalist thinking on international economics claimed that it was based on four guiding or principles:

(1) self-reliant development through domestic and regional orientation;
(2) ecological balance;
(3) solidarity and equalisation of development opportunities;
(4) democratisation of the global economy and protection of human rights [*The Group of Green Economists, 1992: 3*].

No common approach to nature can be discerned in this perspective. At one end of the spectrum some analysts take as their starting points the Western view of science and nature. They therefore attack the underpricing of nature and urge a full environmental costing. The improvement of the environment will only come about, these analysts insist, when domestic and world market prices reflect the environmental costs of production. The objective of trade policies is not only to reflect the real resource cost of the products which enter into foreign trade, but also to limit trade since this, in itself, contributes to a waste of resources [*Morris, 1990: 195*]. Vandana Shiva articulates a critique of the assumptions inherent in Western science and capitalism. She argues that the assumption that technology is superior to nature and can produce limitless growth unconstrained by nature is false [*Shiva, 1991: 24*]. The alternative is a recognition of the inter-relationships and inter-dependence between humans and nature and an awareness of the complexity of nature [*Gaha, 1991*].

Environmentalists object to free trade and believe that trade liberalisation in encouraging economic growth damages the environment. Moreover, production for export markets is held to be more environmentally damaging than production for home consumers. Shrybman argues [*1990: 31*] that 'by putting valuable agricultural resources at the service of export markets, in countries that are not self-sufficient in food, enormous pressures are created for local peoples to over-exploit other resources simply to eke out the barest existence'. And Timberlake [*1985: 69*], in the context of his study of African development, contends that 'planting the best land in cash crops, which almost invariably uses less labour than foodcrops, can push large numbers of subsistence farmers and herders onto marginal land, resulting in desertification'.

Since 1991 environmental activists have made the GATT and the liberal trade regime the focus of their attention [*Thomas, 1992: 104–5; The Economist, 1993: 19*]. The *Economist* suggests that it was the GATT panel ruling, in September 1991, on the United States' ban against imports of tuna from Mexico that sparked the environmentalist challenge to GATT. Thomas charts the new-found activism from July 1991, when a group of environmental and consumer health NGOs sent a joint letter to the Director-General of the GATT voicing concern over the adverse impact of GATT policies on the environment. They voice a number of criticisms of the GATT. First, they argue that GATT is environmentally blind. The organisation falls to take sufficient account of the environmental impacts of trade, and its free trade policy contributes to environmental degradation. Second, they contend that GATT restricts state sovereignty and so prevents countries from taking trade-related measures – for example resorting to countervailing duties, imposing export bans and granting subsidies designed to protect the environment. Third, environmentalists are concerned that proposals in the Uruguay Round to harmonise product standards will force countries with higher environmental protection standards to lower them. Fourth, environmentalists would like international environmental treaties to take precedence over GATT. Unless this is agreed, GATT rules prohibiting discrimination against individual nations may remove one of the most effective measures to protect the environment. Environmentalists also contend that the secrecy surrounding trade negotiations renders the process inherently undemocratic [*The Economist, 1993: 19–24; Thomas, 1992: 100–112; Shrybman, 1990: 30–34*].

Ecology and the International Trading System

The international trading system refers to the complex network of cross-border trade and the national and international rules and regulations designed to supervise this activity. Changes in the structure of global production, the international division of labour, and the rules governing the exchange of goods and services affect the pattern and spread of environmental degradation.

It is now widely accepted that current patterns of trade and development have environmental consequences. The potential gains from trade and the impact of protectionist policies are sallent factors in determining patterns of environmental degradation. The international trading system is thus of crucial importance in the attempt to usher in sustainable development. Although the concept of sustainable development is contested, with no agreed definition [*Pearce et al., 1989: 28–50; 173–85*], the usage of the Brundtland Commission has become widespread. The Commission defined sustainable development as 'development that meets the needs of the present without compromising the ability of future generations to meet their own needs [*World Commission on Environment and Development, 1987: 38*].

Policies to promote economic growth and a rational exploitation of the world's resources consistent with future as well as present needs will be unsuccessful unless the gains from trade are equitably distributed. In the contemporary global economy, this necessitates a reversal in the terms of trade of countries exporting primary commodities, the cessation of protectionist policies by developed countries against the exports of developing countries, and the promotion of successful export diversification strategies by Third World governments. The combined effect of poverty and an unequal trading system perpetuates unsustainable development, environmental degradation and poverty.

Although it is frequently asserted that the international trading regime is one of free trade, it would be more accurate to label it a regime of managed trade. The dominant ideology is that of free trade, but in practice liberal principles are frequently sacrificed in favour of mercantilist interests. Analysis of the environmental implications of the international trading system cannot, therefore, be confined to discussion of trade liberalisation but must also assess the impact of protectionist policies on trading patterns and resource use.

Power, Protectionism and Environmental Issues

A key question facing environmentalists and governments concerns the unilateral imposition of environmental standards or trade bans. The demand for stricter environmental controls in the North raises questions concerning equity and efficiency. The debate on environmental control standards cannot effectively be removed from considerations of power. In the contemporary global political economy it is clear that Northern countries possess greater economic leverage than Southern ones. Thus, the developed states have the potential to impose tighter environmental controls with the effect of restricting the exports of the developing countries in the face of Southern opposition. The problem faced by developing countries is that on one hand, they are unhappy with the prevailing liberal ideology underpinning the international trading system and, on the other, retreat from multilateralism exposes them to unilateral policies which may be more detrimental to their interests.

Post-war international trade in agriculture provides an example of the ability of the richer countries to evade the rules they created, with harmful consequences for the developing world. The impressive liberalisation of trade in industrial products since 1947 has not been applied to the agricultural sector. In this context, it is not surprising that the main stumbling-block to the conclusion of the Uruguay Round is the inability of the negotiators to resolve the impasse over ending protection in agriculture. The exclusion of agriculture from post-war trade liberalisation was the direct result of the farm sector policies followed by the major industrial countries. They erected domestic price support systems to enhance farmers' incomes, maintain food sufficiency and stabilise agricultural prices. This protectionism affected international prices and the pattern of trade and resulted in the developed countries increasing their share of agricultural trade at the expense of the developing countries.

The agricultural protectionism of the developed countries depresses the foreign exchange earnings of many developing countries reliant on the export of primary commodities. The environmental consequences of these policies are twofold. Reduced earnings for the developing countries increases their indebtedness and leads to an 'unsustainable overuse of the natural resource base' [*World Commission on Environment and Development, 1987: 80*] through expanding the acreage given to cash crops or cattle ranching. Furthermore, in shifting production to the developed world, such policies promote the overuse of energy, pesticides and fertilisers in the North [*Porter and Brown, 1991: 136–17*].

The current debate on environmental protection should be viewed in the context of the history of protection in the global political economy and the differential power resources of the various national actors. In other words, the conflict between free trade and protectionism is an inherent feature of the liberal trading system, and the resolution of the conflict owes more to the power of sectional interests than the demonstrable welfare benefits of free trade.

The resort to protectionist devices to limit environmental degradation is likely to win support from commercial interests keen to protect market share. Moreover, it is doubtful whether it will be an easy task to decide if a protectionist measure is genuinely targeted at protecting the environment or in fact is in the interests of domestic producers. Given the unequal power relations in the global political economy the resort to trade bans and other measures may constitute eco-imperialism.

The evidence concerning the efficacy of using international trade to promote environmental goals is disputed. Liberal economists contend that such measures are inefficient and inappropriate. They propose that instead of agitating for trade bans, and other punitive actions, environmentalists should place emphasis on the source of pollution or environmental damage and direct policies to that source.

Environmentalists lament the failure of existing global institutions to support national restrictions taken to protect the environment. Perhaps the most celebrated case concerns the 1991 GATT Panel ruling on the ban by the United States against the import of 'dolphin destructive tuna' from Mexico. Under the Marine Mammal Protection Act the US embargoed tuna caught in purse-seine nets which also entangled and killed dolphins swimming in the fishing area. The US forbade the import of tuna where the number of dolphins killed was in excess of the average number killed by US tuna ships. The GATT Panel ruled that a country could not discriminate on the basis of the process of manufacture of a product. It also ruled that Article XX of the General Agreement did not allow its provisions to be applied extra-territorially [*Arden-Clarke, 1991; Pearce, 1991: 14–21*]

Conclusions

In the post-UNCED period, the salience of international trade for efforts to protect the environment is becoming increasingly recognised. At the present time a clear division exists between advocates of free trade and environmentalists. The World Bank, GATT and liberal economists argue that protection of the environment is better served by liberal trade policies. They contend that the best path to sustainable development is through the decrease in barriers to trade, hence using world resources optimally. Free traders recognise that, in the absence of correct pricing, environmental costs are likely to be excluded, with the result that goods will enter international trade without bearing the full, social cost of production. Liberal economists do not support attempts to harmonise environmental standards since countries possess different environmental absorption capacities, and vary in their preferences concerning the amount of pollution or environmental degradation they are willing to bear. The liberal position is also sceptical concerning the unilateral imposition of discriminatory measures against foreign trade. Such command and control approaches tend to conceal protection for domestic industries. Although liberal economists urge international cooperation to protect the environment, they see little value in trade bans or related measures.

Environmentalists argue that the present international trading system promotes environmental degradation. They oppose attempts at further trade liberalisation. Environmentalists have made GATT the focus of their campaign, arguing that GATT rules and regulations stymie national efforts to protect the environment. Northern NGOs have been in the vanguard of the moves to pressure governments to move unilaterally against foreign products which infringe environmental standards. Environmentalists are also keen on international cooperation, but only where that imposes a harsher regime than existing domestic regulation.

Neither free trade nor protection provides an adequate model for dealing with the problems of environmental degradation. The liberal perspective is seriously deficient because it abstracts from power relations in the global political economy. It may well be economically efficient that pollution from a rich country is dumped in a poor country. The leaders of the poor country may well decide to sacrifice the health and well-being of their population in order to achieve faster economic growth. But to accept (as the example posits), that the international trade in hazardous wastes should result in the poisoning of Third World population is to take a morally bankrupt position. Moreover, to do so means failing to ask questions about structural power and to assume that all choice in the world economy is equally unconstrained.

The environmentalist argument also ignores the centrality of power relations. To attempt to impose identical limits on all countries irrespective of their environmental absorption capacities, or their ability to carry the costs of environmental protection measures or earnings foregone, is to disadvantage certain countries. Unless compensatory mechanisms are in place, the drive for harmonisation will be discriminatory. Moreover, the current structures of the global political economy tend to work in such a way that unilateral measures will be undertaken by the stronger countries. This reinforces existing forms of protection and amounts to a form of eco-imperialism.

The answers are thus to be sought not on the basis of grand theory but through attention to individual cases.

REFERENCES

Anderson, Kym (1992), 'The Standard Welfare Economics of Policies affecting Trade and the Environment', in Anderson and Blackhurst (eds.) [1992: 25–48].

Anderson, Kym and Richard Blackhurst (1992), 'Trade, the Environment and Public Policy', in Anderson and Blackhurst (eds.) [1992: 3–22].

Anderson, Kym and Richard Blackhurst (eds.) (1992), The Greening of World Trade Issues, London: Harvester Wheatsheaf.

Arden-Clarke, Charles (1991), 'The Cruel Trade-Off'. The Guardian, 13 Sept., p.29.

Blackhurst, Richard and Arvind Subramanian (1992), 'Promoting Multilateral Cooperation on the Environment', in Anderson and Blackhurst (eds.) [1992: 247–68].

Chayes, Abram and Anthonia H. Chayes (1991), 'Adjustment and Compliance Processes in International Regulatory Regimes', in Jessica Tuchman Matthews (ed.), Preserving the Global Environment: The Challenge of Shared Leadership, New York: W.W. Norton, pp.280–308.

d'Arge, Ralph C. and Allen V. Kneese (1972), 'Environmental Quality and International Trade', in David A. Kay and Eugene B. Skolinikoff (eds.), World Eco-Crisis: International Organizations in Response, Madison, WI: University of Wisconsin Press, pp.255–301.

Dean, Judith M. (1991), 'Trade and the Environment: A Survey of the Literature', Background Paper prepared for the 1992 World Development Report, World Bank,

Washington, DC, mimeo. *The Economist* (1993), 'Trade and the Environment', Feb. 27, pp.19–24.

Ekins, Paul (1989), 'Trade and Self-Reliance', *The Ecologist*, Vol.19, No.5. pp.186–90.

El-Hinnawi, Essam and Manzur H. Hashmi (eds.) (1982), *Global Environmental Issues*, Dublin: Tycooly International Publishing Ltd. for the United Nations Environment Programme.

The Group of Green Economists (1992), *Ecological Economics: A Practical Programme For Global Reform*, London: Zed Books.

Guha, R. (1991), *The Unquiet Woods: Ecological Change and Peasant Resistance in the Himalayas*, Oxford: Oxford University

Hillman, Ayre L. and Heinrich W. Ursprung (1992), 'The Influence of Environmental Concerns on the Political Determination of Trade Policy', in Kym Anderson and Richard Blackhurst (eds.). *The Greening of World Trade Issues*, London: Harvester Wheatsheaf, pp.195–220.

Magee, Stephen P. and William Freithaler Ford (1972), 'Environmental Pollution, the Terms of Trade and Balance of Payments of the United States', *Kyklos*, Vol.25, pp.101–18.

Merchant, Carolyn (1992), *Radical Ecology: The Search for a Livable World*, London: Routledge.

Morris, David (1990), 'Free Trade: The Great Destroyer', *The Ecologist*, Vol.19, No.5, pp.190–95.

Pearce, David (1991), 'Should the GATT be Reformed for Environmental Reasons?', CSERGE Discussion Paper, GEC 92–01.

Pearce, David *et al.* (1989), *Blueprint for a Green Economy*, London: Earthscan.

Porter, Gareth and Janet Welsh Brown (1991), *Global Environmental Politics*, Boulder, CO: Westview Press.

Runge, C. Ford (1991), Environmental Effects of Trade in the Agricultural Sector: A Case Study, paper prepared for the OECD Environment Directorate, Paris, mimeo.

Runge, C. Ford and Richard M. Nolan (1990), Trade in Disservices: Environmental Regulation and Agricultural Trade, *Food Policy*, Vol.15, No.1, pp.3–7.

Sand, Peter H. (1991), International Cooperation: The Environmental Experience, in Jessica Tuchman Matthews (ed.), *Preserving the Global Environmental: The Challenge of Shared Leadership*, New York: W.W. Norton, pp.236–79.

Shiva, Vandana (1988), *Staying Alive: Women, Ecology and Development*, London: Zed Books.

Shiva, Vandana (1991), *The Violence of the Green Revolution: Third World Agriculture, Ecology and Politics*, London: Zed Books.

Shrybman, Steven (1990), International Trade and the Environment: An Environmental Assessment of the General Agreement on Tariffs and Trade, *The Ecologist*, Vol.20, No.1, pp.30–34.

Thomas, Caroline (1992), *The Environment in International Relations*, London: Royal Institute of International Affairs.

Timberlake, Lloyd (1985), *Africa in Crisis*, London: Earthscan.

Tobey, James A. (1990), The Effects of Domestic Environmental Policies on Patterns of World Trade: An Environmental Test, *Kyklos*, Vol.43, No.2, pp.191–209.

Tobey, James A. (1991), The Effects of Environmental Policy towards Agriculture on Trade, *Food Policy*, Vol.16, No.2, pp.90–94.

Walter, Ingo (1974a), Pollution and Protection: U.S. Environmental Controls as Competitive Distortions, *Weltwirtschaftliches Archiv*, Vol.110, pp.104–13.

Walter, Ingo (1974b), 'International Trade and Resource Diversion: the Case of Environmental Management', *Weltwirtschaftliches Archiv*, Vol.110, pp.482–493.

World Bank (1992), *World Development Report 1992*, New York: Oxford University Press.

World Commission on Environment and Development (The Brundtland Report) (1987), *Our Common Future*, Oxford: Oxford University Press.

The Market for Sulphur Dioxide Permits in the USA and UK

ALAN INGHAM

Economists have long recognised that many environmental problems are due to the absence of property rights and markets. Further, they have argued that the creation of markets in environmental goods will lead to the attainment of optimal levels of pollution at minimum cost compared to the use of standards, or command and control methods. Environmental policy and control has often been in the hands of engineers and scientists, and, because they have usually thought in terms of desirable quantities for the levels of emission of pollutants rather than costs and benefits, perhaps too much emphasis has been placed on the standards approach. Economists have therefore stressed the advantages of market approaches to pollution control ever more strongly using arguments and models of some simplicity to drive the message home. However, because of this, there is the danger that the market approach is being oversold in comparison to what it can do in practice when the assumptions of the simplified models may not apply.

This contribution considers the use of market mechanisms, in particular tradeable permits, in the case of an environmental pollutant: sulphur dioxide (SO_2), the environmental pollutant responsible for acid rain. Attempts have been made in the USA to control SO_2 emissions at minimum cost through various trading arrangements. The commitment of the UK Government to the European Community Large Combustion Plant Directive [*Department of the Environment, 1992b: S11–18*] and its

Alan Ingham is a Lecturer in Economics, Southampton University. The author is grateful to Jasmin Ansar of Pacific Gas and Electric and Alistair Ulph of the University of Southampton for their helpful advice and comments. The article was written whilst a visitor at the Institute of Economics, Aarhus University, Denmark, under the Erasmus exchange scheme. The author is grateful for their hospitality. He acknowledges full responsibility for any errors or omissions.

commitment also to decentralised decision making has led to the exploration of the idea that SO_2 could be controlled in the UK through a system of tradeable marketable permits akin to that currently being developed in the USA [*Corcoran, 1991*].

The study examines the theoretical arguments for such a market system, considers the experience of transactions so far in the United States, looks at why this has not been as expected by many, and finally considers the lessons that might be learnt as to how a market system might be implemented in the UK.

The first section looks at the development of SO_2 control since the Clean Air Act of 1956. Section II then considers the arguments for the use of markets. It starts with the state in which standards, charges, and tradeable permits are all equivalent. By considering the assumptions necessary for this, and the possibility of their being satisfied in practice, we can see that tradeable permits are likely to have considerable advantages over the other methods. Section III then looks at such markets in practice in the USA. The evidence is that markets have not emerged where they might have been expected to have do so, and there is some doubt as to whether they will emerge in any substantial way in the future. The final section draws some conclusions for the implementation of tradeable permit markets in the UK.

Different controls are sometimes compared by their impact on particular goals; for example, environmental effectiveness, minimisation of resource costs, minimisation of administration costs, public revenues, and so on. Here we look at a different way of comparing different policy instruments, that is by the information they require to be implemented for a particular pollution problem compared with the information that is likely to be available, and secondly the consequences for property rights that are implied.

The Control of SO_2 Emissions in the UK

A brief history of the control of SO_2 puts the problem in context. Emissions of SO_2 from the burning of fossil fuels have been known to be an important environmental problem for some considerable time. For example, 4,000 deaths in London in December 1952 have been attributed to poor air quality comprising smoke concentration and SO_2 content [*Department of the Environment/Department of Health, 1981*]. SO_2 concentrations in London had fallen to ten percent of the 1952 figure by 1980. Concentrations are generally much lower now [*Department of the Environment, 1992a*]. In part this has come about through technical change and fuel switching in domestic and transport use. In part it has come about through the operation of the 1956 Clean Air Act which imposed restrictions on fuel use through 'smokeless zones'. Industry has also been regulated by the classification of SO_2 as a 'noxious and offensive gas' for which legislation has required that best practicable means (since replaced by the concept of the Best Available Technology not Entailing Excessive Cost – or BATNEEC) be employed to prevent escape into the atmosphere.

Table 1 shows the dramatic reductions in SO_2 that have occurred in the past 20 years, and also the shift in balance towards coal-fired electricity generating plant. However recent concern about acid rain [*House of Commons, 1984; Department of the Environment, 1990a*] has led to the desire to reduce emissions even further.

TABLE 1

Emissions of SO_2
in Millions of tonnes

	1970	1980	1990
Emissions by Fuel			
Coal	3.34	3.02	2.84
Solid Smokeless	0.25	0.10	0.04
Petroleum			
Motor Spirit	0.01	0.01	0.02
Derv	0.03	0.03	0.04
Gas Oil	0.16	0.09	0.06
Fuel Oil	2.07	1.13	0.73
Refinery Fuel	0.24	0.28	0.02
All Fuels	6.12	4.67	3.77
Emissions by User			
Domestic	0.52	0.22	0.12
Commercial/Public			
services	0.39	0.20	0.09
Power Stations	2.77	2.87	2.72
Refineries	0.24	0.28	0.11
Other Industry	2.12	1.05	0.60
Rail Transport	0.03	0.01	0.003
Road Transport	0.04	0.04	0.06
All Users	6.12	4.67	3.77

Recent technical developments mean that such reductions are possible even with a constant or growing level of output. Examples include: the use of coal with a low sulphur content (0.08 percent);[1] The use of gas (SO_2 free) rather than coal; flue gas desulphurisation (FGD) commonly known as 'scrubbers'; fluidised bed combustion (FBC); and integrated gasification combined cycle (IGCC).

However, these methods vary considerably in cost, so that an important question to ask is which method or combination of methods obtains the target reduction in SO_2 at minimum cost.[2] For example, the cost in 1979 prices of FGD for a 2000 MW plant was thought to add 10–20 percent to electricity generating costs [*Department of the Environment/ Department of Health, 1981*]. Clearly, the question of minimising cost turns on which plants or sectors bear the reductions and how much comes from new investment, how much from retrofitting. The tradition outlined above is for this to be imposed by government and its agencies. This is often referred to as command and control, or *standards*. It amounts to the imposition of a standard specifying what fuels may be burned (as in smokeless zones) or what technology may be used.

Economists have argued for alternatively, for the use of *charges*, such as a sulphur premium or tax. Such a charge encourages the use of low sulphur fuels or sulphur removal techniques by shifting the cost balance in their favour. A third alternative is to introduce a new market in *tradeable permits* to emit SO_2. The number of permits is limited to the amount of SO_2 emissions that the government wishes, and the price that is paid for the permits is what emerges from market transactions.

The use of markets has been advocated in a recent report from London Economics [*1992*] to the Department of the Environment. It estimates that savings of up to £60–80 million per year could be made. Markets in emission permits in the USA are thought to be able to save 25 per cent of compliance costs for the 1990 emission reductions ($1 thousand million on a turnover of $160 thousand million). The main reason is the very different costs of emissions reduction. London Economics reports the following operating costs for flue gas desulphurisation per ton of SO_2 £33.52 for seawater scrubbing; £90.77 for limestone to gypsum; and £205.65 for spray dry absorption (for a full discussion of the magnitudes of damage costs and abatement costs, see Newbery [*1990*]). These costs must be compared with the premium for low-sulphur coal, and the cost of gas. Using the correct mix of technologies is therefore likely to save considerable sums. The central concern of this study is whether this can be realised.

Economic Arguments Advanced for the Use of Markets

Economists typically consider three forms of policy instrument for the control of the environment and pollution. The first is that of standards, or command and control. As we saw in the previous section this has been the favoured approach since 1952. The other methods fall into the category of market instruments, since they use financial incentives rather than quantity restrictions to control behaviour. Such market instruments could be a financial incentive set explicitly by the government. These could take the form of taxes or charges, or subsidies. Alternatively, the financial incentive could be an implicit one produced by using a market in emission permits.

A market in tradeable permits would work by requiring polluters to possess permits for the amount of pollution that they emit. These permits would be initially allocated in some way, possibly by being given to existing users, or alternatively by being auctioned off by the government. Polluters would then acquire the number of permits that they need to have for the level of pollution that they emit by buying them on an open market.

Which of these methods is preferred will depend on the information that the method needs in order to implemented, the property rights implications, and the characteristics of the pollutant being considered. We should not be surprised if different pollutants are best controlled by different methods.

The first task of this section is to outline what information is required, and to show that, not surprisingly, if we have perfect information all methods are equally appropriate in terms of the efficiency of implementation. This is done in section (a). We shall then look at some of the reactions to imperfect information about pollutants. The first, in section (b), discusses recent policies on the control of technology used rather than quantities of pollutants emitted. Section (c) looks at how permit markets may be particularly good in solving some of the problems that arise through uncertainty. Section (d) gathers together the property rights implications.

(a) The Use of Standards and Charges with Perfect Information

Consider an industry which causes environmental damage in relation to the output produced. This is to keep the analysis simple. (A useful discussion of the economic principles is contained in Hahn [*1989*], Barrett [*1986*], Newbery [*1990*], and Tietenberg [*1991; 1992*].) What is the socially desirable level of pollution that we would want the government to maintain by controlling it through the use of one of the methods mentioned above? Suppose the industry consists of a single firm. It is emitting pollution at some level. An economist's approach to the question is to ask whether society would be better off if output and pollution were increased or decreased. This question is answered by considering a single unit of production, and by calculating the value of the damage caused by the pollutant and the social costs of reducing pollution.

We can answer the question by obtaining the environmental costs of extra units of the pollutant emitted (in this case SO_2), or marginal damage cost (MD), on the one hand, and on the other the value of the output produced through those extra units of SO_2, or marginal benefit (MB). We would want to reduce pollution if MD exceeds MB, but to allow increased pollution if MB (the value of the output produced by polluting) exceeds MD (the environmental damage caused). The socially most desirable, or optimal position will be when MD equals MB. If MD increases as pollution increases (environmental damage becomes increasingly costly as pollution increases), and MB falls as output increases (output of a particular commodity is greater when we have small amounts of it), then there is a single quantity that satisfies the condition MB equals MD, and a corresponding value for MB and MD. So the answer to our first question is that we need information about the relationship between the value to society of an extra unit of output at each output level (or MB at all output levels), and the social value of the environmental damage caused by an extra unit of pollution at each pollution level (or MD).

If we have this information we can use any of the policy instruments. In the absence of any regulation the producer would produce as long as profit is positive. However, the optimal amount of SO_2 emissions is one such that any extra emission produces output that is less valuable than the environmental damage caused. This is the amount that we would want the standard to be set at. Alternatively we could charge the producer an amount per unit of SO_2 emitted equal to the marginal damage.[3] Producers will now only emit as long as the value to them of emitting exceeds the charge and this when their emissions are at the level of the appropriate standard. Finally, if the producer had to buy permits, the government would want to ensure that the number of permits bought by the producer cause it to emit the optimal number of units of SO_2, which is the level of the standard, and this will happen as long as the price of permits in the market is that corresponding to the optimal charge.

The different methods may lead to differing financial consequences. The use of charges raises revenue for the government whereas the use of standards does not. The use of tradeable permits leads to payments from those buying permits to those selling and so has financial implications dependent on the initial distribution of the permits. This has been discussed in terms of who has property rights in the atmosphere. In the case of standards or permits it is the producers, whilst in the case of charges it is the government.

We now extend the analysis to the more interesting case where there are two firms in which reducing emissions bears differing costs. It may be that one is a power plant located near to low-sulphur coal, while the other has a plant which is more easily retrofittable with FGD. Suppose they both produce the same output (for example, electricity), and that costs otherwise are the same, so that we are only concerned in ensuring that electricity is generated at minimum cost of emissions. If standards are used, then we have to be sure that we cannot reduce cost by transferring some of the reduction from one plant to another. Giving the same standard to both plants is not a minimum-cost method because the marginal cost of reducing emissions differs, whereas setting a standard for each plant so that the marginal environmental damage equals their own particular marginal cost of reducing emissions *is* a minimum-cost set of standards. Note that if a charge were implemented we would only need to set one, representing the overall marginal environmental damage. Thus the charge has the advantage that we can set a common charge for all producers rather than a whole range of differing standards, potentially one for each firm.

This analysis shows that if we have complete and perfect information it does not matter which method of regulating emissions is chosen from an economic point of view, although for firms with different costs of reducing emissions political considerations may favour the method of charging, which seems like equal treatment, over standards which does not.

This situation changes if information is not perfect. Suppose that the damage costs of extra emissions were constant, and known, but the regulator did not know the benefit to firms from emissions. Setting a charge equal to the damage cost of extra emissions will obtain the correct level of emissions no matter what the marginal benefit is for each firm. On the other hand fixing a standard will require us to know what the marginal benefit is, and may end up being too generous or too restrictive.

Of course, there will also be situations of imperfect information in which setting a standard avoids the information problem whilst a charge does not. If the marginal damage relationship has the property that it is very low below some level of pollution but increases rapidly above that level (for example, a situation where life in a river is extinguished if acidity rises above a critical level), then this leads to a standard of that level at which marginal damage takes off, no matter what the MB relationship is. But the correct tax does require knowledge of this. (This is one of the reasons why many environmentalists advocate standards in preference to charges. They usually forget, though, that if emissions reduction costs vary, then different standards will be required for each plant.)

A similar problem arises if we consider the reduction of emissions from several plants with different cost characteristics. We want to ensure that the marginal cost of reducing emissions is the same across plants, for otherwise a reduction in cost can be achieved. However, if this marginal cost is not known for all the plants, then errors in setting standards will lead to costs not being minimised. The alternative of using a charge avoids this problem, as both firms will choose a level of emissions that leads to marginal cost equalling the charge. If the charge is incorrectly set, however, we may not achieve the level of emissions that we might desire.

The problem with using standards is that we are requiring different standards for all the firms or technologies. In cases where there are many pollutants we could have a different standard for each firm or process and each pollutant. The number of different standards could be very large. Where the standards are set by government agencies, each concerned with a different pollutant, then inefficiencies could arise because no single agency recognises the substitution between different pollutants in the production process. This has led to government interest in integrated pollution control (IPC), in particular control of technology rather than quantities or charges.

(b) Controlling Technology

The concept of BATNEEC[4] is designed with this problem in mind. It works for cases where we do not know what standard should be set, but are able to specify what technology to use. A simple example will illustrate the thinking behind this. Suppose we consider the manufacture of some chemical – a dye for example. There may be three ways of disposing of the waste products generated. One method is to dispose of the waste untreated in a river. This causes pollution, which is felt to be undesirable. Another method is to remove all the undesirable waste. This is perhaps very expensive, and may be thought to be 'going over the top'. A third method is to treat the waste partially so as to remove the particularly noxious components. Technology 1 is perhaps not the best to use, technology 2 is the best but has excessive costs, whilst technology 3 is the best being not excessively costly, and should be the technology chosen. If we are able to assure ourselves that the value of the dye exceeds the pollution costs of technology 3 then we would want industry to use that technology and produce as much of the dye as it deems will maximise profits (providing we can ensure that perfect competition leads the industry to produce an optimal amount). We could achieve the same effect either by calculating a standard of emission or a charge, but we would then need to have information about the details of the technology and its costs to work out what those should be. The nature of the problem is that it is solved by the specification of the technology that should be used.

In the formal definition of BATNEEC, best taken to be the 'most effective in preventing, minimising or rendering harmless polluting emissions', BAT is the adoption of the most emission-saving technology, whilst NEEC is 'can ... be modified by economic considerations where the costs of applying best available techniques would be excessive in relation to the nature of the industry and the environmental protection to be achieved'. BATNEEC is to be expressed as a minimum standard. In the case of costs being low rather than high this minimum standard will be too low. Thus HMIP (Her Majesty's Inspectorate of Pollution, which is to set these BATNEEC standards, needs to have full information to do it correctly. What BATNEEC does do is to recognise at least that in the setting of standards, differences in cost should be taken into account.

However, working out what is best, and what entails excessive cost, may be very difficult in many cases. In the example used it was relatively obvious. In other situations it may be extremely difficult. BATNEEC has been fully discussed by Pearce and Brisson [1993] and by Førsund [1993]. They first comment on the interpretation of excessive cost in terms of 'normal profits' or 'fair or reasonable rate of return' and on the difficulty of defining these, especially for regulated industries. In fact it seems from the official guide in Britain published by the Department of the Environment and the Welsh Office [1991] that one undefined concept is defined in terms of another.

An important observation made is that the level of production of a polluting process will usually be important. Førsund comments that it will always be optimal to reduce the level of production except if there are discontinuities in willingness to pay or in marginal cost (as there was in the example used). If there is a lot of substitution between inputs so that pollution can be varied almost continuously, then we will need to know how much pollution we want to permit, and this may best be done by a charge if we know the damage that pollution does, or a standard if we know that pollution below some level is acceptable but not above it. This means that by focusing on 'end of pipe' technology we are potentially polluting too much and at excessive cost, because a wider view would lead us to consider pollution reduction by output reduction.

BATNEEC may be particularly bad at this because of its emphasis on the firm rather than society. Excessive cost may be interpreted as a cost that would lead the firm to go out of business. But this may be precisely what we wish to happen if that business has particularly poor management with respect to environmental control, is producing a particularly undesirable product or has old plant and equipment. This latter point may lead to particular distortion. If BATNEEC is applied more strongly to new plants or firms than to those with old technology, on the grounds that the latter has an 'excessive cost' of replacing its equipment, then

BATNEEC may lead to competitive advantage being given to old polluting equipment rather than newer less polluting equipment, because the new plant has to go all the way to being best, rather than being just an improvement.

Its emphasis on the firm as the level of control also suggests that the property rights to the environment arising out of BATNEEC be given to firms. As long as they use appropriate technology, then they can do to the environment what they like.

Even the term 'available' is far from clear. Paragraph 5.19 of the official guidance refers to 'a review by HMIP or its consultants of best available techniques around the world. Techniques will be identified which are used in or can be translated into a UK industrial context and which are or can be demonstrated to be commercially viable'. This potentially requires a large amount of information and may lead to BATNEEC being no more informationally advantageous than other methods.

Calculating what is 'excessive cost' will require us to determine the socially optimal level of pollution and to measure the marginal cost of reducing pollution, so that we need exactly the same information as if we were to control the technology or apply a standard. The apparent informational advantage of the BATNEEC approach has evaporated.

(c) Markets as a Solution to Problems of Uncertainty

Suppose now that we are uncertain about both the benefits that firms obtain from emissions, and the damage costs of such emissions. Does the above suggest that we cannot hope to achieve appropriate regulation? This is where the use of tradeable permits is advantageous. The problem is one first posed by Coase [1960]. He considers situations in which one party causes damage to another. His proposal is to create property rights backed up by courts of law and to allow parties to bargain over permission to cause or prevent damage. Coase's contention is that such bargaining will lead to an efficient outcome, no matter to whom the property rights are given. The outcome will depend on who has the property rights, but whether it is the polluting or the polluted party does not effect efficiency. In this case we could think of assigning pollution rights either to those causing pollution or to those suffering it, or maybe the government on their behalf. Either the polluters buy pollution permits from the polluters, and do so as long as the value to them exceeds the value to polluters, or the polluters buy the permits from those potentially polluted, and again will do so as long as the value to the polluter exceeds that to the polluted. Trades will take place as long as the level of output and pollution gives rise to MD and MB being different. After all, if trades have taken place in a perfect market MB will equal MD. So the level of pollution will be that which would be the optimal standard and the permits will trade at a price equal to the optimal charge. Thus the market in tradeable permits leads to the same outcome as charges or standards under perfect information.

The main difference is in the amount of information that is needed. If the market satisfies the assumptions required for their correct functioning (and these assumptions are quite stringent and unlikely to be satisfied – see below, then no one requires any information beyond the value of the permits to themselves. The government could issue a number of permits equal to the initial level of emissions (or maybe more) to firms, to individuals, or to itself. The government buys, or retains, permits as long as the value of the damage caused by the level of pollution exceeds the price. If it does not, it sells. Correspondingly, firms buy permits if the value to them – that is, the profits they obtain by emitting the pollution – exceeds the price. If individuals feel that the government is not buying enough permits on their behalf they can themselves buy them, and again this requires that the damage they suffer exceed the price of permits.

The attractiveness of this solution is that the only information that needs to be transmitted is the price of permits. We can allow for differing plants to have differing costs of reducing emissions, and they will all buy permits up to the point where the marginal cost of reducing emissions equals the price of the permit. So we can be sure that the overall cost of reducing emissions will be minimised [*Montgomery, 1972*]. Further, by either issuing just enough permits, or intervening to buy up some, the government can achieve its target reduction. If others, either environmental groups within the UK or foreign governments, believe this reduction to be insufficient for the damage caused, then they can buy up the permits themselves. We can be sure that these further reductions are warranted as the purchasers are having to 'put their money where their mouth is'.

These are some of the reasons why tradeable permits and the use of market mechanisms have been encouraged in the USA [*Tietenberg, 1991*] and proposed for the UK [*London Economics, 1992*]. However, the market approach is not without its problems, as we shall see when we examine the American experience. A whole set of problems, which have been used to criticise the Coase approach, surround the assumptions necessary to ensure that the market will lead to an optimal outcome. These are, first, that we have a large number of buyers and sellers who individually have no market power, and have no transactions costs. Secondly, they are also presumed to act in their own self interest. In particular, there is no monopoly power in the permit market[5] and the buyers and sellers are not regulated by the government. Neither of these assumptions is likely to hold within Britain with the market as it is proposed. As can be seen from Table 1 the permits are likely to be bought by electricity generators using coal, so that there are likely to be at most two possible purchasers – National Power and PowerGen. Further, the allocation of permits is likely to be either through 'grandfathering' (the allocation of permits based on historic emissions levels) or by purchase from the government through auction. In either case the trade in permits is most likely to be between one buyer and one seller. Morever, the industry is highly regulated through the price cap on electricity. Whilst this works indirectly through the Regional Electricity Companies (RECs) we can not assume that the two power generators are maximising profit in a competitive world. So whilst there are situations in which marketable permits will work efficiently, given the information available, there will be situations in which the tradeable permits approach has no advantages over other methods, and may be even worse.

(d) The Implicit Property Rights of Various Instruments

Our discussion so far has been based on questions of efficiency. These are concerned with achieving an optimal level of pollution at least cost. Different methods do imply different property rights. Taxation gives the government an implicit property right to the environment, on behalf of society. Subsidies give implicit property rights to polluters, as society has to buy them off. Standards share property rights between society and the government, in that polluters have rights up to a certain level, and society in the rest. For markets, it depends how the permits are allocated. If they are auctioned off, then this is tantamount to society selling its rights to polluters. If permits are allocated by past use, as in 'grandfathering', then we are ascribing property rights to polluters.

In a perfect world we could separate the question of efficiency from ownership of the environment. A tax levied on polluters could be returned to them in such a way that the introduction of an environment tax does not make them worse off. Similarly, subsidies paid to polluters to reduce their emissions could be clawed back from them. In practice, though, it may be difficult to implement these corrective policies, so that the choice of policy instrument may imply particular ownership rights in the environment. Thus the discussion about policy instruments may reflect as much the property right implications as the efficiency characteristics. Or the efficiency advantages of a method of control may hide a decision concerning property rights in the environment.

Tradeable permit markets have the advantage that the allocation of property rights is made transparent through the rules used for the initial distribution of permits. So we might expect that the discussion of efficient methods for control can be carried out independently of the discussion of the ownership of the environment.

To see what traders might emerge we now turn to the American experience.

The American Experience in Using Tradeable Permits Since 1970

Whilst the USA has had clean air legislation since about the same time as the UK the different structure of power generation has led to a different approach being used. In 1970, whereas the British government could pursue policy by issuing directions to the CEGB, the American administration introduced legislation appropriate to the decentralised nature of its power industry and also to the vast size of the country. A brief and probably simplistic description of the 1970 legislation follows (see Hahn and Hester [*1989*] for more details).

First the Environmental Protection Agency (EPA) was set up to oversee the policy. Secondly, the USA was divided into 247 regions, some at risk from acid rain, some not. Thirdly, states had to have their own implementation plan (SIP) and also had to implement the EPA standards through the issue of permits. Emissions, fourthly, may be traded through Emission Reduction Credits (ERCs) which are property rights to emit, and are created through reducing emissions levels below a baseline level. Finally, firms may engage in four types of trade. The first of these is *offsets*. If a new emission source locates in a region at risk (a non-attainment area), it has to obtain ERCs either internally within the firm or from another firm in that region. The second is *bubbles*, by which existing sources may increase emissions by obtaining ERCs either internally within the firm or from another firm operating in the same region.[6] Through the third – *banking* – states may allow for ERCs to be transferable over time, so that ERCs owned but not used one year may be used in future years by the firm banking the credit or by another purchasing it. The fourth is *netting* – as when a firm may increase emissions at one source if it decreases them at another so that the net effect does not correspond to the magnitude of emissions from a new major source.

The experience of the use of these was that netting was used a a great deal. Hahn and Hester quote 900 sources using netting in 1984 and 60 sources using offsets, which is thought to exceed the extent to which bubbles and banking have ever been used. Yet it is bubbles and banking that form the heart of the market trading system. Hahn and Hester provide several explanations why the markets that were expected in the form of bubbles and banking have not emerged. They centre around the layers of bureaucracy imposed on the markets. The fact that banked credits were by arrangement with the states led firms to feel that the credits could not be relied on. Firms suspected that if a state fell into difficulties then it could cancel the banked credits. Thus the literature contains lengthy discussion on what the 'property rights' in such banked credits really are. Bubbles are set up by firms themselves and require approval either from the EPA or from part of the SIP. This means that there is a large transaction cost involved in forming a bubble, and bubbles have only been formed when the cost savings have been large. The general impression given is that whilst there was the opportunity for markets to emerge, they did not generally do so, and this was mainly due to the cost of organising agreements and of negotiating with both states and the EPA.

The lack of the use of market schemes has led to much discussion about the model used to justify market methods. The argument that claims that permit markets work depends on simultaneous trades occurring between agents who can easily locate each other. This, however, is the classic paradigm of a market that is now being challenged by developments in game theory such as those put forward by Rubinstein and Wolinsky [1990], where the market trading process is modelled as one that starts with matching traders who then trade with each other.

The consequences of this for the permits markets is discussed by Atkinson and Tietenberg [1991]. They recognise that whereas the model used to generate results on the desirability of a market mechanism requires trades that are multilateral and simultaneous, in fact the process has been bilateral and sequential with restrictions imposed on the process by the SIPs. They model the consequences of using various trading rules for the cost reductions obtained by using tradeable permits rather than command and control.

Reducing emissions has a cost for each firm. There is a matrix of transfer coefficients for the pollution from sources to receptors and SIP constraints on the pollution at those receptors. The PA rules do not permit these constraints to be exceeded. However, they also forbid trades that might increase the pollution levels at any source, even though that source may be well below the required pollution levels.

Various trading rules are considered, ranging from those in which must information about the potential trades is used to one in which rather little information is used. In all of these, trades take place in emission reduction credits between sources so as to comply with the SIP standards. Essentially, sources with low abatement costs trade with those with high abatement costs. Most sources need to reduce to meet the SIP standards but maybe not all. However, those that could increase their emissions and stay within the requirements are prevented from doing so by another EPA rule that does not allow any trade to lead a source to increase its emissions. It is thus saying that everyone has to reduce but maybe some more than others. The trading processes allow for multiple outcomes, with the outcome chosen being dependent on the trading rules. For it to happen that there is full information, and all trades take place simultaneously, there has to be some distortion in the trading process. Essentially, it is that when two traders meet, they trade as much as possible and the trading process may not allow for this to be corrected. So that if an excess of trade takes place there may be no way for it to be corrected.

The 'high-information simultaneous' case is one where a trading process is designed to minimise cost by a simultaneous re-allocation of emissions, but with the EPA restriction that no-one can increase emissions. The 'high-information sequential' case is one in which the firm with the lowest marginal cost of reduction considers its trades first knowing who potential purchasers are. It trades with the firm with the largest cost difference to equalise marginal cost, if this is possible, but no trade violating EPA rules is allowed. If a trade is not feasible it is scaled back by five percent for up to 20 times until either a feasible trade is found or no trade takes place. The trading process then moves to the next best seller in the sequence. Compared to these full information cases are 'Partial information trading rules' where information about the location of traders is limited. Two rules are applied. The first is where the firms with the lowest marginal costs trade first. The second is where the order of trading is random. As well as this there is the question about whether the matching of traders takes into account the restrictions of the EPA. When they are taken into account before matching occurs, this is referred to as the *ex-ante* case. If matching takes place before feasibility, it is known is the *ex-post* case. For the more stringent secondary standards the percentage potential cost savings are as in Table 2.

This table shows that the EPA rule forbidding increases in emissions loses a third of the potential savings, and that the sequential nature of trades loses a further six, even with full information. Partial information can reduce this to a quarter. Trading does reduce cost, but in situations where a lot of trades may be necessary only about a quarter of the savings expected from the least cost benchmark may be achieved.

A widely quoted table, for example, London Economics [*1992: 87, Table A2*], suggests that least cost – the absolute minimum with perfect allocation – can be up to a twentieth of command and control cost. These two results suggest that the tradeable permit cost may be nowhere near this level of reduction. It does seem that in advocating tradeable permits the costs of this are taken to be least cost, so that a comparison is made

TABLE 2

Least Cost Benchmark	100%
SIP Benchmark	0%
Full Information	
Simultaneous	66%
Sequential	50%
Partial Information	
Low MC ex ante	39%
Low MC ex post	18%
Random ex ante	25%
Random ex post	17%

between an actual value and a theoretical minimum. A more valid comparison would be between the costs that actually arise out of command and control and tradeable permits. Nevertheless the scheme has been calculated to have led to significant cost savings. Hahn and Hester quote figures for cost savings of $12 thousand million from netting, $500 million from bubbles, with savings from offsets being large but not easily measured, and savings from banking being small.

A somewhat different reason for a short fall in expected trades, but one also based on a trading model than does not have perfect competition features, is provided by Malueg [1990]. Malueg considers a situation in which the output market of the polluting firms that are trading permits is not competitive. This is the case for electricity generation, which is the main industry involved in SO_2 production. Even though the permit market may be competitive, and there are no trading costs, then some firms will be worse off if command and control is replaced by tradeable permits, and it is even the case that overall welfare may fall. The reason for this is that in the oligopolistic output market the changes in costs that arise from the change in policy instrument cause a reshuffling of output between the firms, and it is not certain that output is directed towards the cheaper firms. In the Malueg model the level of output will change as the environmental control policy changes, whereas for the models used to justify tradeable permits output is taken as fixed.

In order to obtain these results there must be some difference between the cost changes for different firms. However, in electricity generation this is likely to be the case, as firms will have different ages of equipment and use different fuels, some of which are very much affected by changes in policy instruments – such as high-sulphur coal – whilst some are completely unaffected, as in the case with natural gas.

It is also the case that regulation of the rate of return will reduce the incentive to engage in trading permits. Imposing a ceiling on the rate of return that a utility may make increases the capital that the utility uses. It may well be that one way the utility does this is to over-invest in scrubbers. This may well lead to no firms entering into the permit market.

This mechanism was modified in 1990 by amendments to the Clean Air Act and stricter emissions reductions. These amendments changed the previous system (see Corcoran [1991], and Linder and Comer [1991] for further details and discussion) by allowing trades in permits nationally, requiring 111 large generating plants to reduce emissions by 2.5 lbs per mm-BTU, and subjecting emissions to state-imposed ceilings. Further extra allowances are available for early compliance.

The first trades under the new rules took place in May 1992 when the Wisconsin Power and Light Co. sold 10,000 permits to the Tennessee Valley Authority for $250–$300 per ton (Wall Street Journal, 11 May 1992). Wisconsin is one of the cleanest operators and Tennessee one of the dirtiest. This trade is quite small, though, compared to the magnitude of emissions. Commenting in The Energy Daily, 8 July 1992, on a purchase of 25,000 permits at a price of $250–$350, which Ohio Edison made from Alcoa, Disbrow, the Chairman of American Electric, observed that these trades would last American Electric for three weeks in the light of their having to reduce emissions by 600,000 tons. Of course we might expect that the purchase of permits will form just part of the strategy towards emissions reduction. A survey of strategies conducted by IIS is shown in Table 3 (see The Energy Daily, 8 July 1992).

TABLE 3

Compliance Strategy	% of Phase 1 Utilities	% of Other Utilities
Switch to Low Sulphur coal	71	32
Switch to other fuel eg gas	39	24
Install new scrubbers	23	10
Purchase emission allowances	16	13
Use dirty plants less	13	12
Improve efficiency of scrubbers	10	19
Retire plants	10	3
Adopt other clean up technology	6	9
Other	3	12
Now meet phase 1 standards	10	–
Already in compliance through 2000	36	–

The other aspect of these trades is that the prices are much lower than was predicted, generally in the range of $400–800 [*Niemeyer, 1991*] (The range quoted here is derived from the premium on low sulphur coal and the cost of scrubbers.) AER*X, an emissions brokerage, in its publication *Air Credit Advisor*, has published price projections from market surveys. In 1991 it reported respondents as being willing to buy allowances at $421 and sell at $950, whereas in its issue of the second quarter of 1992 it reported utilities as being willing to purchase at $175 and sell at $600.

The EPA has extended the use of market-based schemes from allowing firms to trade with one another to auctioning off air pollution allowances by the Chicago Board of Trade. This auction was for allowances that had both been allocated to the 110 utilities and were surplus to their requirements (95,000 phase 1 and 30,000 phase 2), and some new permits (50,000 phase 1 and 100,000 phase 2). It should be added that this forms a very small part of the total permits to be issued (for emissions after 2000 there will be 8.9 million so this auction represents three per cent of the total only).

The utilities were able to specify minimum prices for the auction, but the new permits sold by the EPA had no reserve price. The results of these auctions were reported in The *Financial Times* for the 29 and 30 March 1993. Of the total of 275,000 permits only 150,010 were sold. So virtually none of the permits already allocated were sold. Further, the price obtained for the EPA's permits was extremely low, the average being $439, with a range of $122 to $450. These prices are both substantially below the cost of scrubbers, and the fines imposed for exceeding emission allowances ($2,000 per ton). However they are in line with the AER*X survey figures for 1991 reported above, where the willingness to pay for allowances was calculated at $421.

There were 171 bids, so there was widespread interest outside the utility companies. Purchasers included brokers five (per cent) who may have been acting *incognito* for utility companies as a way of avoiding publicity, some by environmental interest groups making token purchases, coal companies, and smokestack industries, as well as the power companies. The main conclusion to be drawn from this experience is that the attempt by the Chicago Board of Trade to set up a series of auctions and then a futures and options market all based on private sales of permits with reserve prices looks as if it is unlikely to succeed.

Why did these attempts to trade permits appear to have failed? The basic reason is that there is a wide spread between the prices at which permit holders are willing to sell, and the prices at which potential purchasers are willing to buy. The fact that there is a spread is not too surprising. First there is the usual reason for a bid-ask spread in asset prices.[7] There is some risk in holding an asset. The greater the risk in holding the asset the more the return required. This risk is in part due to the fluctuation in prices that may occur, depending on the strategies that utilities adopt and the demand for electricity. The utilities also may feel that there is some risk that banked permits may be cancelled if states exceed their emissions limits.

This risk can be insured if appropriate futures markets or forward contracts exist. A futures market in SO_2 emission allowances has been proposed by the Chicago Board of Trade (see The Derivative Products and New Ventures Group, Kidder, Peabody and Co. [*1992*]), although it is not expected to begin trading until 1993. It is also the case that a large spot market is needed to support the futures market. So it is thought that utilities in the USA will tend to use forward contracts, although these will not realise all the gains from trade in the insurance market that might be available.

A further reason is the capital cost of installing scrubbers or other pollution reduction methods. If permits are allocated on a 'grandfathering' basis then for a utility to have permits to sell it must install scrubbers or adopt some other means of reducing emissions. This requires it to finance the new equipment as well as having the extra costs of running the scrubbers. The price it sells the permits at must cover both of these costs. On the other hand if it can buy permits at a price less than the cost of operating its existing scrubbers then it will switch those off and increase its emissions using the purchased permits instead.

This is one criticisms of the use of permits. The amount of emissions will be the number of permits that are in the hands of the utilities. Thus if there are a large number of permits in circulation, so that the price of them falls, then utilities will buy up permits, switch their scrubbers off and so emissions will be higher than they otherwise might be. Of course, this could be a desirable state. Scrubbers are expensive to operate, use limestone from scenic areas, and produce vast amounts of waste – gypsum – of an inferior type to that obtained naturally.

It should not be forgotten that there is also a cost in terms of adverse public relations. SO_2 is a local pollutant, so that the purchase of emission permits by a utility in a particular area advertises the fact that local inhabitants are to experience a worse environment than they otherwise might. Of course this may come with the benefit of lower electricity prices, but also higher profits for the utility company, which may not be fully appreciated by local residents. Trades that have taken place in Wisconsin, Tennessee and Pennsylvania have led to adverse reaction from local consumer and environmental groups. The *Financial Times* article referred to above also commented on adverse publicity for Lilco, a

New York utility that sold all its permits to Amax Energy, a high-sulphur coal producer which proposed to supply these permits with its coal in the Mid West. If the Mid West utilities used high smoke stacks then the acid rain would appear in New York and the Adirondacks. This is another reason to doubt the wisdom of a market-based approach for a local pollutant.

Advocating the Use of Tradeable Permit Markets in the UK and What They Might Do

Recent government statements indicate that UK policy is changing from one of standards to either BATNEEC or market instruments. In this section we shall look at the arguments put forward for this and the impacts possible for the UK in practice. The overall direction has been indicated by the two white papers *This Common Inheritance* and *This Common Inheritance – The Second Year Report*. The reasons given for the change in policy are, first, that direct regulation is complicated, slow to devise and enforce, and imposes greater costs on industry. Secondly, market instruments are more flexible and cost effective, and allow for fine tuning of controls to make them more effective and efficient. The London Economics [*1992*] study is referred to as the basis for a tradeable permits approach for acid rain. We have already seen that many of the advantages that arise in a perfect theoretical model may not arise in practice. We shall consider here what is expected from market instruments and whether it may be possible for them to deliver.

First we should reiterate the fact that the cost saving may be nowhere near the 22 multiple referred to in London Economics [*1992*] and elsewhere. This is based on an inappropriate comparison of what an actual standard which may be poorly designed can do compared to a perfectly working market. As we saw in the discussion of tradeable permits in the USA, these markets have been far from perfect. However the reasons for imperfection of markets will be different in the UK case. The UK market will consist of two large potential purchasers, the main coal-fired electricity generators National Power and PowerGen, as well as the smaller generators tied in with the Distribution Companies and maybe some environmental groups. It is hard to imagine that the different players will not be able to find each other or do so imperfectly as in the Atkinson/Tietenberg story. Further it is not possible to imagine that there will be the differences in costs that Malueg uses, nor the role of a dominant player as imagined by Misiolek and Elder.

We would imagine though that there will be a strategic component to the permit market. By buying permits and thereby raising their price a firm can increase its rivals costs as in Salop and Scheffman. By precommitting to different levels of capacity they can also influence their own costs and make credible statements about intended output. The oligopolistic nature of the electricity generation business and the fact that the distribution companies are regulated but not the generators means that it will be difficult to discover what strategies will be followed. It would be surprising if there were no strategic component. It seems from the USA that a reaction to the difficulties of strategy might be to opt out altogether and go for technology which means that a firm is independent of the permit market through the use of gas or the installation of FGDs. Thus the imposition of a permit market could lead to maximum cost rather than minimum cost. The dash for gas that has been observed in the UK in the past year may be an example of that.

To understand, therefore, what the implications of a permit market will be we will need to understand what are the strategic aspects of trades. This might be rather difficult. By contrast, a system of charges does not allow for any extra strategic behaviour than that already present. As we saw above charges are almost equivalent to tradeable permits apart from the informational basis. Both charges and permits will require monitoring, one to levy the charge the other to ensure that the permits are not being exceeded. It may be that for permits spot checks only might be necessary, but for charges self-reporting with similar spot checks could be used. Both raise revenue and if both systems are working correctly then the amount raised should be the same. Of course if we were to replace an imperfectly functioning permits market by charges then the amount raised would change. Both systems could be made to correspond to a variety of property rights. It may be harder to organise the return of levied charges in a neutral way, than to decide on ownership of environmental property rights through different allocations of the permits. Both systems return the same information about the reaction of emissions to price. Charges do it by reporting an emissions quantity based on the charge set. Tradeable permits do it by giving a permit price based on the number of permits issued.

Where they do differ is in the information required to set them up. Tradeable permits have the advantage that they can ensure that a given total is not exceeded except by firms breaking the law. For charges some adjustment process will be needed to bring emissions in line with the required total. Further, if demand and technology are changing then it may be difficult to stay within some required amount. Finally, sulphur dioxide emissions do cause problems if they exceed an amount given by critical loads so that a quantified approach is to be preferred.

There is the further possibility of a 'double benefit' arising out of a permit market. In an oligopolistic output market for which there is the possibility of pre-commitment by means of investment then there are incentives to over-invest. This has a social cost. Suppose that the pre-commitment now occurs through the purchase of permits, and that the allocation of permits restricts and shuffles the output so as to solve the strategic output game (this would require some restriction on permits being traded at the time that production is taking place, since otherwise there would be no pre-commitment). Once this is done, costs of production are minimised so that production is efficient, given the allocation of permits. What is being over-invested in are pieces of paper – the permits – rather than real physical capital. Of course the permits will be inefficiently allocated and this will cause too much pollution reduction, over-investment in SO_2 abatement technology, and a switching of fuel to gas. Whilst there is a cost to this there is also a benefit from having SO_2 levels even lower than we otherwise might have. Presumably it is always the case that less is better than more. This claim would need to be carefully investigated. It is certainly possible that using excessive gas and having too many FGDs may be more costly than too much generating capacity of all sorts. However, it is also possible that not all inefficiencies will be equally socially undesirable.

Conclusions

The message from this last section is that markets have not developed in the USA to anything like the extent expected. Most of the trades undertaken are within plant/firm trades that arise out of the very strict and inflexible system adopted in the USA (see London Economics [*1992: Annex A*]). There are several reasons for this. First, the markets were overlaid until 1992 with substantial negotiation with the EPA and individual states. This has led to high transactions costs in organising trades. Second, utilities are regulated and so may install scrubbers as the best way to satisfy the utility regulators, so that the excessive cost of scrubbers should be seen as a cost due to utility regulation rather than a cost in terms of environmental standards. Third, utilities have been suspicious about the property rights they have in banked permits. Fourth, the trade of permits may have costs of negative publicity from pressure groups. Fifth, to decide correctly on the choice between the purchase of permits and installing scrubbers depends on the future price of permits. This risk could be hedged if futures markets existed, but they will not if spot markets are thin.

What does this imply for the use of emission permit markets in the UK? London Economics expects that savings of £60–80 million per year could be made from 2003 onwards. However the scale of the reductions in the EC directive for the UK and the very high share of coal-fired electricity plant in UK SO_2 emissions means that trades in permits will be dominated by those between National Power and PowerGen. It is unlikely therefore that a futures market would arise. They could come to long-term agreements through forward contracts, but these might be seen by the regulator as constituting an anti-competitive practice, as it could be used to enforce a cartel agreement between the two.

The spatial dimension of SO_2 emissions has been emphasised in the White Papers and the London Economics report. However, as London Economics do admit, the EC LCP directive only addresses the spatial problem through reduction in aggregate emissions. If the two companies' coal-fired plants were situated in different parts of the country, then a requirement that there should be different numbers of permits for plants threatening vulnerable areas from those that do not would lead to the efficient solution in which coal is burned where it does least damage. However it should be recognised that negative publicity may result. Indeed, it already exists (*North Wales Weekly News*, 6 Nov. 1992).

If markets can be established, they are a very attractive way of ensuring a given level or reduction in a least-cost way, in both ensuring that polluters adopt the correct avoidance strategy, and in minimising regulatory and monitoring costs. However there are severe problems in situations where the number of polluting firms is small, and where they are regulated utilities. The American experience is not particularly encouraging so far. Trades that have taken place are those which either would be unnecessary under the more flexible pollution control in Britain, or are supported by the existing structure. Whether correctly functioning markets can be established in Britain remains open to question.

Finally, the important message is that the system of control ought to be chosen in relation to the degree of competition that is actually going to occur, rather than to that which is assumed in models designed to sell the tradeable permits package.

NOTES

1. British coal averages 1.5 per cent. The world range for sulphur content is 0.5 per cent to 11 per cent.
2. It is also important to ask what the magnitude of benefits from the reduction is. There is considerable uncertainty about the nature of some of the damage from acid rain, and the location of emissions sources causing that damage. We shall regard the governments targets as being given; the question being how best to achieve those. For example of comment on damages, see *The Independent*, 29 Oct. 1992, p.5.

3. The discussion taking place at present both in the USA and UK concerns the use of permit markets rather than standards. However, charges are used in several countries, for example France, Japan and Norway (see London Economics [1992].

4. See Department of the Environment/Welsh Office [1990]. For a discussion of the development of pollution control in Britain, see Silberton [1993].

5. Hahn [1992] shows that if one of the firms has market power then total abatement costs are only minimised if it is given exactly the number of permits as it would need for the first best-cost minimisation. The degree of inefficiency due to this market power increases as the number of permits awarded diverges from the first best optimal number. Thus in a first best world with market power we might observe no trades taking place.

6. The use of the term 'bubble' is somewhat different to its use in Britain, where bubble is defined to be the area or firms within which emission permits may be traded. Thus the bubbles in Britain discussed are National Power and PowerGen, All of England and Wales including Electricity Generation and Industry, England and Wales plus Scotland.

7. See the spread on foreign currency at banks. AER*X sees the presence of the bid-ask spread as evidence for risk aversion by the utilities. This is not so. The spread will be determined by the risk premium, which is the insurance premium that an individual would be prepared to pay to avoid the risk in fluctuating asset price. This is determined by the degree of risk aversion but also by the return to holding the asset and the variance of returns of that asset.

REFERENCES

Atkinson, S. (1983), 'Marketable Pollution Permits and Acid Rain Externalities', *Canadian Journal of Economics*. Vol.16, No. 4, pp. 704–22

Atkinson, S. and T. Tietenberg (1991), 'Market Failure in Incentive Based Regulation: The Case of Emission Trading', *Journal of Environmental Management and Economics*, Vol.21, pp.17–31.

Barrett, S. (1986), *The Use of Market Mechanisms in the Regulation of Air Pollution*, UK Centre for Economic and Environmental Development.

Coase, R. (1960), 'The Problem of Social Cost', *Journal of Law and Economics*. Vol. 3, No.1.

Corcoran, E. (1991), 'Cleaning Up Coal', *Scientific American*, May, pp.70–80.

Department of Environment/Department of Health (1981), *Coal and the Environment*, Report of Commission on Energy and the Environment, London: HMSO.

Department of Environment (1990), *This Common Inheritance: Britain's Environmental Strategy*, Cm. 1200, London: HMSO.

Department of Environment and the Welsh Office (1991), 'Integrated Pollution Control: A Practical Guide' (mimeo).

Department of Environment (1992a), *The UK Environment*, London: HMSO.

Department of Environment (1992b), *This Common Inheritance: Britain's Environmental Strategy Second Report*, Cm.2068, London: HMSO.

Derivative Products and New Ventures Group, Kidder Peabody & Co. (1992), 'Hedging, Pricing and Trading Title IV SO_2 Emission Allowances: An Introduction' (mimeo).

Førsund, F. (1993), 'BAT and BATNEEC: An Analytical Interpretation', Discussion Paper, Department of Economics, University of Oslo.

Hahn, R. (1984), 'Market Power and Transferable Property Rights', *Quarterly Journal of Economics*, Vol.99, pp.753–65.

Hahn, R. (1989), 'Economic Prescriptions for Environmental Problems: How the Patient Followed the Doctor's Orders', *Journal of Economic Perspectives*, Vol.3, No.2, pp.95–114.

Hahn, R. (1992), 'Economic Incentives for Environmental Protection: Integrating Theory and Practice', *American Economic Review*, Vol.82, No.2, pp.464–8.

Hahn, R. and G. Hester (1989), 'Where Did All the Markets Go?: An Analysis of EPA's Emissions Trading Program', *Yale Journal on Regulation*, Vol.6, No.1, pp.109–53.

House of Commons (1984), *Acid Rain; Fourth Report from the Environment Committee*, Session 1983–84 HC Paper 446, London: HMSO.

Linder, K. and E. Comer (1991), 'Economic Regulation of Allowance Trading', *Electric Perspectives*, Sept./Oct., pp.30–32.

London Economics (1992), *The Potential Role of Market Mechanisms in the Control of Acid Rain*, Department of the Environment Environmental Economics Research Series, London: HMSO.

Malueg, D. (1990), 'Welfare Consequences of Emission Credit Trading Programmes', *Journal of Environmental Management and Economics*, Vol.18, pp.17–31.

Misiolek, W. and H. Elder (1989), 'Exclusionary Manipulation of Markets for Pollution Rights', *Journal of Environmental Management and Economics*, Vol.16, No.2, pp.156–66.

Montgomery, W. (1972), 'Markets in Licenses and Efficient Pollution Controls', *Journal of Economic Theory*, Vol.5, No.3, pp.395–418.

Newbery, D. (1990), 'Acid Rain', *Economic Policy*, Oct. 11

Niemeyer, V. (1991), *Emission Trading: Effects on Utility Planning and Operations*, EPRI, Palo Alto, CA.

Pearce D.W. and Brisson I. (1993), 'BATNEEC: The Economics of Technology-Based Environmental Standards', *Oxford Review of Economic Policy*, Vol.9, No.4.

Rubinstein, A. and A. Wolinsky (1990), 'Decentralized Trading, Strategic Behaviour and the Walrasian Outcome', *Review of Economic Studies*, Vol.57, No.1, pp.63–78.

Salop, S. and D. Scheffman (1983), 'Raising Rivals' Costs', *American Economic Review Supplement*, Vol.73, No.2, pp.267–71.

Silberton, A. (1993), 'Economics and the Royal Commission on Environmental Pollution', *National Westminster Bank Review*, forthcoming.

Tietenberg, T. (1991), 'Economic Instruments for Environmental Regulation' in D. Helm (ed.), *Economic Policy Towards the Environment*, Oxford: Blackwell, pp.86–110.

Tietenberg, T. (1992), *Environmental and Natural Resource Economics*, 3rd edn., New York: HarperCollins.

The United Nations' Role in Sustainable Development

MARK F. IMBER

Overhauling and coordinating the UN's internal organisation to reflect the change in consciousness from environment and development as two separate areas to sustainable development as an integrated policy is a formidable task. The newly created Commission on Sustainable Development has been charged with the tasks of UNCED follow up and national reporting, as well as aspects of UN system coordination. The role of UNEP has been strengthened. The UNDP has an important role to play; its finances far outstrip those of UNEP. New money for sustainable development, meagre though it is, is to be channelled through the Global Environmental Facility which is a cause for concern among developing countries suspicious of its ties with the World Bank. Perhaps more fundamental than organisational constraints are the financial constraints on the implementation of sustainable development policies. Unless the flow of resources via debt repayment from South to North is halted and reversed, even a streamlined UN system will have only a very limited impact on sustainable development.

Great Expectations

The United Nations is both the best and the worst place in which to conduct multi-lateral diplomacy on environmental questions. It is the only arena in which all states can meet on the basis of sovereign-equality, negotiate and agree new norms of behaviour and even adopt binding

Mark F. Imber is Lecturer in the Department of International Relations, University of St Andrews, Fife Scotland, KY 16 9AL. Research for this article was supported by the ESRC, Grant No. ROOO 23 2457. The author is also grateful to many colleagues in the BISA-Global Environmental Change Seminar for their comments on earlier versions of this work.

conventions on a range of issues. However, representation is strictly limited to *states*. Therefore entire nations and most indigenous peoples are excluded, and the role of NGOs is strictly marginal. Also, the organisation is dominated by intellectual and structural obstacles which make it difficult to overcome the 'sectoral' as opposed to 'integrated' approach to sustainable development. Finally the gulf between declaratory standards and their implementation grows wider as many member-states' willingness to finance what they vote for, and to submit to verification and compliance procedures in conventions which they adopt, reveal the strains of confronting the *full* agenda of sustainable development. Beyond the reaping of a few green votes in the panic summer of 1988, facing up to the *actual* as opposed to *rhetorical* obligations of sustainable development will prove harder.

The UNCED process, like that of the Stockholm Conference on the Human Environment 20 years earlier, showed both the best and the worst of the UN's potential as an arena for change. On the positive side, the framework conventions adopted on climate change and biological diversity attracted the most public attention. However, the former was flawed to meet American demands and excluded *any* quantitative commitments. The negotiation of a framework convention on climate change (FCCC) continues. The latter convention on bio-diversity was not signed by the US because of objections to its financial implications, particularly compensation for commercial exploitation of natural products in pharmaceutical industry. Later, however, the US announced it would sign. The anticipated third convention on forestry could not be agreed and an anodyne 'non-legally binding authoritative statement of principles' represented the point at which consensus rested. Less well publicised was the agreement to initiate negotiations on a desertification convention, and the adoption of separate but UNCED-inspired resolutions in the 1992 General Assembly on the protection of straddling and highly migratory fishstocks, and the special needs of small island states.

The Rio Declaration on Environment and Development, a brief statement of consensus, demonstrated the manner in which two separate thought processes, one relating to environment and the other to development, had met but not married. However, the *circa* 500 pages of *Agenda 21* with over 2,500 national and international policy commitments in over 150 programme areas, made by over 170 states, comprised the most specific undertaking of its kind to date [*Washington Weekly Report, XIX–6, 1993*]. It provided for action at sub-national, national and international levels and, controversially, created two mechanisms for monitoring compliance which will be implemented over the next few years. One is the standard UN-system provision for a follow-up conference in 1997, while the other is for the implementation of national reporting procedures. The latter has led to comparisons being drawn between the UNCED process and the work of the UN Commission for Human Rights. Both tasks, follow-up and national monitoring, fall to the newly created Commission on Sustainable Development (CSD).

Overhauling the United Nations Internal Organisation

On the principle 'physician heal thyself' UNCED adopted, in Chapter 38 of Agenda 21, a series of measures for the overhaul of the UN's internal organisation to match the shift in consciousness from 'environment' and 'development' as separate issues to 'sustainable development'. The strong preference of the Anglo-Saxon delegations in the preparatory process was to achieve this objective without either creating any new organs, or committing net additional resources. To the surprise of UN watchers, inured to the 1980s Reagan–Thatcher atmosphere of 'no new agencies, no new money', the case for creating a Commission on Sustainable Development (CSD) was made convincingly and successfully during the period between the New York preparatory meeting and the opening of the conference, that is between March and June 1992. An extensive discussion below will detail the structure and functions of the CSD, as it was established after debate in the United Nations General Assembly (UNGA) in October–December 1992 and further debate and elections in the Economic and Social Council (ECOSOC) during February 1993.

The Tasks of the CSD

Besides the task of follow-up and national reporting, the CSD has also been burdened with aspects of UN-system coordination. This may prove to be beyond its means for reasons that will be elaborated below. UN-system coordination shares certain characteristics with black holes in outer-space. All who venture in are torn apart by forces beyond their comprehension, whilst no sight or sound of their struggles or screams emerges to deter others from following. A harsh critic might suggest that rather than being a revolutionary recognition of the concept of sustainable development, the CSD is, in fact, being asked to follow where others have been asked to go, more or less boldly, before: the Administrative Committee on Coordination (ACC), the United Nations Environment Programme (UNEP), the Committee of International Development Institutions on Environment (CIDIE), the Designated Officers on Environmental Matters (DOEM) and even ECOSOC.

Despite arguments at Rio in favour of making the CSD a UNGA organ, and therefore potentially universal, it emerged as a functional commission of ECOSOC (ECOSOC itself had been established by the UN Charter as 'the principal organ to coordinate the economic and social work of the UN').[1] As such, its membership is limited to 53. ECOSOC elects the 53 members for three-year terms from a regional formula, giving Afria 14, Asia 11, Latin America and the Caribbean 10, Eastern Europe 6 and WEOG 13. Elections were held on 16 February, and shortly thereafter the first CSD 'bureau' was created with Razali Ismail of Malaysia as chairperson and Rodney Williams (Antigua and Barbuda), Hamadi Khouni (Tunisia), Bedrich Moldan (Czech Republic), and Arthur Campeau (Canada), as the four vice chairpersons one from each of the regions. In addition to the 53 member states, any other UN member is able to attend as an observer. Furthermore, and consistent with the UNCED process, the CSD has adopted rules for NGO participation which are more generous than those usually operated by ECOSOC. In short, any NGO accredited to the UNCED will be able to apply for NGO status at the CSD, subject to review to be undertaken over the next two years on the whole question of NGO participation. The NGO's themselves fall into at least four distinct types. Global campaigning groups such as FOE, Greenpeace and WWF, scientific-professional networks, thinly disguised producer-cartel groups under bland names such as the Uranium Institute, and the political fringe (the fringe of the fringe), comprising single-issue groups.

The work of the CSD will be organised over the five years running up to the UNCED review-conference. It has adopted a provisional agenda in which certain clusters of issues will be discussed annually, while a separate list of issues will be worked through, several each year, thus covering the 2,500 recommended national and international actions cited in the adoption of *Agenda 21*. Furthermore the CSD will receive the national reports of 181 UN members. Since the CSD is only expected to convene for a two-week period in advance of ECOSOC each year, it is clear that the bulk of its consideration will rest in the hands of its intersessional 'bureau' and permanent staff assigned to CSD from the new Department of Policy Coordination and Sustainable Development (see below for more details on this).

The issues to be addressed on an annual basis have been grouped as follows:[2]

A. Critical elements of sustainability, including international co-operation and domestic policy coordination, combating poverty, consumption patterns and demographic issues.

B. Financial resources and mechanisms.

C. Education, science and technology (to include bio-technology, technology transfer, public awareness and scientific training).

D. Decision-making structures, including the integration of environmental and developmental planning (which might be described as the sub-text of all sustainability questions, including the reorganisation of the UN's own capacities in these fields), and also international institutional and legal questions.

E. The roles of major groups ('major groups' is UN-speak for the role of women, youth, indigenous peoples, NGO's, local authorities, workers and trade-unions, business and industry, scientists and technologists and farmers. Each is addressed by a separate chapter of *Agenda 21*).

The issues to be addressed on the rolling programme, probably starting in 1994, will be organised thus:

F. Health, human settlements and fresh water. *Human* misery will be increasingly concentrated in the great cities. Twenty-two large cities are expected to reach a population of 25 million each during the 1990s, a list headed by São Paulo and Mexico City. Whereas New York, Paris and London each took over 150 years to grow to their eight million size, Mexico City will add that number to its population in just 15 years [*Myers, 1990: 82*].

G. Land, desertification, forests and biodiversity, including integrated as opposed to sectoral approaches to the management of fragile ecosystems and the conservation of biological diversity.

H. Atmosphere, oceans and freshwater. The global issue of the atmosphere is joined with oceans, so defined as to include enclosed and semi-enclosed seas such as the Black Sea and perhaps, curiously in view of F above, the protection of fresh water resources. The link is that river pollution, such as that of the Rhone and Po, are major sources of in-shore marine pollution.

I. Toxic chemicals and hazardous wastes. This cluster includes the two politically sensitive issues of the illegal trade in toxic waste and the safe disposal of radio-active waste. In the case of the former, buying a Third World country may be cheaper than buying land-fill sites. In the latter case, the fundamentalist argument concerns the choice between re-processing and spent-fuel storage. Plutonium has a half life of 24,000 years; no human system of government has maintained continuous law and order and record keeping for more than perhaps 800 years on a generous assessment of the Roman Republic and Empire.

Chapter 38 made a number of additional proposals for UN reform in pursuit of sustainable development. Reflecting the new ethos, the framework in which this is to occur stresses not only 'the principles of universality, democracy and transparency', but also 'cost-effectiveness and accountability' [*Agenda 21: Ch. 38.2*]. In addition to the creation of CSD, *Agenda 21* also provided for the creation of a High Level Advisory Board [*38.16*]. The HLAB is envisaged as a group of experts, appointed in their individual capacity, not as representatives of states, nor dependent for their selection upon any regional formula. Numbering between 15 and 25, the Board will act as personal advisors to the UN Secretary General and will meet prior to the sessions of the CSD.

Strengthening the United Nations Environment Programme

A particularly important achievement of the Rio Conference was recognition of the work and role of the United Nations Environment Programme (UNEP) and the commitments given in Chapter 38.I.1 to enhance and strengthen the role of the programme. Created in 1972 as a direct result of the Stockholm Conference, UNEP has been the agency in which the environmental hopes and fears of the entire UN system have been invested. Within this system, UNEP has been assigned primary responsibility for the promotion of environmental awareness.

Established as a small secretariat in Nairobi,[3] UNEP has both suffered and gained from its size and location. Away from the intrigue and careerism of the UN headquarters, it is also isolated from the struggle for influence. Autocratic in his managerial style, the charismatic Dr Mustapha Tolba has for 16 years enthused the staff of approximately 250 with direction and, by UN standards, a high degree of professionalism and commitment. UNEP has created a role for itself, usually described as 'catalytic and coordinating'. This author has written more extensively elsewhere on the implications of this dual mandate [*Imber, 1993: 58–67*]. Suffice it to say that whereas the role of catalyst (that is, providing modest financial resources and high quality scientific input to pioneering and cross-sectoral projects) has been generally well regarded,[4] the task of coordinating the environmental work of numerous and practically independent UN agencies, most larger and longer established than, UNEP, has proved a labour of Sisyphus. This never-ending story was recognised by the creation of the CSD, which will quite properly liberate UNEP from the burden of coordination. It now becomes one more UN organ to *be* coordinated, *by* the CSD (see below).

The most widely acknowledged activities of UNEP are those that concern global environmental data gathering and dissemination. The Earthwatch programme consists of the Global Earth Monitoring System (GEMS), a reconnaissance satellite-based data-gathering system, and Global Resources Information Data-base (GRID). GEMS–GRID contributes data to the International Referral System for Sources of Environmental Information (INFOTERRA). UNEP also administers the International Register of Potentially Toxic Chemicals (IRPTC), and the Convention on International Trade in Endangered Species (CITES). Having taken a prominent role in bringing parties together on the question of ozone-layer depletion, an expansion of these responsibilities has been the early stages of administering the Ozone Fund created in connection with the Montreal Protocol. Before responsibility was wrested from it by the General Assembly in December 1990, UNEP had also taken the lead, bequeathed by the IPCC, on negotiations for a framework convention on climate change. It continues to provide a major technical input to this process despite the creation of an International Negotiating Committee (INC) under General Assembly auspices.

Agenda 21 sets out a manifesto for growth in UNEP, although careful to use the financially reticent language of 'an enhanced and strengthened role' [*Ch. 38. 21*]. UNEP is specifically re-confirmed in it catalytic role, within the UN systems, also in promoting policies, and developing new techniques in the fields of accountancy and economics not currently strengths of the programme. UNEP is further charged with the coordination of scientific research, its dissemination, and 'raising general awareness and action in the area of environmental protection with the general public, non-governmental entities and intergovernmental institutions' [*Ch. 38. 21 para. c–g*]. More specifically, Chapter 38 gives UNEP the lead responsibility for the development of international environmental law, environmental impact assessments, regional co-operation, technical advice to governments in collaboration with the United Nations Development Programme (UNDP), and (a particular initiative of Dr Tolba's), a role in environmental emergency planning [*Ch. 38. paras, h–n*].

The UNDP and Other Agencies

Equally explicitly, Chapter 38 places other burdens directly on UNDP which as the other half of sustainable development, in fact outranks UNEP within the system, by the single criterion which counts: financial donations. Taking the pre-Rio budgetary cycle, UNDP was in receipt of $948 million in 1988, compared to UNEP's meagre $31 million for 1987, just 3.2 per cent of the money donated to the larger programme.[5] UNDP's tasks are defined as having lead-agency status for capacity building at local, national and regional levels. It is to mobilise donor resources, strengthen its own programmes and assist recipient countries in coordinating their follow-up to the UNCED [*Ch. 38. 24 and 38. 25*].

Other provisions in Chapter 38 assign further duties to the full range of appropriate UN agencies: the United Nations Conference on Trade and Development (UNCTAD), the Sahelian Office, the specialised agencies and the international financial organisations are each appropriately cited [*Ch. 38. 27–41*].

However, for sustainable development to represent a culture-shift rather than an additional slogan, the UN system will require more than the paper-commitments of the Agenda 21. It will require an overhaul of the mechanisms for coordination, and massive net additional funding. The lesson of the last decade is that whereas finance will definitely *not* be forthcoming without structural reform, such reform is unlikely. As we shall see, in global terms, compared to other financial flows, the picture is bleak.

The Global Environmental Facility

The principal source of new money linked to UNCED is the Global Environmental Facility (GEF). This tri-agency fund brings together UNEP, UNDP and the World Bank. It is significant both for its innovation and for its attempt at integrated rather than sectoral action. Sums of around $2.5 thousand million have been mooted, but very specific limitations apply to GEF money. Projects must have global benefits and be unlikely to be funded unilaterally, especially by LDCs; and they must fall outside the scope of conventional bilateral overseas development aid. GEF funds are available only to countries with a per capita income of less than $4,000 in 1989.

GEF was launched in 1990, for an initial three year trial period, as a result of cooperation between the agencies. Initially funded to the tune of $1.3 billion, GEF was to operate by a combination of grant-aid and low interest loans. It was the focus of both favourable publicity and controversy during the UNCED. The innovation and size of resources devoted to GEF was promoted by the Group of Seven (G7) developed countries as evidence of their commitment to sustainable development. However, to the Group of 77 (G77) developing countries the size of the fund and the number of caveats attached to its operation was evidence of the weak and partial commitment of the G7. Also its location within the World Bank was a cause of great concern and suspicion, especially regarding transparency and accountability. Although climate change, ozone layer protection and maritime pollution issues are eligible for funding, adaptive strategies for climate change, or the mass of issues central to Third World urban life, must continue to receive national, or bi-lateral funding. The greatest single obstacle to this sort of commitment on the part of the LDC's remains the draining effects of the net transfer of wealth from South to North that has been created by the debt crisis.

Coordinating the Coordinators?

Superficially there has been progress. Most obviously, the creation of the CSD represented a late conversion to the cause of 'one-more-agency' after a decade of resistance from the US and UK leadership of the Geneva-group of donors. Since 1986, reform in the UN has been led by financial stringency, cost-cutting, zero real growth and an accountant's concern for cost-effectiveness. There is nothing intrinsically wrong with financial stringency in organisations of international government responsible for the dispersal of several billion dollars of overseas development assistance (ODA). The problem arises when such stringency becomes a policy objective in its own right rather than a measure of efficiency. By the late 1980s, the intellectual credibility gap and the double standard involved in some attacks on UN financial rectitude became substantial. The Reagan administration demanded consensus procedures within the Committee on Programme and Coordination, which was granted after 1986, and a further detailed review of the Secretariat's structure was undertaken by the Committee of 18 [*Taylor, 1988: 226–34*]. However, throughout this period, the US use of financial penalties against the UN became the single largest cause of the financial crisis faced by the organisation. After 1988 the source of the difficulties shifted from the White House to Congress, when successive bills introduced by President Bush to make good the arrears of several years foundered on Congressional opposition. The US used a combination of withholdings, late-payments and arrears to become by the end of 1992 the largest debtor in the UN system (withholdings are monies withheld from the UN by legislation or executive decision, such as the US share of UN monies spent on abortion programmes by the United Nations Family Planning Agency (UNFPA); late payments are monies paid after the 60–day deadline required by the UN, but within the two-year deadline, after which monies owed are properly termed arrears). In September 1992, the extent of US payments outstanding for more than 12 months stood at $554 million. The cash-flow of the UN was more affected by the further $624 million due in 1992, that was still owing nine months into that year. [*Washington Weekly Report, XVIII, 1992*]. Furthermore, despite the much touted US claim to be unfairly carrying 25 per cent of the assessed budget of the organisation, the decline of the US contribution to multilateral programmes was so great as to rank only eighteenth in ODA *per capita,* in 1992 [*World Resources, 1992–93: 236–7*], at 0.2 per cent of GDP.

The UN Secretariat was substantially reduced in staffing and re-organised into larger departments, one with specific responsibility for the UNCED, by a series of reforms initiated by Boutros Boutros Ghali after February 1992 and completed by the end of that year. On 3 December 1992, the Secretary General announced the creation of the Department for Policy Coordination and Sustainable Development (mentioned above) under the direction of Under-Secretary General Desai. It is this Department which will in turn provide the staff for both the CSD and the High Level Advisory Group of individual experts. Although the CSD has been created to undertake the task of coordinating sustainable develop-ment policy, it will in turn be subject to the coordinating efforts of ECOSOC and of the sub-committee structure, the 'Inter-agency com-mittee on sustainable development'. Ultimately the buck stops at the UN General Assembly, which is the principal organ to which all except the Security Council are accountable. Chapter 38 confirms the role of the Assembly as 'the highest level intergovernmental mechanism ... the principle policy making and appraisal organ on matters relating to the follow-up to the conference' [*38. 9*]. In addition to receiving the annual report of ECOSOC, the Assembly may also table an annual debate on the Rio follow-up, either in plenary, or in its Second Committee. The UN's way of streamlining itself seems dubious.

The Burden of Debt

The North-to-South flow of capital projected by GEF is swamped by the reverse flow amounting to approximately $40 thousand million per annum, South-to-North, which is paid by the world's poorest states in interest charges on the $1,300 thousand million debt currently borne by the Third World [*Miller, 1990: 25*]. If this flow of capital could be halted, or even reversed, this would provide the greatest single source of funds for sustainable development and for the implementation of programmes of soil conservation, sewage treatment, child survival, public health-care, public transport investment and energy-efficiency amongst the poorest third of the human population. It would also provide the best chance of persuading Third World governments to comply, nationally, with inter-national agreements. Despite much adverse publicity and hype surround-ing the Mexican and Brazilian defaults in 1982, the overwhelming majority of debt *is* serviced, and the private sector banks risk little as they derive some tax advantages from accounting provisions made for the tiny proportion of debt that does fail.[6]

Susan George has calculated that the Third World has to date transferred to the North, in real prices, a sum equivalent to *six* Marshall Plans
[*George, 1991: xv–xvi*]. The structural adjustment packages used by the
IMF and the World Bank to manage the debt crisis have had a catastrophic human and environmental impact. The economic gains of the
period 1960–1980 in Sub-Saharan Africa, and parts of Latin America
have been reversed by 'negative growth' and the net export of capital
during the latter half of the 1980s. The rate of child mortality from
preventable diseases in the developing world has been estimated at 12.9
million per annum [*World Resources Institute, 1992: 82*]. Of course not all
of these deaths are directly attributable to the impact of the debt burden,
but UNICEF, in logging the 37 poorest countries that have halved
expenditure on public health during the last decade, attribute 500,000
child deaths to this factor alone for 1988 [*Jolly, 1989: 51–2*]. WRI traces
the full extent of diarrhoea, respiratory infections and whooping cough,
also maternal anaemia and vitamin A deficiency [*WRI, 1992: 82–5*]. On
the linkage between deforestation and debt, George makes extensive use
of Norman Myers' data, to demonstrate a correlation between the biggest
debtors and most rapid rates of tropical deforestation, especially in
relation to Brazil, Mexico, India, Indonesia, Nigeria, Venezuela and
Philippines [*George, 1991: 10*]. Myers himself is more cautious concerning this correlation, and cites additional factors in population pressures,
systems of land tenure and the general neglect of peasant agriculture
[*Myers, 1990: 372–99; also 1992: 430–54*].

The reasons for the debt crisis and its negation of sustainable development are deep rooted and diverse. The decade of disappointment was a
decade of slower growth in the North, of softer commodity prices, and of
continuing protectionism against semi-manufactures and agricultural
produce despite the rhetoric of GATT and achievements in liberalising
North-North trade. Miller also explains that the effects of the Volcker
shock – that is, the rise in US interests rates after 1979 – created
historically high rates across the world. It was also a decade in which, as
shown above, ODA fell to its smallest recorded percentage share of the
developed countries' GDP.

Elaborate schemes have been advanced for debt relief – that is, re-
scheduling – and for debt-conversion, including the attractive but marginal impact of so-called debt-for-nature swaps.[7] However, the depth of
the crisis requires debt forgiveness and cancellation on a massive scale.
Not only does the debt burden blight lives and the environment, but the
people responsible for borrowing and spending it are not those now being
required to repay it. Some of the North's favourite dictators and reliable
clients borrowed the money. It is the children of their democratic

successors who are re-paying it, with interest, every day of their short and blighted lives.

Conclusion

Can the UN, after the cold war's end, confront environmental security with the same degree of vigour and new thinking that has accompanied the shift towards new and imaginative actions in the field of peace-keeping? Not only has the scope of such operations been extended, but new skills such as humanitarian relief, election supervision and the quasi-imperial reconstruction of civil society as in Somalia and Cambodia have been added. Environmental security – that is, action to protect the eco-system from threats to its sustainability – deserves, intellectually and financially, a similar degree of attention.[8] The financial crisis of the UN peacekeeping budgets shows that the costs of war can be more readily summoned than the costs of maintaining the peace. Any attempt to extend the concept of security into preventive actions concerning the preservation of the environment will be even harder to establish. Whereas $9 thousand million was raised for the 1991 war in the Gulf, largely by subscription from the non-combatants Japan and Germany, the UN was owed $800 million of its $3 thousand million peacekeeping accounts at the close of 1992. The Secretary-General has suggested that some part of the $1,000 thousand million expended on defence globally might be converted to the purchase of environmental security. This requires a paradigm shift in how societies define their security. The Secretary General cited mass-migration of refugees, population pressures and barriers to trade among the causes of 'poverty, disease famine, and oppression', which create insecurity and tensions between states.[9] One day of global defence expenditure would fund GEF for one year.

The range of very credible threats to ecological sustainability is grow-ing: desertification, international water-rights disputes, food-security, the prospect of mass-migrations of refugees caused by environmental degradation and the disruption of economies and life-styles are not fanciful, but fit with the low-to-medium scenario for climate change over 50 years associated with IPCC. This is to do no more than mention, without analysis, the disputes that range over population pressure – that is, whether to place greater emphasis upon the weight of Third World numbers or the consumption patterns of the northern minority.

Deudney, whilst warning of the dangers of mixing national security and environmental security vocabularies, provides a very telling summary of the mind-shift that is required to address the latter agenda. The dif-ferences may be summarised thus [*Deudney, 1990: 463–5*]:

National Security	*Environmental Security*
specific threats	diffuse threats
others as enemy	ourselves as enemy
intended harm	unintended harm
short time scales	long time scales

Two cheers for Rio. It took from 1950 to 1989 to revive the great scheme of collective security in the UN. And then many got cold feet when they read what was actually in Article 42. Rio has really done little more than establish the existence of sustainable development as a totem. Definitely more important than the two flawed conventions adopted are the novel procedures for sub-national, national and intergovernmental review contained in *Agenda 21*. At the apex of these proposals are the ambitious plans for an expanded UN role that has been discussed here. As with all questions of UN reform there is no shortage of imaginative paper-work. The most important constraint is political will. The sole criterion by which to measure *that* is evidence of financial support from the G7 and OECD powers, which, despite the exigencies of the contemporary recession are far and away the most able to fund sustainable development. Most obviously this can be achieved by embracing an expanded concept of environmental security that includes some diversion of conventional defence expenditures and imaginative treatment of the debt burden.

NOTES

1. ECOSOC comprises 53 elected members drawn from the General Assembly. Eighteen join and leave in rotation each year after a three-year term (see *Basic Facts About the United Nations*, New York: United Nations, 1987, p.9).
2. The following list is only slightly adapted from that produced by Tom Bigg of the UK–UNA Sustainable Development Unit in March 1993 (see also Kathy Sessions in *Washington Weekly Report* of the UNA–USA, XIX-6, 5 March 1993).
3. The term 'small secretariat' is derived from the General Assembly resolution which created UNEP, and which in the absence of any other formal statute serves as the constitution of the programme (see *UNGA*, 2997 (XXVII), Section II, para. I).
4. See in particular the report by the United States General Accounting Office (GAO), *United Nations; United States Participation in the Environment Programme*, General Accounting Office, NSAID, 89–142, Washington, DC, 1989. Whilst by no means uncritical in respect of the very wide spread of projects undertaken, and the proportion of programme support costs expended, the GAO was generally supportive, describing procedures as 'a reasonable framework for financial management and accountability' (p.19).
5. Data are complicated by the UN organs operating a biennial funding system, and by the existence of extensive trust funds and reserves as well as straight cash donations to the two programmes (see GAO, 1989, p.9; also *United Nations: US Participation in the UN Development Programme*, GAO, NSAID 90–64, Feb. 1990, Washington, DC, p.29).
6. For extensive discussion of the debt issue see George [*1992*] and Miller [*1990*]. George

in particular argues the environmental impacts of debt servicing, and the tax arrangements available across a number of OECD countries which offer substantial protection to private-sector bank debts.

7. Vallely in particular notes the marginal role of debt-for-nature swops as presently practised. See Vallely [*1990: 299–319*]; also Miller [*1990: 62–3*].

8. The literature on environmental security is well discussed by Caroline Thomas [*1992: 115–54*]. On the role of the UN Security Council see Imber [*1993: 67–70*].

9. These remarks and comparisons are contained in the report prepared by the Secretary General at the invitation of the Security Council, which places a discussion of new peacekeeping activities into the wider context of the period since the end of the cold war. See Boutros-Ghali [*1992: 6–7*].

REFERENCES

Agenda 21, UN A/CONF. 151/4 Part IV.

Boutros-Ghali, Boutros (1992), *Agenda for Peace*, New York: United Nations.

Deudney, Daniel (1990), 'The Case Against Linking Environmental Degradation and National Security,' *Millennium*, Vol.19, No.3, pp.461–76.

George, Susan (1991), *The Debt Boomerang*, Boulder, C. Westview Press.

Imber, Mark (1993), 'Too Many Cooks? The post-Rio Reform of the UN', *International Affairs*, Vol.69, No.1, pp.55–70.

Jolly, R. (1989), 'The Human Dimensions of International Debt', in Adrian Hewitt and Bowen Wells (eds.), *Growing Out of Debt*, London: Overseas Development Institute for the All Party Parliamentary Group on Overseas Development Institute, pp.52–63.

Miller, Morris (1990), *Debt and Environment, Converging Crises*, New York: United Nations.

Myers, Norman (1990), *The Gaia Atlas of Future Worlds*, London: Robertson McCarta.

Myers, Norman (1992), 'The Anatomy of Environmental Action: The Case of Tropical Deforestation', in Andrew Hurell and Benedict Kingsbury (eds.), *The International Politics of the Environment*, Oxford: Oxford University Press, pp.430–54.

Taylor, Paul (1988), 'Reforming the System: Getting the Money to Talk', in Paul Taylor and John Groom (eds.), *International Institutions at Work*, London: Pinter pp.220–36.

Thomas, Caroline (1992), *The Environment in International Relations*, London: RIIA.

UNEP (1991), 'Global Environmental Facility', in UNEP, *Our Planet*, Vol.3, No.3, (Nairobi: UNEP), pp.10–13.

Vallely, Paul (1990), *Bad Samaritans*, Sevenoaks: Hodder & Stoughton.

Washington Weekly Report, United Nations Association of the United States of America, Washington, DC.

World Resources Institute (1992), *World Resources 1992–93; A Report by the World Resources Institute*, Oxford: Oxford University Press.

Letting the Genie Out:
Local Government and UNCED

JOHN GORDON

When the role of local government in UNCED follow-up, and more generally in promoting sustainable development, is examined, and when Agenda 21 and the Framework Convention on Climate Change, together with, parallel commitments under the EC's Fifth Environmental Programme, are also taken into account, it must be concluded that increased involvement by local government in international environmental issues is probably inevitable. But its effectiveness in different countries will be greatly influenced by broader factors such as the relative centrality of sustainable development in national policy process, the overall health and vigour of local government, and the nature of the relationship between local and central government. Britain faces particular problems in this area which are likely to damage the effectiveness of local government's contribution.

The Political and Legal Framework

Over the last decade increased public concern regarding the environment and increased recognition of the link between environment and development has encouraged local government in many countries to work together more closely to share their experience in local environmental problems and to promote direct co-operation between municipalities in North and South and (after the fall of communism) East and West. One early milestone in this process was the Cologne Appeal, issued in September 1985 by representatives of NGOs and local authorities from nine European countries calling for North–South co-operation in specific areas at local level to address poverty, growing economic dis-

John Gordon is Deputy and Policy Director of the Global Environment Research Centre at Imperial College, London.

parities between developed and developing countries and increased third world environmental destruction.

Against this background of growing awareness and cooperation, an alliance of international municipal bodies determined to get local government written into the Rio outcome and lobbied accordingly.[1] The key bodies were the so-called 'Group of Four': the International Union of Local Authorities (IULA), the United Towns Organisation (UTO), the Summit of the World's Major Cities and Metropolis. The Group was partly coordinated by a newer Canadian-based body, the International Council for Local Environmental Initiatives (ICLEI). Conferences and declarations multiplied. Numerous meetings were held at national and international level. The IULA Oslo Declaration of June 1991 contained local government's major pre-UNCED bid for a place in the sun, while the Curitiba World Urban Forum on the eve of UNCED in May 1992 produced a Common Declaration to Rio on behalf of the cities and local municipalities of the world. Of all the constituent groups involved in UNCED, local government was undoubtedly one of the most vocal.

Disappointingly, the only mention of local government and local communities in the Rio Declaration on Environment and Development, in Principle 22, is unsatisfactory.[2] But the far greater prize of a separate chapter in Agenda 21 was achieved. Chapter 28 (Agenda 21's shortest) recognises that because so many of the problems and solutions addressed by Agenda 21 have their roots in local activities, the participation and co-operation of local communities will be a determining factor in fulfilling its objectives. Local government's role is recognised both as planner and implementer of relevant policies and as educator and mobiliser of local public opinion. One objective is immediately enhanced international co-operation between municipalities. Far more important, the chapter establishes that there will be a dialogue between each local authority and its citizens, local organisations and local business which would lead to the adoption of a 'Local Agenda 21'. The importance of consultation, consensus-building and awareness-creation are emphasised. A deadline of 1996 is given for the completion of this process, although with the stipulation that this covers 'most local authorities' rather than all of them.

By contrast neither the Framework Convention on Climate Change nor the Convention on Biological Diversity mentions the role of local government or even of local action. Responsibility for implementation is given exclusively to 'the Parties' (Climate Change Convention) and 'Contracting Parties' (Biodiversity Convention) – in other words to the traditional sole actors in international agreements, national states. In terms of political process therefore the Conventions are a far less innovatory form of international agreement than Agenda 21 with its persistent emphasis on the need for a far wider range of institutional actors outside central government to be involved if UNCED follow up is to succeed.[3]

A corollary of some importance for local government should be noted. The Conventions when ratified and in force will be legally binding. Agenda 21 by contrast is not designed to have legal force. Rather, John Major and other world leaders assembled at Rio committed themselves (in the wording of its preamble) to 'a global partnership for sustainable development' reflecting 'global consensus and political commitment' at the highest level. The participation of local government in Rio follow-up has therefore a political rather than a legal base. Its effectiveness will be heavily dependent on the level of parallel post-Rio political commitment by the British government, political parties and public opinion.

UNCED Follow-Up by Local Government

Local government awareness of the need for its direct involvement in promoting sustainable policies and practices both in its own backyard and overseas has greatly increased as a result of UNCED. But with one major exception (Local Agenda 21) the predominant pattern is one of expanding activities and networks which were already in existence before UNCED. The range and scope of these globally is enormous, but from the perspective of 'Northern' local government can be divided into two broad categories: domestic and international. The former refers to action to raise awareness of people locally of the need for change in their behaviour patterns in order to promote sustainable development at local level, the promotion of relevant policies and practices for local sustainable development, and the promotion of local reductions in greenhouse gas emissions and of public awareness of the need for this. The latter refers to awareness-raising at local level of global issues and campaigning on these, specific cooperation with partner municipalities in developing countries or East Europe through twinning and linking, technical assistance (for example, secondment of staff) and projects, and specific action to help partner municipalities reduce greenhouse gas emissions.

Some broad general considerations stand out. First, there is a strong link between national and local approaches. All other factors being equal, the more generally aware a country is of the importance of environmental and North-South issues (and they usually go hand in hand) the more likely it is that its towns and cities will wish to be involved and the more likely it is that effective local and national policies will reinforce each other. Thus it is not surprising that the main lead in the local government field has come from Northern Europe and North America.[4]

Second, the more autonomous, financially secure and self-confident local government is, the more likely it is to be able to 'deliver' both locally and internationally. The climate of central-local government relations is therefore extremely important. We shall return to this point later in the UK context. Third, local government activities relating to sustainable development on the one hand, and actions to address global warming on the other, are largely being run separately from each other. This parallels the separation at national and global level of follow-up to Agenda 21 on the one hand, and the Climate Convention on the other. Fourth, there is (as we shall see) much exciting and innovative work being carried out both locally and internationally by local government to reduce CO_2 emissions and thus address global warming. But there seems to be almost no parallel internationally promoted work by local government in the field of preserving biodiversity, despite the argument of many environmentalists that it is only through cooperation with local communities that fragile eco-systems and the species that inhabit them can be preserved.

Against this background we consider current activities from three perspectives. The first is that of national frameworks for civic action. The second is that of the international organisations, networks and programmes established by and run by local authorities. The third is specific programmes set up to promote Local Agenda 21s and energy policies to reduce greenhouse gas emissions. In all these instances we shall concentrate on the most promising innovatory programmes, since these will give us the best idea for how activities might most usefully be expanded in the future.

National Programmes

A recent report on local initiatives for sustainable development [*Towns and Development, 1992a*] suggests that while in around 1980 there was only a small number of North–South local initiatives in a small number of countries, there are now many thousands of activities throughout the world. It estimates that five countries now have more than 100 links or twinnings: the US around 700, Germany around 600, the UK around 300 and France and the Netherlands around 200 each. The most common types are project-based, or linkages devoted mainly to cultural, social and sporting exchanges. While very little analysis appears to have been done on the quality and effectiveness of these exchanges, it is quite clear that some are far more effective than others in terms of the degree of commitment deployed, the resources behind them and the impact on

participating communities. Particularly impressive are municipal programmes in Germany, the Netherlands and Canada. These are now
briefly described.

In *West Germany* prior to reunification, 500–700 out of a total of 3507
local communities were involved in development cooperation (but very
few in the GDR). A far smaller number, perhaps 80–100, are assessed as
having serious programmes. The majority of these are concerned either
with providing finance for projects or with providing training for
Southern local administrators. Programmes appear loosely linked
nationally, with three major local grouping government bodies involved.
Federal help is available for some projects, but towns and cities themselves provide considerable sums from their own budgets (for example,
the Berlin 1991 budget for international cooperation was 900,000 DM).
Co-operation with local NGOs and others, for example in joint fund-
raising and awareness-raising campaigns, is common. A number of cities
run outstandingly innovative projects. Bremen, for example, has not only
networked with other local groups to raise over 100 million DM for
project aid to linked Southern municipalities, but has also, in cooperation
with local technical institutions, run pioneering projects to help African
cities install bio-gas plants and promote other relevant technologies.

The *Netherlands* has probably the most comprehensive involvement of
national municipalities of any country in the world – with some 430 out of
650 municipalities (including all 40 towns with more than 60,000
inhabitants) involved. As with Germany relevant local budgets are often
sizeable (for example, 1.6 million guilders for Rotterdam and 500,000 for
Amsterdam in 1992). Co-operation between local authorities and other
local groups is the rule. Co-operation with national government (including co-funding) for development education is a particular strong feature
and has helped make the Dutch one of the most environmentally conscious people in the world. Considerable efforts are made by the bigger
cities to evolve international policies which are then integrated into urban
sectoral policies. Links with Nicaragua dating from the 1980s are particularly well developed. Delft's involvement in these links led to its taking
the lead some years ago in establishing a consortium of European cities,
with the help of EC co-funding, to install an improved drinking water
supply for 25,000 inhabitants of the Nicaraguan town of Esteli at a cost of
over one million guilders. Another striking example has been cooperation between the small town of Nordwijn (25,000 inhabitants) and
Burkino Faso over the past 15 years. This has raised about 1.3 million
guilders for educational and agricultural projects.

Canada stands among the world leaders in two key areas in integrating
national and local programmes – for promoting sustainable development

abroad, and in evolving structures at local as well as regional and national level to promote sustainable development at home.

The main Canadian coordinating body for international activities is the Federation of Canadian Municipalities (FCM), with 600 members. Of these 40 have formal linking arrangements with the South. With financial support from the Canadian International Development Agency (CIDA), FCM now runs three North–South co-operation programmes. Municipal Professional Exchange arranges the exchange of senior managerial and technical staff. Africa 2000, with some 32 Canadian cities participating, arranges technical support and small scale project funding for African towns. The Chinese Open Cities programme brings Chinese local officials and businessmen to Canada for secondment, seminars or study tours. FCM is also encouraging Canadian cities to reduce their CO_2 emissions by 20 per cent by the year 2005. A number of Canadian municipality to municipality projects are considered by outside observers to be outstandingly effective. One example is the small-scale link between the village of St Elizabeth in Quebec (population 1,600) and the village of Sanankoroba in Mali (population 4,000), financed partly under the Africa 2000 Programme and designed to help build up technical knowledge, management skills and food self sufficiency. This appears to have been remarkably successful, not least in helping secure fuller participation by the women of Sanankoroba in village decision-making and a more equitable division of work between women and men.

The second area of Canadian activity of particular interest is in creating mechanisms for dialogue at local, provincial and national level on achieving sustainable development on the home front, through the Canadian Round Table mechanisms. Originally established in 1990 in the context of national discussions on Canada's Green Plan, the Round Tables embody an attempt to improve and inform the decision-making process for sustainable development at all levels of society. They are specifically designed to promote 'stakeholder dialogue' between key interest groups, and thus build consensus on future economic and environmental policies. Whilst still relatively new, they offer a valuable glimpse of the sort of institutional and political innovation needed to make a reality of sustainable development. Over 200 Round Tables now exist at local level and the number is growing fast.

International Organisations and Programmes

The international picture is complicated. UK local authorities have strong links, through their designated body the Local Government International Bureau (LGIB), with the Council of European Municipalities and Regions (CEMR) at the European level and with the

International Union of Local Authorities (IULA) at the global level. All these organisations in turn work closely with the International Council for Local Environmental Initiatives (ICLEI) founded in 1990 as an associate of CEMR and IULA with the objectives of helping local authorities develop solutions to their environmental problems, organising the exchange of relevant information and experience across national boundaries and instituting joint development and pilot projects internationally. These groupings are strongest in North Europe, North America, Japan and English-speaking developing countries.

As so often in international affairs another potentially rival, predominantly francophone, organisation exists – the United Town Organisation (UTO). This was originally established under left-wing political auspices to promote contacts between cities in East and West Europe. But it has largely shaken off its earlier political tendencies and is now strongest in the Mediterranean areas, Latin America and francophone Africa. It operates on a broad range of fields of interest to local authorities. UTO-IULA relations have in the past been bad but are now improving. These two organisations, working together with the Summit of the World's Major Cities and Metropolis in the 'Group of Four', see themselves as spearheading local government involvement in UNCED follow-up. Regular 'Summit discussions' between the four groups are planned to reinforce this co-operation.

A rather different but also important organisation is Towns and Development, a consortium of European local authorities and NGOs, supported by the North-South Centre of the Council of Europe and by the EC, which work together to raise awareness of global issues at local level. Towns and Development pioneered the concept of 'community-based development initiatives'. Its 1985 Cologne Conference and Appeal did much to make local communities more conscious of their global role, while their October 1992 Berlin Conference, 'Local Initiatives for Sustainable Development', launched a Berlin Charter and Action Agenda designed to galvanise local government and local groups to greater action in the wake of UNCED. Unlike ICLEI, however, it does not promote joint programmes, nor is it now specifically involved in action to develop Local Agenda 21s or to reduce CO_2 emissions.

Internationally ICLEI appears to be the only association with a specific programme for Local Agenda 21s. This initiative has three components. It is encouraging its member to establish their own Local Agenda 21 campaigns, defined as 'any participatory, local effort to establish a comprehensive action strategy for sustainable development in that local jurisdiction or area', based on four basic principles and on four basic planning elements.[5] These in turn reflect the ICLEI definition of sustainable development at the local level: 'Sustainable development is development that delivers basic environmental, social and economic services to all residents of a community without threatening the viability of the natural, built and social systems upon which the delivery of these systems depends'.

The second component is national campaigns. National and regional associations of local authorities are encouraged to launch their own national campaigns to encourage this actively at local level and at the same time to seek funding from national governments (as, for example, already agreed for Australia, Finland and the UK). One particular recommendation is for each country to establish a national model programme which provides technical and financial support to selected municipalities to help them establish successful models of local planning for sustainable development. Others can then copy or adapt.

The third strand is the Local Agenda 21 Model Programme. ICLEI is seeking proposals from local authorities worldwide to participate in a model programme of 21 municipalities (four from Africa, five from Asia and the Pacific, one each from the Caribbean and the Middle East, four from Latin America and two from North America). Funding is being raised to provide support for the model programmes that will be selected. So far all three initiatives are in the early stages.

In the UK the national campaign to promote Local Agenda 21s is managed by a steering committee drawn from the UK local authority associations and will be serviced by the Local Government Management Board (LGMB). At the time of writing (May 1993) it was too early to report concrete results.

Local Climate Action Campaigns

Local government interest in promoting sustainable energy policies at local level and more specifically in reducing local emissions of CO_2, predates UNCED. Such cities as Amsterdam, West Berlin and Helsinki were pursuing long-term policies to promote energy efficiency and conservation throughout the 1980s. Canadian cities were being urged to reduce their CO_2 emissions by 20 per cent by 2005 in 1990. More comprehensively, ICLEI's Urban CO_2 Reduction Project was launched in 1991 involving collaboration between cities in Denmark, Germany, Finland, Turkey, Canada, the US and Costa Rica.

None the less UNCED, and in particular the Climate Convention,[6] have given a major boost to local government concern and involvement in this area. It has given rise to ICLEI's Cities for Climate Protection initiative, and launched the Municipal Leader's Summit on Climate

Change and the Urban Environment held at the UN in New York in January 1993. This aims at strengthening municipal commitment to measures and policies that reduce emissions of greenhouse gases, to provide an analytical framework to help municipalities to do this, to encourage and publicise innovative local projects for reducing energy and to provide a common voice for municipalities in national climate action plans and future discussions at the Framework Convention. In more detail it centres on formulating and implementing local action plans for reducing CO_2 emissions in five stages (identifying local energy use patterns, evaluating, identifying and ranking measures to reduce emissions, establishing a specific reduction target and developing policies and programmes to implement reduction measures). Key factors identified include pattern of energy supply, distribution and use; the relationship of demand to lifestyle and attitudes; land use; and transportation infrastructures.

Under ICLEI's auspices, four campaign initiatives are being pursued. The first is 'green fleets' to reduce CO_2 emissions from municipal vehicles and municipal employer travel. Municipalities joining this initiative pledge to reduce relevant energy use and CO_2 emissions by 20 per cent over 10 years. Denver in the US is providing the model. The second initiative is 'energy buildings' to reduce energy use and CO_2 emissions in municipally-owned buildings. Recommended strategies include building retrofits, high efficiency lighting and control systems, on-site co-generation and renewable energy technologies. Municipalities joining the initiative are pledged to reduce relevant energy and CO_2 emissions by 20 per cent over ten years. The third initiative is the Energy Partners Programme designed to help municipalities in the North exchange energy management expertise with municipalities in developing countries and East Europe. Two sources of assistance are proposed: Energy Partners Consulting is to draw on the expertise of professional staff in local government and in municipal utilities, and the Energy Partner Fund is to pay for technical assistance and training. Municipalities joining the initiative pledge to make enough staff and funding available to be able to co-operate effectively with at least one partner municipality in the South or East Europe. Finally, 'Energy Collaborations' provides funding for work in municipalities to develop advanced and analytical techniques and innovative municipal energy policies.

In parallel, national inter-city projects exist or are being set up in a number of European countries. These include the Municipal Climate Protection Campaign in Germany, the Carbon Resolution in Britain (aimed at getting local authorities to sign up for a 30 per cent reduction in CO_2 emissions from their area by 2005 and to develop a comprehensive strategy for this), Cities against the Greenhouse Effect in Italy and the Dutch Union of Climate Alliance Cities. None of these initiatives is, so far at least, integrated with Local Agenda 21 initiatives.

Finally, in this section it may be worth giving just two examples of the sort of projects that are currently under way. Both are from Germany.

Saarbrucken's energy programme is based on energy saving (with local finance available from households and business to enable them to pay for higher quality insulation and equipment), renewable energy (with solar energy provided from both municipal and private sources) and the widespread use of combined heat and power (CHP). In municipal buildings energy use has been reduced by 45 per cent by comparison with 1980, CO_2 emissions by 60 per cent. All municipal swimming pools are, or shortly will be, heated by solar power. Overall CO_2 use has been reduced by 15 per cent since 1980, and further major reductions are planned. This has secured Saarbrucken one of the 12 awards in the UNCED's Local Government Honours Programme.

Freiburg (im Breisgau) has pursued similar policies, but with variants. It was the first city in Germany to introduce differential levels of charging for electricity use divided into three time zones, and one of the first to insist that housing on all land bought or leased from the city should meet extremely high energy efficiency standards. Its relative success in integrated transport policy is remarkable and highly relevant in the CO_2 reduction context. By expanding public transport (notably trams), subsidising low fares, extending bicycle path networks, imposing high charges for parking, and speed and other traffic restrictions in all streets and through other means, the growth in motor vehicle users has been held almost constant while the amount of journeys have risen sharply. Long-term policy is that local public transport, the bicycle and the car (which still accounts for 47 per cent of journeys made) should each account for a third of the journeys made.

Freiburg is also of interest as the Western partner, together with the Freiburg-based Oko Institute, of a unique twinning project with Lviv in the Ukraine. Under this, the German partner advises its Ukrainian partner in retrofitting existing blocks of municipal flats and on designing new prefabricated housing units, and on higher standards of energy efficiency. It also part finances this process and otherwise helps develop the city's energy conservation strategy.

The European Community Dimension

Before considering the broad implications of local government involvement in sustainable development on global post-UNCED activities, it is worth briefly looking at the parallel EC dimension. The Community 'equivalent' of Agenda 21 is the Fifth Action Programme on the Environment, adopted in late 1992 by the EC Council of Ministers. It sets out Community environmental objectives, policy and implementation programmes for the period 1992–6, but is designed to set the framework for environmental policy until the end of the century. In the same way as Agenda 21 for the first time pulls together and develops global policies on environment and development in the UN system, so the Fifth Action Programme for the first time in Community history provides a framework for integrating previously incompatible sectoral EC policies, and is specifically designed to help provide a European framework for the realisation of Agenda 21.

Five key sectors are identified for integrated approaches to sustainable development; agriculture, energy, industry, transport and tourism. The overriding importance of shared responsibility between national, regional and local government, business and the general public is recognised on the basis of the principle of subsidiarity. The special responsibility of local and regional authorities in, for example, the areas of land use planning, economic and infrastructure development, control of industrial pollution, waste management, transport, public information and education and internal auditing, is clearly identified. The Programme also states that local authorities must have the resources necessary to implement their responsibilities. A series of 19 detailed tables sets out long-term policies and reduction targets indicating where appropriate where local authorities should be involved in over 70 different policy actions.

The linkage between national follow-up on UNCED and on the Fifth Action Programme is obvious. So are the potential synergies. In theory EC commitments, which member governments traditionally take (or at least claim to take) seriously, should reinforce similar commitments in the UN system, which governments traditionally take lightly. In practice, however, this may not happen. The Fifth Action Programme is a Commission document which has not been discussed in detail or amended by member states. Commitment by the British and other EC governments to it is limited to general endorsement in the Council of Ministers. Any specific Commission proposals based on it will, in the traditional way, need to be negotiated separately through the Council machinery. By contrast every word of Agenda 21 and the Rio Convention was negotiated between national governments, and all are committed to it 'at the highest political level' (see above). Similarly, neither local government nor NGOs were consulted on the Action Programme, whereas by contrast they were very much included in UNCED (with, as we have seen, an alliance of local government groups virtually writing chapter 28 of Agenda 21). They do not therefore 'own' the Action Programme in the way they 'own' Agenda 21, and in consequence are – so far at least – far more committed to the latter.[7]

More fundamentally, it is not perhaps unduly cynical to wonder how far the overall pattern of economic integration to which the Community is committed with the completion of the Single European Market, is compatible with the concept, let alone the reality, of sustainable development. For all its strengths the Fifth Environmental Action Programme is far less likely to be a turning point in the Community's history than UNCED in the history of the UN system and of global co-operation.

Some Broader Issues

Having selectively analysed how local government has become increasingly involved with international environmental issues we now turn to the underlying causes of this development, to the constraints on local government and to some of the possible longer term political consequences. There are two main reasons why local and international concerns are increasingly linked. First, policies which need to be agreed by the international community to address global environmental degradation and sustainable development involve influencing a far wider range of activities than those addressed in diplomatic negotiations in the past. Most of these take place at the local level. Current estimates suggest that local authorities will be responsible for implementing about 40 per cent of the EC's Fifth Action Programme and that over two thirds of Agenda 21 commitments cannot be delivered without the commitment and cooperation of local government.[8] Local government, along with a range of other bodies, is therefore an essential partner in the pursuit of sustainable development. The need is, of course, not just for action by local government alone, but also to incorporate the activities of local government into a broader national framework [*Stewart and Hams, 1992: 27*].

The second major factor relates to process rather than to content. Sustainable development is conceived of in Agenda 21 as a decentralised and participatory process. Implementation is seen as best and most appropriately carried out at the local level, where the knowledge and experience is, and where the action has to be taken. While admittedly Agenda 21 is neither fully consistent on the point nor pushes it to its possible logical conclusion, the emphasis is more on local and community-based action taking place within an enabling national framework than on traditional 'top–down' approaches which put the national state centre stage and ignore or downgrade the role of other institutions and groups.

In Britain many local authorities have been actively involved in international cooperation and awareness-raising and are excited by the possibilities that UNCED has opened up. None the less they are severely handicapped in contrast with local authorities in other European countries where relations between local and national government are less stressed. Whitehall policies over the past decade have forced local government into a very short time-frame governed by strict financial constraints. Key concerns all too often centre on which local services are to be 'saved' and which cut, and by how much to meet externally imposed financial ceilings. Long-term overall perspectives have largely gone by the board. With the current government rethink on relations with local authorities, the situation may perhaps begin to change. Some of the most environmentally regressive policies of the past (for example, guidelines on land use policies which favoured out of town superstore developments) are being revised. Even so, constraints on local government in terms, particularly, of freedom to pursue appropriate local transport and energy policies, remain crucial. Financial constraints and deregulation of local bus services make investment in integrated and environmentally friendly public transport systems extremely difficult. British cities cannot go nearly as far as Freiburg and other German, Dutch and Nordic cities in persuading their citizens to make less use of their motor cars.[9]

British towns and cities are indeed making efforts to increase energy efficiency and energy savings in municipally-owned housing and public buildings. But these are uphill individual efforts rather than part of an overall national strategy as is the case in, for example, the Netherlands. Local government has no direct involvement in energy supply nor has it so far been able to develop a dialogue with the electrical supply utilities established by electricity privatisation. A whole range of policy options, including the building and operation of municipal CHP stations which are common practice in continental Europe remain almost unknown in the UK, despite their strong economic and environmental advantages. Only some of the impressive range of long-term policies for energy efficiency, conservation and hence CO_2 emission reductions which such cities as Amsterdam, Helsinki and Hanover have very successfully followed for years are available to British local authorities. This in turn will inevitably greatly handicap national efforts to meet targets under the Climate Convention.

A further major impediment lies in the British system of government, in particular the enormous imbalance in power and self-confidence between national and local government and the secretive nature of the Whitehall decision-making process. In such a system it is extremely difficult to achieve the cooperation, dialogue and interdependence between different tiers of government and between 'major groups' which Agenda 21 envisages as a precondition for sustainable development.

It would however be one-sided to suggest that all the problems of British local government stem from inappropriate Whitehall policies or poor relations with central government. The best local authorities have shown what can be done within existing constraints. The gap between them and the worst is enormous. Many councils are still hardly aware that the environment is an issue, let alone know or want to hear about sustainable development. Local action to draw up Local Agenda 21s is likely to meet with a very mixed reaction. In some areas it will be wholehearted and impressive. In others, councils will go through the motions of consultation unenthusiastically. And in others the call is likely to go straight into the waste paper basket. In such circumstances, the willingness and ability of other local groups to step in and mobilise local opinion will be crucial. But, overall, a ragged national response seems inevitable.[10]

As a contrast to the situation in the UK, as one British local government official specialising in sustainable development has pointed out,[11] there is the example of Denmark, where local authorities have far wider financial autonomy and practical responsibilities (including either direct provision of or regulation of energy, water and sewage services). A rolling 4–year plan with a 9 to 12–year time horizon is designed to ensure that development remains within the environmental capacity of the local area. All proposed developments are subjected to assessment on grounds of environmental sustainability, including the relationship between transport and land use. Conflicts between local and national government are rare, with good relations encouraged by a frequent interchange of staff.

Thus despite the genuine enthusiasm in many UK local authorities for UNCED follow up, the modest achievements of such authorities as Leicester, Sheffield and Strathclyde at home and the pioneering efforts of East Staffordshire and others in North–South co-operation, the UK results so far seem rather less impressive than those achieved in countries where relations between local and national government are better and where the former have greater freedom of action.

Another more technical factor is the absence of a broader political and financial framework for encouraging British local government involvement in overseas co-operation. Previous legal uncertainties on the extent to which local authorities were able to develop co-operation are being resolved following queries by the Audit Commission (in the context of the Local Authority Links Scheme for Central and East Europe funded by the FCO Know-How Fund). A Private Member's Bill is going through

Parliament at the time of writing (1993) with government and all-party support, under the name of Jim Lester MP, to give local authority clearer and broader powers to engage in international work. But the Bill will not provide additional financial resources for this purpose and in present financial circumstances it is quite unrealistic to envisage local authorities following the example of, say, Amsterdam, Utrecht or Berlin in making substantial sums available from their own budgets.

A final difficulty is uncertainly over the international status of local authorities. While their role as a pressure group will probably continue to expand, local authorities understandably and perhaps logically look for a formal role in EC and UN institutions. In the former much effort is currently going into trying to ensure direct municipal representation on the proposed Committee of the Regions (often in the teeth of indifference or hostility from national governments) and more generally in arguing for the concept of a 'Europe of the regions' with greater direct popular participation. Institutional innovative possibilities are at present fewer in the UN system. Despite recognition at UNCED of the need for far greater involvement by non-central governmental organisations (NCGOs) in the UN system, the system still gives overwhelming pride of place to nation states. All other bodies are generically lumped together as NGOs and given a generally ineffective consultative role. While the newly-created UN Commission on Sustainable Development is tasked with ensuring more effective NCGO input, there seems at present no possibility of a separate local government 'seat' on it. The main local government organisations are at present giving this issue low priority. But in the longer term pressures for institutional reform in the UN system which allow for direct municipal representation are likely to grow.

Conclusion

The future pattern of local government involvement in UNCED follow up is inevitably linked to broader developments. If neither government nor public opinion put sustainable development at centre stage of national policy, and UNCED follow-up remains on the political margins, then for all the singing and dancing local government and Local Agenda 21s will not be able to get very far in the near future. Should however national and international opinion be re-energised, perhaps under the impact of further large-scale and threatening ecological destruction, much faster progress can be made.

Either way the long term need is for a more effective integration of local and national policies which recognises that the pursuit of sustainable development is a multi-level process involving equal partners, and that policies at all levels must be mutually reinforcing. Key elements of such a strategy in Britain would be the following:

There should be a closer integration of current local government efforts to prepare Local Agenda 21s with the national process, coordinated by the DOE, for reporting to the UN Commission on Sustainable Development on national progress towards sustainable development. In parallel, the government might encourage British local government to help local authorities in developing countries and East Europe develop their own Local Agenda 21s.

Secondly, local government should be involved as a major partner in the UK's national response strategy for reducing greenhouse gas emissions in the context of the Climate Change Convention, in terms both of cutting emissions nationally and of helping partner towns abroad. This might include UK government encouragement and co-funding for British local government participation in the ICLEI Cites for Climate Change Programme abroad and in the 'Carbon Resolution' at home.

Thirdly, then should be a similar involvement by local government and regions in implementation of the Biodiversity Convention at home and abroad.

Fourthly, local government should be acting not just autonomously and in conjunction with national governments but also as a catalyst for mobilising local communities. It should therefore cooperate more with other local groups (for example, NGOs, business, community associations and universities) in joint programmes to help towns in developing countries (following, for example, the example of many German and Dutch towns in joint fund-raising for specific projects).

Government should recognise, fifthly, that these activities are a valuable, and permanent, future of UNCED follow-up and they should provide co-funding accordingly under either the ODA or DOE budget.

Finally, the effectiveness of international co-operation carried out by local government should be regularly assessed to ensure that local and national funds are well spent in much the same way as national aid programmes are periodically appraised. Additionally appraisal of the best Dutch, German and Canadian programmes could be extremely useful in terms of helping shape future British local government programmes.

However, more effective local involvement also presupposes fundamental changes in other areas of national policy. Sustainable policies at the local level must work with, rather than against, the grain of national policies. The role of the motor car cannot be restricted in, and by, cities if the Great Car Economy and an ever-expanding system of roads and motorways remains the national paradigm. Local government cannot pursue effective energy efficiency and conservation policies unless their efforts complement national energy policies. If they continue to be denied the range of powers their continental opposite numbers have in areas vital to local sustainable development they must be able to form a partnership with other relevant agencies (such as electricity utilities, bus companies, environmental regulatory bodies) so as to be able to draw up and implement Local Agenda 21s. If they are to do this, fundamental changes in the way these agencies currently operate are necessary. This problem can only be resolved in agreement between national and local authorities.

It must, however, be doubted whether such an agreement is feasible in Britain's current political climate. The concept of sustainable development, with its emphasis on action by local communities, on a 'bottom-up' approach and on building local and national consensus for the difficult decisions ahead is hard to reconcile with Whitehall's domineering approach to local government and resistance to pressures from below. It may well be that a breakthrough will only be possible if broader pressures for political and constitutional reform, generated for quite other reasons, succeed.

While Britain has her own difficulties in integrating local and national efforts, few if any countries have yet got an adequate framework for such integration. Almost everywhere local authorities are preparing Local Agenda 21s in cheerful isolation from the national strategies for sustainable development which their governments are drafting for the UN Commission on Sustainable Development. The latter, in its turn, has so far made no effort to incorporate discussion of the local dimension or to invite international local government bodies to be key participants in its future work programme. Neither individual governments nor the Inter-governmental Negotiating Committee for a Framework Convention on Climate Change appear interested in discussing action to limit green-house gas emissions at sub-national level. Technical assistance, grants and loans from the World Bank, Global Environmental Facility and the EBRD are still almost exclusively reserved for national governments.

In other words nation-states, despite Rio, still consider themselves as the only important actors on stage. By contrast local government, along with the other 'major groups' identified in Agenda 21, is seen as having an ill-defined supporting role. As this article has suggested this approach is outdated and short-sighted. Local government and local action are essential elements in UNCED follow-up. Unless they can be integrated fully into the international political process prospects for success will be small.

NOTES

1. And met with an open door. Western governments, including the UK, were generally receptive. Maurice Strong, UNCED's Secretary General, commented in one of his speeches, 'No organisation or group is more important than local authorities when it comes to following up the Brazil Conference'. Mrs Gro Harland Brundtland, Norwegian Prime Minister, speaking at the opening in June 1991 in Oslo of the World Congress of the International Union of Local Authorities (IULA) said 'We must think globally when we act locally. Local authorities across the world are by definition closer to local problems. But the fact that these local problems cannot be seen in isolation from the global trends or challenges of our time is clear to us all. That is why local authorities must see their role in a wider global perspective.'

2. It was tied to 'indigenous' people, traditional communities and cultures and implicitly seen as very much apart from rather than part of the national state.

3. This was however almost certainly an incidental result of proceeding on separate negotiating tracks, different priorities in different interest groups and lack of time to check and ensure consistency of coverage and commitments in all Rio texts (what the French call 'la toilette de textes') rather than deliberately planned.

4. It is however worth noting that the motivation behind many international initiatives has varied considerably. While probably the majority has been for 'mainstream' reasons of addressing the economic and environmental problems of poorer countries others have been more specifically political. The reason why there were so many US and European co-operation projects with Nicaragua in the 1980s was not because Nicaragua was particularly poor but for reasons of political solidarity against the policies of the Reagan administration. Many of the twinning links developed by the United Towns Organisation (UTO) in the same period were for the declared purpose of promoting peace and solidarity between like-minded, and generally very left-wing, municipalities. And the driving force behind the work a number of German cities are doing to help promote energy efficiency in cities in East Europe and the CIS is in part strong dislike of nuclear power and the wish to make East European countries less dependent on dangerous and outdated Soviet-built RBMK and VVER nuclear power stations.

5. The basic principles are defined as multi-sectoral, cross-disciplinary, participatory and elegant. The basic elements are seen to be a community consultation process, sustainable development auditing, target setting and the development and use of clear meaningful and measurable indications (see ICLEI [1993a]).

6. Despite, as already noted, the fact that it contains no specific provision for action at the local level and talks exclusively in terms of national plans and targets.

7. This observation is made on the basis of personal participation in discussions on both programmes involving local government, NGOs, the EC Commission and the British government.

8. Cited respectively in two publications by the Local Government Management Board [1992: 1; 1993: 28].

9. The results of Mrs Thatcher's determined assaults on local authorities freedom to run their own transport policies are still with us. Sheffield, for example, was forced in the mid-1980s to dismantle its integrated subsidised and heavily used public transport system. The result is that the use of private cars in the city has sharply increased and with it of course Sheffield's carbon emissions. Cambridge's plans to limit cars into its city centre (which still need Parliamentary approval), may if implemented mark the beginning of change.

10. This analysis is based on recent discussions with representatives of local community environmental action groups from a number of cities in England and Wales.
11. Janice Morphet comments that 'the powers available to UK local institutions and environmental agencies seem almost toothless in comparison with the Danish system'. The good news is that they are seeking to export their experience and values to other EC member states, including the UK.

REFERENCES

Berlin City (1992), *Energiekonzept Berlin: Entwurf für die Offentlichkeitsbeteiligung*, Berlin.
Bosworth, T. (1993), 'Local Authorities and Sustainable Development', *European Environment*, Spring.
City of Copenhagen (1993), *Review of the Reduction of CO_2 Emissions in Copenhagen in the Years 1988 till 2005*, Copenhagen.
Energiebedrijf Ansterdam (1989), *From Energy Conservation Strategies to a Sustainable Energy Economy – 15 Years Energy Saving Experiences in Amsterdam*, Amsterdam.
Energiebedrijf Amsterdam (1992), *Energy in Amsterdam: Planning for Energy Saving and Environment*, Amsterdam.
ICLEI (1992a), *Curitaba Commitment*, Freiburg.
ICLEI (1992b), *The Urban CO_2 Reduction Project*, Freiburg.
ICLEI (1993a), *The Local Agenda 21 Initiative: ICLEI Guidelines for Local Agenda 21 Campaigns*, Freiburg.
ICLEI (1993b), *Cities for Climate Protection: An International ICLEI Campaign*, Freiburg.
IULA World Congress (1991), *Oslo Declaration on Environment, Health and Lifestyle*, June.
Local Government Management Board (1992), *Agenda 21: A Guide for Local Authorities*, Luton.
Local Government Management Board (1993), *Towards Sustainability: The EC's Fifth Action Programme on the Environment: A Guide for Local Authorities*, Luton.
Morphet, J. (1993), 'Danes Make the Running in Search of Green Plans', *Planning for the National and Built Environment*, 29 Jan.
National Round Table Review (1992), *Round Tables in Canada*, Spring.
Netherlands Ministry of Housing, Physical Planning and Environment and Association of Netherlands Municipalities (1993), *Preventing Climate Change: Urban Action in the Netherlands*, The Hague.
Roseland, M. (1992), *Towards Sustainable Communities: A Resource Book for Municipal and Local Governments*, Ottawa: Canadian Round Table on the Environment and the Economy.
Smith, V. (ed.) (1990), *Partnership with Developing Countries – A Practical Agenda for Local Authorities*, London: Local Government International Bureau (LGIB).
Spiers, D. (1992), *African Connections: Local Government Overseas Links – A Chief Executive's View*, Luton: Local Government Management Board.
Stewart, J. and T. Hams (1992), *Local Government for Sustainable Development*, London: LGIB.
Towns and Development (1992a), *Local Initiatives for Sustainable Development – 49 Examples*, London: LGIB.
Towns and Development (1992b), *The Berlin Charter and Action Agenda*, Oct., The Hague.

International Environmental Regimes: Verification and Implementation Review

OWEN GREENE

Verification issues have received relatively little attention in relation to international environmental regimes. Yet they are potentially important for a wide range of existing and emerging regimes. Perceptions of 'verifiability' can be a key factor in determining whether key actors are prepared to participate in a regime. Thus, the rules of the regime may be shaped to increase (or decrease) their verifiability. Moreover, the development of verification and implementation review processes – formal and informal – is likely to be an important factor in improving the overall effectiveness of international institutions. The significance of these issues is examined systematically, drawing extensively on the experience of existing and emerging environmental regimes.

In most established environmental regimes, implementation review procedures are inadequately developed and poorly implemented. In many cases, governments seem comfortable with international arrangements that will not help others to monitor too closely the extent to which they are implementing their commitments. This situation is unsatisfactory from the perspective of those who wish to increase the effectiveness of international environmental institutions. There are a number of ways in which international implementation review processes could be developed, drawing upon precedents. It is important, for example, that these take into account the key role that non-state actors play in implementing environmental regimes, as well as their potentially important monitoring role.

Verification issues have received relatively little attention in relation to international environmental agreements. Yet there are a number of reasons to believe that they may be important. This study examines the significance of verification and implementation review processes in the

Owen Greene is at the School of Peace Studies, Bradford University. This study is based on work carried out as part of a project supported by the ESRC's Global Environmental Change Programme, and the author gratefully acknowledges that support.

development and effectiveness of international environmental regimes, and discusses ways in which the role of such processes can be developed in the future.[1]

Verification is a process for assessing compliance with the terms of an international agreement. The process includes: monitoring, data-collection and information exchange; data analysis; and, on the basis of this analysis, assessing the extent to which the parties to the agreement are meeting their obligations. As such, verification processes aim to deter non-compliance: that is, to encourage states to implement their commitments properly and to report accurate information. They provide a mechanism for either removing or confirming suspicions of non-compliance. Thus they can build confidence in the regime, encouraging broader participation and further regime development. Alternatively, verification procedures aim to bring evidence of non-compliance to the attention of regime participants in a timely way, so that they can take appropriate actions to persuade the culprit to mend its ways or to protect their interests.

Implementation review is similar to verification, though it is a somewhat broader notion. The term is perhaps more diplomatically acceptable in environmental politics: it carries fewer connotations of suspicions about deliberate non-compliance and more of cooperative attempts to monitor and improve implementation. It refers to the processes by which regime participants exchange and review information relating to the implementation of agreed measures, and assess progress toward the objectives of the regime. Implementation review procedures include arrangements for reports from member governments and other recognised participants to be regularly exchanged and audited. They provide a framework within which compliance can be reviewed, lessons can be learned, and members can identify areas where further resources or rule changes are needed to improve the effectiveness of the regime. By increasing transparency, verification and implementation review processes can promote public debate and increase the scope for environmental groups and other non-state actors to exert pressure to improve environmental performance.

Verification and implementation review processes can be either formal or informal. Many international institutions include explicitly-agreed verification or implementation review procedures. However, informal processes may also be involved, including independent monitoring by governments, 'informal' reviews by groups of parties, meetings of 'experts', and a wide range of non-governmental monitoring and review processes involving all sorts of interested groups. This is a reflection of the fact that a 'regime' can involve a broad international social institution establishing norms, rules and practices that constrain and prescribe the activities, and shape the expectations, of all types of actors involved in a particular issue area. In an effective regime, the formally-agreed institutional procedures are embedded in a wider complex of processes that maintain and shape its implementation and development.

Perceptions of 'verifiability' can be a key factor in determining whether key actors are prepared to participate in a regime. Thus, the rules of the regime may be shaped to increase their verifiability (or to decrease it, if the participants want to avoid being committed to more than vague statements of intent). Moreover, the development of verification and implementation review processes may also be an important factor in improving the effectiveness of international institutions. *Effectiveness* in this context is the extent to which a regime alters the behaviour of its participants in line with its objectives.

The next section aims briefly to locate and discuss the potential role of verification and implementation review in international regimes. The subsequent section then examines different aspects of the role of verification and implementation review in environmental regimes, and makes comparisons with arms control and disarmament agreements, where verification issues have typically been important. The issues discussed include: the significance of verifiability during environmental treaty negotiations; implementation review processes in existing environmental regimes; the role of non-state actors in implementing environmental agreements; and ways in which implementation review procedures can be structured to increase their effectiveness.

The Role of Verification in International Regimes

It is obviously important for an international regime that its key participants normally comply reasonably well with its main requirements. However, this does not necessarily mean that verification is important for the regime. Sometimes agreements are so vague that no one knows in practice what the rules are, making assessments of compliance impossible. In other cases, the rules of the regime may be entirely compatible with what all of its members would choose to do independently, irrespective of the compliance of others or, perhaps, of the existence of the regime itself. In such cases, there is likely to be a high level of compliance with the regime even without verification arrangements, and participation in the regime is unlikely to depend upon its verifiability.

Verification issues become potentially significant where the benefits of participating in a regime depend to some extent on the compliance of other members with its main rules. In this context, three main types of interest structures (or 'games') can be distinguished. The characteristic role of verification in regimes in each of these is analysed below. In practice, of course, regimes cannot easily be placed within one of these categories. Thus the following discussion aims only to clarify the ways in which the role and significance of verification or implementation review in international regimes, including environmental regimes, can be expected to vary according to underlying patterns of power and interests.

In the first of our three categories, one or more states may negotiate an international agreement with rules that they would independently want to adopt anyway, but where the benefits would be increased if other actors were also persuaded to participate. The International Whaling Convention's moratorium on commercial whaling may provide an example of this. In the mid-1980s, a number of Western whaling states which were unilaterally moving towards ending their whaling activities joined with non-whaling nations on the International Whaling Commission to pressure Japan, Norway and the Soviet Union into accepting an international moratorium [*Porter and Brown, 1991: 78–82*].

In such cases, compliance by 'leading' participants will not depend greatly on the existence of effective verification systems, since by definition they believe that the rules of the regime reflect their independent interests or preferences. However, leading members of the regime will want to encourage compliance by more reluctant participants, who may only have been induced to join by economic or other incentives or by the threat of reprisals.[2] To discourage 'reluctant' parties from pocketing the incentives (or avoiding reprisals) while neglecting implementation, the leading participants have an interest in being able to monitor and assess their compliance. The effectiveness of such verification systems may have a significant effect on the degree of compliance amongst 'reluctant' participants.

Where the regime has been formed by a hegemonic state, this state may have the capacity to carry out desired monitoring and verification tasks nationally. However, as 'institutionalists' such as Keohane [*1984; 1989*] and Young [*1989; 1992*] emphasise, international regimes may not depend on coercion or enforcement by hegemonic power or even by coalitions of a few great powers. Medium and small powers and non-state actors may be important leading participants in developing international regimes. In these cases, such actors have an interest in embedding verification processes in international institutions, where monitoring, implementation review and responses to non-compliance are managed collectively. Such verification procedures might be applied equally to all regime members, to avoid accusations of discrimination, encourage broader participation in the regime, and build mutual confidence. In any case, the situation may change; initially reluctant participants may come to support the regime rules, while some leading parties may lose their enthusiasm for the regime.

A second type of situation resembles *coordination games* [*Stein, 1990*], where the benefits of complying with the rules of the regime depend upon the compliance of an 'adequate' number of other participants. The parties have shared 'aversions' to certain outcomes, and aim to co-operate to avoid them. However, there are several acceptable sets of regulations, and parties are relatively unconcerned about which of these are actually agreed. Attempts to establish common international standards can fall into this category; parties most want to avoid a situation where there are incompatible national standards, and are willing to compromise to achieve agreement on international standards. Ausubel and Victor [*1992: 28*] argue that many international shipping standards designed to limit oil pollution are examples of this; the parties most want to avoid a situation where co-operation fails and they face different standards at each port.

Such international agreements may nevertheless prove difficult to negotiate, as has been demonstrated by European Community negotiations for establishing common technical standards for a single European market. The actors may have interests in promoting different systems of rules. However, once the regime is established, it is to a large extent 'self-enforcing'. Any party that chose to break with the regime would suffer self-inflicted costs, and the most effective response by remaining members of the regime (provided there was still 'adequate' participation) would be to continue to comply with the agreed rules. Moreover, in these situations non-compliance tends to be relatively transparent or obvious from the disruption it caused. Therefore, demand for specific verification procedures may be low.

The situation is quite different for *collaboration games*, where there are benefits in cooperation but they depend on the compliance of others and there are incentives to cheat or defect [*Stein, 1990: 32–6*]. The 'prisoner's dilemma' is a classic illustration of situations in which each party has incentives to free-ride and there are substantial costs in contributing to a collective good when others have defected, but where everybody suffers if more than one key party defects or attempts to free-ride.

In such situations, analysts from the 'realist' perspective are sceptical about the possibility of establishing enduring regimes in an international system of sovereign states. Any agreements will be unstable; there are incentives to defect and, in the absence of an effective supranational authority (or hegemonic power) to enforce compliance, the main response to non-compliance available to remaining parties is to withdraw, or threaten to withdraw, from the regime. Nevertheless, from this perspective there remains some scope for states to come to collaborative agreements, provided they are carefully designed to ensure that the potential benefits of collaboration outweigh the perceived risk posed by free-riding or defection by other parties.

Verification issues are potentially very important in this context. Parties may only be willing to participate in 'verifiable' regimes. Effective verification processes can deter potential free-riders, build confidence in the regime, and provide timely warning of serious non-compliance by a participant so that other parties can take appropriate measures to persuade it to reform its behaviour or to protect their interests.

If there is a substantial risk that non-compliance would be exposed in a timely way, the incentives to cheat will be much reduced; not only is a free-rider strategy less likely to succeed, but also the costs of exposure can be substantial. Although tough international sanctions are rarely formally imposed on a non-compliant state unless it is already marginal or a 'pariah' [*Chayes and Chayes, 1991: 288–90*], limited sanctions are possible, particularly from those who are most adversely affected. Non-compliance with one regime may be reciprocated by refusals to co-operate in other areas. States which gain a reputation for free-riding or treaty violation risk being treated as undesirable partners for future co-operation.

From the 'institutionalist' perspective, 'realists' underestimate the potential for establishing effective international institutions. Although they accept that states and other powerful actors tend to pursue their own interests, institutionalists argue that international institutions can shape the ways such interests are defined. Moreover, participating governments are subject to a wide range of influences and pressures that can reduce their incentives to free-ride or defect; a well-designed regime can enhance the effectiveness of such pressures. Policy-makers tend, for example, to try to avoid gaining a reputation for breaking agreements or contravening widely-accepted norms. They are also sensitive to pressures from a range of international, domestic and transnational constituencies, particularly in democracies. Embarrassment with the nickname 'the dirty man of Europe' in the late 1980s is probably an important reason why Britain has become more positive about international rules to limit marine pollution [*Stokke, 1992: 7*].

Thus, from the institutionalist perspective, 'realists' take too narrow a view of the potential role of verification in enhancing the effectiveness of international regimes. Appropriate monitoring, reporting, and implementation review processes can increase transparency about the way that international agreements are being implemented and thus increase pressures for full compliance [*Young, 1992: 176–8; Chayes and Chayes, 1991: 290–304*]. Transparency and implementation review can also facilitate institutional learning, and promote acceptance of the norms and practices of the regime throughout international society. It can enhance the capacity of the international institutions to respond to changing circumstances and to situations where inadequate compliance is due to neglect, inadvertance or lack of national capacity for effective implementation. Demands that vague statements of intent be turned into verifiable commitments could play an important role in efforts to transform weak or symbolic agreements into more substantial regimes. Moreover, monitoring and implementation review arrangements can both facilitate the development of expert 'epistemic' communities (which may be key factors in regime development) and improve their capacity to influence policy-making.[3]

Verification and International Environmental Regimes

Over 350 international environmental agreements have been made [*Fischer, 1991: 9*], of which at least 120 are multilateral and have legal substance and contemporary relevance [*Sand, 1992: 501–38*].[4] In several cases substantial international institutions have developed. Little systematic research has been carried out into the role of verification and implementation review in environmental agreements. However, it is possible to make some initial generalisations.[5]

Verification Issues and Environmental Treaty Negotiations

The first of these generalisations is that verification issues have not usually been very prominent in negotiations to establish environmental agreements, or in government decisions on whether or not to sign environmental treaties. In this respect the contrast with arms control and disarmament regimes is striking. Most major arms control agreements have been profoundly shaped by verification concerns from the beginning of their development. The areas of control and the precise treaty obligations have typically been selected for their 'verifiability' as much as for their military or strategic significance.

One potential explanation for this contrast is that there are structural differences between the situations in which environmental and arms control regimes typically have to develop. Perhaps a relatively large number of environmental agreements have been largely symbolic, or have simply involved commitments that are compatible with policies that all parties would have independently chosen to implement. Similarly, a relatively high proportion of more substantial environmental regimes may be self-enforcing, with little or no incentive to free-ride or defect.

However, arguments that there are fundamental structural differences between the requirements for environmental and arms control regimes can be greatly exaggerated. Arms control agreements have developed in a wide range of situations, including many where the incentives to cheat are low or where the security policies of participating states would probably not need to change greatly if one party were to defect. Moreover, there seem to be many environmental regimes where there are potentially serious concerns about free-riding or non-compliance.

Nevertheless, it is easy to understand why verification may seem to be relatively important for arms control agreements. The risk that undetected cheating may lead to threatening imbalances in military capabilities would be much more worrying for governments than the threat posed by rival states covertly producing CFCs or breaking CITES rules relating to endangered species of wildlife. The potential costs of continuing to comply with an environmental regime while another member defects are generally perceived by governments to be lower, and slower to develop, than in the arms control area.

Thus verification processes for environmental regimes may be considered adequate by member states even if there is a significant chance that substantial non-compliance may not be detected for some time. Moreover, the potential benefits of defection may be relatively low, reducing the incentives to free-ride and hence reducing the need for the confidence-building or deterrence functions of effective verification procedures. Furthermore, arms control typically involves negotiations between adversaries, in situations of mutual tension and suspicion. In contrast, many environmental protection regimes are negotiated between countries with good political, economic or social links, or at least with reasonably friendly relations. In this context, there is more likely to be a presumption of trust and good faith. Finally, the transparency of many environmentally-relevant activities may typically be greater than military measures, which tend to be veiled in secrecy.

In some cases, the lack of prominence of verification issues may reflect a conscious decision by leading partipants in negotiations to postpone the issue until later. There is always a tension in the regime-building process between achieving wide participation in a weak convention and achieving a convention with strong verifiable obligations which some key states are not willing to join. 'Reluctant' states will be more willing to sign a convention, and even accept relatively strong commitments, if they feel that they will be able to avoid full implementation without serious risk of formal exposure. In such contexts, negotiators of 'leading' states may prefer to defer attempts to develop formal verification procedures until after broad partipation in the regime and support for basic norms has been achieved.

Nevertheless, they may still have significant verification concerns and seek to address these through informal mechanisms pending the establishment of adequate formal verification procedures. For example, developed states may gain some reassurance about each other's compliance by making use of the many information sources and consultative processes that are already available to them, and if necessary they can establish new information exchange networks outside the official institutions of the environmental regime. Where they have induced 'reluctant' developing states to join a global regime by establishing additional aid mechanisms, OECD governments can insist upon monitoring how this aid is used by means of the standard procedures of the World Bank or other funding agencies.

Whether or not concerns about verifiability have been critical for decisions about whether to participate in environmental regimes, there are reasons to believe that they have influenced regime design. In the Montreal Protocol, for example, a state's 'consumption' of each controlled substance (such as CFCs or halons) was defined as production plus imports minus exports because these three factors could be more reliably monitored than consumption [Benedick, 1991]. Similarly, limits on states' carbon dioxide emissions from burning fossil fuels are being singled out for possible negotiated limits in the climate change convention partly because they can be relatively reliably calculated according to an agreed methodology using energy statistics and other available data [Fischer et al., 1990]. In contrast, it is intrinsically very difficult to calculate carbon dioxide emissions from deforestation with any reliability; the proportions of methane and carbon dioxide emitted from burning areas are highly sensitive to transient local conditions. For this reason, if states want to negotiate regulations that would limit greenhouse gas emissions due to deforestation, they will be well advised to do so indirectly, for example by regulating forest areas [Greene and Salt, 1992; Lanchbery, Salt and Greene, 1993]. Changes in forest areas could be monitored reasonably reliably using a combination of satellite and aerial surveillance and ground inspections.

There is some direct evidence that verifiability has actually increased compliance in practice. Experience of compliance with International Maritime Organisation (IMO) and MARPOL regulations provides a useful example. Their regulations limiting oil pollution from tankers take two forms [Ausubel and Victor, 1992: 8-9]. Operational regulations relate to the conduct of tankers at sea, for example restricting the rate at which they should discharge oily water into the ocean. *Technological* regulations relate to tanker design and equipment, and port facilities. The former are typically intrinsically difficult to monitor reliably, relying mainly on self-reporting by ship captains. The latter can be reliably monitored through routine inspections, since non-compliance is transparent and the costs of dismantling required equipment (or fitting substandard equipment) between inspections is high. Reportedly, compliance with the technological regulations is very good, whereas experts suspect (no-one knows) that compliance with inconvenient or costly operational rules is often quite poor [*Mitchell, 1993*].

Implementation Review Procedures

Where it is appropriate to the main treaty rules, most environmental agreements have some requirement that the parties collect data relevant to implementation and provide regular reports. In most such cases, only data produced and reported by the partipating states themselves can formally be considered during implementation review.[6] Moreover, the reporting requirements for states in environmental regimes are often rather vague.[7]

Even where the reporting requirements are relatively precise, compliance with them has often been rather poor, even in high profile regimes such as the Montreal protocol [*Greene, 1992*]. For example, by the end of 1991, many states had not even provided complete 'baseline' data for production of controlled substances such as CFCs for 1986 and 1989, let alone their data for 1990 [*Greene, 1993*]. Performance in other major regimes is even worse; in the cases of the London Dumping Convention, MARPOL, and CITES, less than 30 per cent of member states provided reports in 1990 [*US General Accounting Office, 1992*].

Amongst those agreements with reporting obligations, only a minority establish explicit procedures for reviewing submitted reports. In such cases, the formal assessment of implementation is typically carried out solely by states parties. The international secretariats to whom the states send their reports are generally strictly limited in what they can do with them. Mostly, they collate and summarise them, but are not permitted to carry out independent analysis.

To the extent that the above generalisations are valid, they indicate that many governments have tended to resist or neglect the development of effective implementation review processes associated with environmental agreements. It is easy in general to understand why states and other powerful actors can often share an interest in limiting the effectiveness of international institutions. More specifically, governments may negotiate agreements primarily to placate domestic constituencies and to symbolise their concern for the environment. Aware that full implementation may involve uncomfortably high political, economic or social costs, their demand for effective verification procedures in such cases is bound to be low.

The Role of Non-State Actors in Implementation

An important variable for regimes is the extent to which non-state actors are involved in implementation. In this respect, environmental regimes are typically very different from arms control agreements. States' defence and security policy-making and implementation is normally unambiguously controlled by central government. The mechanisms by which governments can ensure that military activities change in accord with state policy are mostly well established and relatively straightforward. In contrast, most environmentally-relevant activities are carried out by private non-state actors, semi-autonomous state industries or agencies, or local authorities. The governments who sign international agreements thus face the complex task of successfully regulating or altering the actions of many domestic or transnational actors within their jurisdiction.

In this context, we can develop the conclusions of the preceding subsection. The relative complexity of domestic implementation of environmental regimes means that much non-compliance can be due to governments 'turning a blind eye' to activities within their jurisdiction which they do not directly control, or failing to devote sufficient resources to enforce relevant regulations effectively. This is perhaps a tempting strategy for deliberate non-compliance. It is relatively deniable (being a sin of *omission* rather than *commission*), and accusations of government non-compliance would be hard to substantiate; everybody accepts that domestic enforcement of regulations can only be imperfectly effective. Questions of national sovereignty can be raised if foreign governments try to criticise a state's domestic regulatory system.

However, such non-compliance might not mean that a government joined a regime entirely in bad faith. Governments frequently sign international agreements without being fully aware of the implications of implementing the rules, which may not be due to come into force for some time. Once they turn their attention to implementation, governments may be reluctant to offend powerful domestic interest groups or to devote sufficient resources to achieve full compliance. Once the decision has been made to join the regime, political leaders may tend to leave implementation to lesser authorities that lack the power to overcome domestic resistance or to direct necessary resources.

In these contexts, verification and transparency systems could have an important role in exposing inadequate implementation and helping to ensure that the political costs of non-compliance outweigh the costs of ensuring effective implementation in each member state. They could encourage continuing high-level political concern with domestic implementation.

In some cases, states may genuinely lack the capacity to ensure effective domestic implementation. Countries in which the state apparatus is weak may lack the power or regulatory capacity to enforce regime rules domestically. Poor states may lack the necessary information-gathering and inspection networks, or the economic or social capital required to make necessary changes. Fear of exposing such lack of capacity to the international community may sometimes help to explain resistance to independent monitoring systems and effective verification procedures. However, systems that help to identify such lack of capacity can obviously play an important role in regime development. The rules may be revised so that such states are capable of implementing them, or international resources may be directed to help with implementation. In practice, a substantial proportion of funds from the Interim Multilateral Fund and the Global Environmental Facility has been used to help developing states to develop adequate national monitoring, data-collection and recording systems to improve implementation of environmental regimes.

Finally, the fact that many environmental regimes must largely be implemented by non-state actors and semi-autonomous state agencies may further help to explain why governments have been relatively unconcerned about establishing reliable verification systems before joining environmental regimes. In many cases, most of the potential costs of implementing the agreement will not be borne by central government. The government ministries responsible for negotiating the agreement may be relatively unaware or unconcerned about the extent of such costs, or the potential for free-riding. The non-state actors that could be most affected by free-riding may be only one of many lobby groups trying to influence government policy. They may often only become aware of the potential implications of an environmental regime after it has been established.

Making Implementation Review More Effective

As discussed above, most regimes depend on data reported by governments for information on implementation. There are endemic problems with interpreting and comparing different states' reports. Unless the data required from states is specified in detail, reports are bound to be incomplete, ambiguous on key points, or incompatible. Moreover, much can depend on the precise methodologies used to collect and calculate national reported data. Each state's internal monitoring and data-collection systems have evolved in their own way. Seemingly minor technical differences of definition or methods of analysis can lead to substantial discrepancies in results. For this reason, the development of agreed methodologies for preparing national greenhouse gas inventories has been central to the implementation of the framework convention on climate change.

Through the development of common methodologies and data-collection practices, much can be done to improve the usefulness of government reports for implementation review. It is also clear that most states could benefit from assistance in developing reliable national monitoring systems. Nevertheless, monitoring and implementation review processes that depend entirely on data reported by states on their own activities are clearly prone to serious reliability problems. Governments have an interest in omitting embarrassing information, and in massaging their data to disguise inadequate implementation. Left to their own devices, they may also not take adequate steps to ensure the reliability of data submitted to them by the appropriate domestic actors. For example, the task of monitoring compliance with international fishing quotas has often been undermined by the unreliability of reported data [Petersen, 1993: 280–84]. Individual fishers had an incentive to under-report their catches, and most governments had little incentive to cross-check the data.

Two ways of improving the reliability of the information on which implementation review is based are to use information from sources other than the governments concerned, and to establish independent international monitoring systems. In relation to the first point, there is normally a wide range of potential supplementary sources of information, ranging from international organisations such as the OECD, World Bank, and UN Food and Agriculture Organisation (FAO), through other national governments, to non-state actors such as trades unions, companies, environmental pressure groups, and individuals. The significance of non-state actors in implementing environmental regimes implies increased scope for informal monitoring systems to play a significant role in implementation review. The role of environmental organisations is well known. However, companies may also have an interest in exposing non-compliance by their competitors. They may also have greater access to relevant information than many governments or environmental organisations.

In principle, transparency about the environmental performance of each state would be improved if implementation review procedures were designed to allow consideration of all such data from non-governmental sources. The problem is that much of this additional information may also be unreliable or difficult to interpret, posing the risk of increasing confusion and undermining the overall effectiveness of the implementation review process. Thus, mechanisms are needed to assess and filter such information before it is used in judgements about compliance. In regimes where any such mechanisms exist, the most widely used is to permit only states parties to introduce supplementary information. Governments can make use of information from any sources they choose if they wish to challenge the accuracy of another state's reports.

There are, however, a number of problems with emphasising this approach. Few states are likely to allocate sufficient expert resources to assess all the relevant data and compare it with other states' reports. If a government did receive and recognise reliable information showing inaccuracies in another country's report, it would usually be reluctant to incur the diplomatic costs of issuing a challenge. The exception would be when it wanted for other reasons to embarrass that country, in which case it may be tempted to use any information to issue a challenge, however dubious it may be. Thus, the process would be inadequate and vulnerable to subordination to broader political concerns. It would fail to exert consistent pressure on governments to ensure that their reports on implementation were reliable and adequate.

A more effective approach would be to establish an international secretariat or body of experts tasked with routinely carrying out a technical review of national reports, taking into account information from other sources as it deems appropriate. As far as possible, such a technical review body should be shielded from direct political pressures. Where it identifies omissions or inconsistencies in a national report, or it has questions relating to methodologies used or compatability with other available information, this body should at least be able to request further information or clarification from relevant national governments. Preferably it should be able to send appropriate representatives to make visits to facilities or officials in the country concerned.

This should be a non-confrontational but persistent and structured 'apolitical' process. Apparent inconsistencies should be treated as subjects for clarification or further investigation, and not as indications of deliberate non-implementation. The revised national reports that emerge from this process would be submitted for overall assessment of implementation by the regime's appropriate political authority. A separate report from the international review body (and perhaps other recognised organisations) might also be submitted alongside the revised national reports. As much as possible of the information in these reports should then be publicly available, to enhance the role of international and non-governmental organisations in the overall implementation review process.

Some existing regimes have established implementation review institutions similar to this model. The International Atomic Energy Authority (IAEA) system for monitoring inventories of fissile materials corresponds to it quite closely [Fischer, 1989]. So do the review systems for International Labour Organisation conventions and for the International Covenant on Civil and Political Rights [Plant, 1991: 7–10]. As yet, however, such examples are harder to find in the environmental area. To some extent, the International Union for the Conservation of Nature (IUCN) plays the independent technical review body role discussed above within CITES. The European Environment Agency, due to be established by 1994, will play this role in relation to the implementation of environmental policies within EC states. The model would arguably be appropriate for a wide range of environmental regimes, including emerging ones such as the climate change convention [Fischer et al., 1990; Greene, 1991: 27–30].

Government reports are likely to continue to be the main source of information on implementation of most environmental regimes. To a greater or lesser extent, states already have the infrastructure necessary for gathering relevant data or monitoring activities within their areas of jurisdiction. The costs of establishing extensive parallel independent networks specifically to monitor implementation of an environmental regime would be prohibitive in many issue areas, even if political resistance to them could be overcome.

However, there are some cases where governments have come to accept (and even rely on) international monitoring systems for monitoring implementation. A prime example is the Co-operative Programme for Monitoring and Evaluation of the Long-Range Transmission of Air Pollutants in Europe (EMEP). EMEP maintains an international network for monitoring and assessing the chemical composition of rain, which can be used to deduce overall emissions of acid-causing substances from a particular country [Ausubel and Victor, 1992: 20]. EMEP is formally part of the convention on the Long-Range Transmission of Air Pollution (LRTAP), which has mainly been concerned with limiting the acid-rain problem in Europe. Similarly, the environmental data collected from a wide range of sources for the Global Environment Monitoring System (GEMS) promises to make an increasingly important contribution to environmental assessment and implementation review [Gosovic, 1992].

Conclusion

The potential role of verification issues and implementation review processes in the development, character and effectiveness of international environmental regimes is often underestimated. Although, unlike the arms control area for example, they have not typically been prominent in negotiations to establish environmental conventions, concerns about verifiability have shaped the character and rules of such regimes. Moreover, verification and implementation review processes, formal and informal, can play an important role in strengthening international environmental institutions and in enhancing their effectiveness. The increased use of independent data on implementation to supplement and correct national reports, combined with measures to establish independent review bodies to make the review processes more systematic, searching and open, could help substantially to increase the effectiveness of international environmental regimes.

NOTES

1. The author gratefully achnowledges valuable discussions on several of the issues raised here (mainly in relation to climate change) with Julian Salt, John Lanchbery Wolfgang Fischer, Werner Katscher, Gotthard Stein, Juan-Carlos Di Primio, and David Victor, held in the context of an ESRC project, research collaboration with VERTIC and Forschungszentrum Julich GmbH, and preparations for an IIASA project on the effectiveness of international environmental regimes.

2. Sand [*1990; 1991*], for example, emphasises the significance of 'selective incentives' in encouraging participation in international environmental institutions, by which fringe benefits help to persuade parties to participate in a programme or adhene to a standard which they would otherwise find unacceptable.

3. Peter Haas [*1990*], for example, has emphasised the importance of the collective beliefs of transnationally organised networks of knowledge-based communities – 'epistemic communities' – in the development and effectiveness of international environmental institutions, drawing mainly on his studies of the politics of international environmental management of the Mediterranean Sea.

4. More or less comprehensive outlines or surveys of international agreements relating to the environment can be found in Burhenne [*1974*], UNEP [*1989*], Sand [*1992*], and Scovazzi and Treves [*1992*].

5. This is based on my own preliminary review of environmental regimes combined with three recent outline reviews by Fischer [*1991*], the US General Accounting Office [*1992*] and Ausubel and Victor [*1992*].

6. In fact, as Andresan [*1992: 114*] and others have pointed out, this tends to be the case in most issue areas.

7. This was true, for example, of almost all of the sample of 13 major international environmental agreements whose formal obligations were reviewed by Fischer [*1991*], relating to: transboundary sea, river and air pollution; and conservation of whales, salmon, and endangered species.

REFERENCES

Andresen, S. (1992), 'International Verification in Practice: A Brief Account of Experiences from Relevant International Cooperative Measures', in E. Lykke (ed.) *Achieving Environmental Goals: The Concept and Practice of Environmental Performance Review*, London: Bellhaven, pp.101–18.

Ausubel, J. and D. Victor (1992), 'Verification of International Environmental Agreements', *Annual Review of Energy and the Environment 1992*, Vol.17.

Benedick, R. (1991), *Ozone Diplomacy: New Directions in Safeguarding the Planet*, London: Harvard University Press.

Burhenne, W. (1974), *International Environmental Law: Multilateral Treaties*, 5 vols., Berlin.

Chayes, A. and A. Chayes (1991), 'Adjustment and Compliance Processes in International Regulatory Regimes', in J. Tuchman Mathews (ed.), *Preserving the Global Environment: The Challenge of Shared Leadership*, New York: W.W. Norton, pp.280–308.

Fischer, W. *et al.* (1990), 'A Convention on Greenhouse Gases: Towards the Design of a Verification System', *Berichte des Forschungszentrums Julich; 2390*, Julich: Forschungszentrum Julich GmbH.

Fischer, W. (1991), 'The Verification of International Conventions on Protection of the Environment and Common Resources', *Berichte des Forschungszentrums Julich; 2495*, Julich: Forschungszentrum Julich GmbH.

Fisher, D. (1989), 'The IAEA Safeguards Model', in H. Schiefer and J. Keeley (eds.), *International Atomic Energy Agency Safeguards as a Model for Verification of a Chemical Weapons Convention*, Arms Control Verification Occassional Papers No.3, Canada: Department of External Affairs.

Gosovic, B. (1992), *The Quest for World Environmental Cooperation: The Case of the UN Global Environment Monitoring System*, London: Routledge.

Greene, O. (1991), 'Building a Global Warming Convention: Lessons from the Arms Control Experience?', in M. Grubb and N. Steen (eds.), *Pledge and Review Processes: Possible Components of a Climate Convention*, London: Royal Institute for International Affairs, pp.21–33.

Greene, O. (1992), 'Ozone Depletion: Implementing and Strengthening the Montreal Protocol', in J. Poole and R. Guthrie (eds.), *Verification Report 1992: Yearbook on Arms Control and Environmental Agreements* London: VERTIC, pp.265–75.

Greene, O. (1993), 'Limiting Ozone Depletion: The 1992 Review Process and the Development of the Montreal Protocol', in J. Poole and R. Guthrie (eds.), *Verification Report 1993: Yearbook on Arms Control and Environmental Agreements*, London: Brasseys, in press.

Greene, O. and J. Salt (1992), 'Limiting Climate Change: Verifying National Commitments', *Ecodecision*, Vol.7.

Haas, P (1990), *Saving the Mediterranean: The Politics of International Environmental Cooperation*, New York: Columbia University Press.

Keohane, R. (1984), *After Hegemony: Cooperation and Discord in the World Political Economy*, Princeton, NJ: Princeton University Press.

Keohane, R. (1989), *International Institutions and State Power*, Boulder, CO: Westview Press.

Lanchbery, J., Salt, J. and O. Greene (1993), 'Limiting Climate Change: Verification of Compliance with Treaty Commitments to Limit Greenhouse Gas Emissions from Forests and Land Use by Remote Sensing', *Berichte des Forschungszentrums Julich*, Julich: Forschungszentrum Julich GmbH, forthcoming.

Mitchell, R. (1993), 'International Oil Pollution of the Oceans', in P. Haas, R. Keohane and M. Levy (eds.), *Institutions for the Earth*, Cambridge, MA: MIT Press, pp.183–248.

Petersen, M. (1993), 'International Fisheries Management', in P. Haas, R. Keohane and M. Levy (eds.), *Institutions for the Earth* Cambridge, MA: MIT Press, pp.249–305.

Plant, G. (1991), 'Pledge and Review: Survey of Precedents', in M. Grubb and N. Steen (eds.), *Pledge and Review Processes: Possible Components of a Climate Convention*, London: Royal Institute for International Affairs, pp.5–14.

Porter, G. and J.W. Brown (1991), *Global Environmental Politics*, Boulder, CD Westview Press.

Sand, P. (1990), *Lessons Learned in Global Environmental Governance*, New York: World Resources Institute.

Sand, P. (1991), 'International Cooperation: The Environmental Experience', in J. Tuchman Mathews (ed.), *Preserving the Global Environment: The Challenge of Shared Leadership*, New York: W.W. Norton, pp.236–79.

Sand, P. (1992), *The Effectiveness of International Environmental Agreements: Survey of Existing Legal Instruments*, Cambridge: Grotius Publications.

Scovacci, T. and T. Treves (eds.) (1992), *World Treaties for the Protection of the Environment*, Milan: Istituto per l'Ambiente.

Stein, A. (1990), *Why Nations Cooperate: Circumstances and Choice in International Relations*, London: Cornell University Press.

Stokke, O. (1992), 'Environmental Performance Review: Choices in Design', in E. Lykke (ed.), *Achieving Environmental Goals: The Concept and practice of Environmental Performance Review*, London: Bellhaven, pp.3–24.

United Nations Environment Programme (1989), *Register of International Treaties and Other Agreements in the Field of the Environment*, UNEP/GC.15/Inf.2, Nairobi: UNEP.

United States General Accounting Office (1992), *International Environment: International Agreements are Not Well Monitored*, GAO/RCED-92-43, Washington, DC: General Accounting Office.

Young, O. (1989), *International Cooperation: Building Regimes for Natural Resources and the Environment*, London: Cornell University Press.

Young, O. (1992), 'The Effectiveness of International Institutions: Hard Cases and Critical Variables', in J. Rosenau and E. Czempiel, *Governance without Government: Order and Change in World Politics*, Cambridge: Cambridge University Press, pp.160–95.

The Politics of Climate Change after UNCED

MATTHEW PATERSON

Progress on responding effectively to potential global warming has been inadequate from an environmental point of view. The potential for an improved response at the international level will depend on a number of factors, including the ability of Bill Clinton to deliver his pledges and the political developments within the European Community. But the most important constraint will be the near-term future of the world economy. Should the world pull out of its current recession, then the political feasibility of more aggressive abatement programmes will be greatly enhanced. Without this improved response, many alarming projections of the potential impacts of global warming may be realised. Abatement attempts to date will make little impact on the growth of atmospheric concentrations of carbon dioxide. Consequences for developing countries will be particularly severe. The recession will both limit the likelihood of abatement programmes in the North, and also limit the potential for technology transfer to limit the future growth of emissions in many developing countries.

This study will assess the prospects for an improved international response to the problem of potential global warming, against the background of the UNCED Framework Convention. It begins by outlining some features of the framework convention, signed in Rio in June 1992. Secondly, it looks at some developments since Rio that will affect the way in which the international community responds in the near future. Thirdly, it looks at some implications of these developments; at the

Matthew Paterson was at the Department of Political Studies, University of Stirling, but is now at the Department of International Relations, Keele University. An earlier version of this study was given as a paper to the Postgraduate colloquium in the Department of Government at the University of Strathclyde. The author is grateful for the comments made by many of those present. He is also grateful to Michael Grubb of Chatham House for some particular pieces of information, and to Jo Van Every for her constructive criticism.

policies and targets so far adopted by states; and at how the impacts of global warming may or may not have been alleviated. Finally, the study considers some underlying reasons that help explain why the development of climate politics has not been as rapid as some might have wished. While recognising a certain autonomy of political events, notably the election of Bill Clinton, the focus in this concluding section is on the role of the world recession, starting roughly in 1990, in slowing developments and in potentially constraining them in the future. The focus on the world economy helps correct a bias present in many writings on global warming which imply that climate politics can be separated from other areas of international political life.

The Current Position: The Framework Convention and Rio

Climate change was propelled on to the international agenda during 1988.[1] Over the following four years there followed frenetic activity on the issue: a huge international scientific assessment of the nature of the problem in the Intergovernmental Panel on Climate Change (IPCC); a series of international conferences at which various states pledged their commitment to respond to the problem; and finally, formal negotiations towards an international Convention on the issue, organised through the Intergovernmental Negotiating Committee for a Framework Convention on Climate Change (INC). This Committee, established by the UN General Assembly, started meeting in February 1991, and produced a Convention which was signed by 155 countries at the UNCED in Rio de Janeiro in June 1992.

Many commentaries have been written on the Convention.[2] Most criticism has focused on the inadequacy of the commitments contained in it, in particular those undertaken by industrialised countries to limit their greenhouse gas emissions. The view of the environmental non-governmental organisations (NGOs) is most aptly summed up by the headline in their newsletter, produced once the final text on industrialised country commitments on greenhouse gases had been negotiated: 'True Trash!' (*ECO*, 8 May 1992; p.1). This final text committed industrialised countries only to enacting 'policies and take corresponding measures on the mitigation of climate change ... with the aim of returning individually or jointly to their 1990 levels these anthropogenic emissions of carbon dioxide and other greenhouse gases not controlled by the Montreal Protocol' [*United Nations, 1992: Articles 4.2 (a) and (b)*].

Set against the IPCC's assessment that 60 per cent reductions in CO_2 emissions would be needed to stabilise atmospheric concentrations of

CO_2 at current levels, this does indeed seem a meagre commitment. There has been disagreement over the meaning of the formulation. David Fisk, Chief Scientist at the Department of the Environment and head of the UK delegations to the climate negotiations, claimed that the wording is 'indistinguishable' from an absolute guarantee to stabilise emissions (*The Guardian*, 12 May 1992). On the other hand, Clayton Yeutter, Bush's Counsellor for Domestic Policy, wrote that 'the word "aim" was carefully chosen, it does not constitute a commitment, binding or otherwise' (quoted in *ECO* (UNCED Issue), June 1992). Added to this is the dropping of the year 2000 from the sentence. It is clear that the wording is significantly weaker than that proposed by the European countries. Fisk's interpretation is wishful thinking at best. None the less, Hare [*1992*] is correct to point out that industrialised countries are committed to adopting measures that can stabilise emissions.

However, as the Alliance of Small Island States (AOSIS) and several NGOs pointed out, even the firm commitment to stabilise emissions of CO_2 and other greenhouse gases by 2000 preferred by most industrialised countries (with objections by the USA) would not significantly alter future increases in atmospheric concentrations of CO_2. It was only the AOSIS states that repeatedly pressed for industrialised countries to commit themselves to actual reductions in emissions. The commitments made unilaterally by many industrialised countries (most commonly to stabilise their CO_2 emissions at 1990 levels by the year 2000), would, according to the International Energy Agency (IEA), only reduce *projected* CO_2 emissions for the year 2000 by about four per cent [*IEA, 1992: 31 (Figure 1)*].

Another widespread criticism of the Convention was on North–South issues. The negotiation of these issues focused primarily on the necessity of significant financial and technological transfers to take place if developing countries were to be able to undertake any meaningful commitments in the Convention or in any future agreements. The outcome was one where although developing countries were able to get across their point that any commitments undertaken by them would be purely dependent on such transfers from the North, they (along with some sympathetic states in the North) were unable to persuade most Northern countries to commit themselves to significant transfers. The wording in the Convention text is simply that Northern countries (excluding the former Soviet bloc countries) will provide financial assistance to enable developing countries to compile 'national inventories' of the sources and sinks on their territory, and for measures the latter may undertake to mitigate climate change [*United Nations, 1992: Articles 4.1, 4.3 and 12.1*]. The important phrase is that Northern countries will meet the 'full agreed incremental costs' of such undertakings by developing countries. The Convention thus provides little incentive for developing countries to try to limit the rate of growth of their emissions, as few schemes are likely to be implemented unless industrialised countries agree to meet the costs.

Although significant weaknesses in the final wording of the Convention must be acknowledged, it does provide an important framework for future developments in two respects. On the one hand it provides an outline of the measures that the international community felt were required to respond to the threat of global climate change. While criticised by many for being too weak on controlling greenhouse gases, the Convention does provide a basic set of types of measures which need to be implemented if climate change is to be slowed. In this sense it is a framework for future developments. On the other hand, it also provides an elaborate institutional system for future negotiations. The negotiators knew that while there was an immediate expectation on them to produce an agreement which committed states to slowing global warming significantly, the problem was essentially a long-term one in that it could not be solved in one round of negotiations. Thus they also provided a framework for future negotiations and developments. These institutions include not only the standard Conference of the Parties, Secretariat, and so on, which merely acknowledge that negotiations on climate change will continue in the future, they also involve the creation of several other bodies. These include a 'financial mechanism' (Article 11), anticipating that financial transfers are likely to be crucial to the success of any future agreements; a 'subsidiary body for scientific and technological advice' (Article 9), anticipating the need to keep the future negotiation well informed about changes in scientific knowledge about global warming; and a 'subsidiary body for Implementation' (Article 10), which will review the information submitted by states about their greenhouse gas inventories and policies implemented.

The negotiators for the Framework Convention also believed that it would be necessary to continue negotiations before the Convention formally enters into force. This is 90 days after the fiftieth state has ratified or acceded to the Convention (Article 23), which is unlikely to be for a few years. The report to the UN General Assembly on behalf of the INC by the UN Secretary General estimated it would take about two years, so that September 1994 was a 'prudent working hypothesis' for when the convention is likely to enter into force [*UN General Assembly, 1992a: 6*]. They agreed therefore an interim procedure: that, with the consent of the General Assembly, the INC would continue meeting until the Convention enters into force [*INC, May 1992a, Annex II: 28–9*]. This was approved by the UN General Assembly [*UN General Assembly, 1992b*]. The INC's continued mandate is to

> prepare for the first meeting of the Conference of the Parties; to contribute to the effective functioning of the interim arrangements; and to promote a coherent and coordinated programme of action in support of the entry into force and implementation of the Convention, paying particular attention, in that context, to capacity-building in developing and other countries [*INC, 1992b: 6*].

This seems specifically to exclude the negotiation of protocols or the renegotiation of the control articles (Article 4.2).

The INC has continued to meet since UNCED. Its first meeting after Rio was an organisational one held on 7–10 December 1992 in Geneva. The Draft Report gives little information about the outcome. *ECO* (10 Dec. 1992, p.2) reports that most of the time was spent on organisational matters. The INC's working group structure was reorganised so that Working Group I would deal with 'commitments and review of information, methodologies, and modalities for the first CoP [Conference of the Parties]', while Working Group II would deal with 'financing, rules of procedure, and institutional issues'. Thus it seems that the inability to negotiate protocols prior to the Convention entering into force, mentioned above, has been entrenched. Some states, such as Germany and the Netherlands, did call for 'action beyond a simple review of information' but this form of action has not come into the formal business of the INC [*ibid*]. In general, it seems that there was a reiteration of the North–South conflict and that future meetings would focus on financial questions and the Global Environmental Facility.

Future Directions

Beyond the institutional inertia at the international level, several conditions have changed which will be far more important in affecting the future development of international negotiations on the issue. In the main, these are domestic political developments within the main industrialised countries: the USA, the EC and Japan. Scientific developments, which drove the issue in its early stages, are now not particularly important, because the importance of scientists was dependent, among other things, on the relatively low level of politicisation of the issue. Similarly, the impetus from freak weather seems to have declined to an extent. 1992 was a significantly cooler year than those previous to it (*New Scientist*, 9 Jan. 1993, p.10), although this seems to be clearly associated with the eruption of Mount Pinatubo the previous year. While this is obviously consistent with an underlying warming trend, it allows breathing space for greenhouse sceptics or those wishing to ignore global warming.

Clinton: The (Partial) Autonomy of Politics

The first, and most obvious, of these political developments are those in US politics, in particular the election of Bill Clinton as president. All five potential Democratic presidential candidates criticised Bush heavily during the race for the nomination for his refusal to commit the US to stabilisation, and all five committed themselves to such a target. Clinton himself stated that he would commit the US to stabilisation at 1990 levels by 2000, 'with "serious consideration" given to cuts of 20–30 per cent by 2005' (*ECO*, 18 Feb. 1991). During the campaign he endorsed 'strict fuel economy standards for cars, taxes to encourage energy conservation and efforts to protect endangered species. He also promoted renewable energy sources over nuclear and fossil fuels [*Charles, 1992*]. However, Charles also notes that his actual environmental record as Governor of Arkansas is mixed [*ibid: 13*].

It is, however, Clinton's choice of Al Gore as running mate that means that the US position on climate change is likely to change rather radically in the near future. Gore is widely regarded as one of the most progressive US politicians on environmental issues generally, and has expressed strong views on the climate change issue. Attending the climate negotiations in Geneva in December 1991 (before he was Clinton's running mate), he claimed that Bush's approach to global warming was 'the worst abdication of leadership ever' (quoted in *ECO*, 18 Dec. 1991, p.1). He introduced, along with Majority Leader Mitchell, a 'Global Climate Protection Act' into the US Senate in May 1992, which would have committed the US to stabilisation (*ECO*, 8 May 1992, p.4). Gore himself claimed that he 'emphasised the environment more than any other issue during the campaign' (quoted in Gwynne and Taylor [*1992*]). He made sure that the Democrats' campaign stressed that 'sound environmental policies can be an engine of growth that will help the American economy compete with Germany and Japan in the 1990s [*Linden, 1992*], countering Bush and Quayle's more simplistic jobs-versus-the-environment dichotomy.

It may be too early to assess fully the implications of Clinton's election. However, some things are clear. It will signal a significant change in presidential attitudes to the issue and changes in policy areas which affect it. At the international level, this will mean a convergence of views among the industrialised countries, which may facilitate a stronger agreement being signed on CO_2 in the relatively near future. Of course the pace of a

CO_2 protocol seems to have been limited by the institutional remit given to the INC, as noted above.

Two aspects of Clinton's early period in office are of note. Firstly, his commitment in general to environmental issues has been emphasised. He has established a White House office of ecological coordination, led by Gore; he has promised to introduce legislation to bring the Environmental Protection Agency (EPA) up to Cabinet level; and in the short term, he has drafted environmental provisions to go into the North American Free Trade Agreement (NAFTA) (*The Guardian*, 9 Feb. 1993, p.10).

Secondly, he has included a broad-based energy tax in his economic plan. This was to be designed to raise $71.4 thousand million over five years to contribute to his aim of reducing the federal budget deficit. Driven more by fiscal than environmental pressures, it is to be an energy rather than a carbon tax, based on the heat content of the fuels (*Financial Times*, 19 Feb. 1993, p.5). Nevertheless, the intention is also to stimulate energy conservation and efficiency, a factor emphasised even by Lloyd Bentsen, Treasury Secretary (*The Guardian*, 19 Feb. 1993, p.10). The tax will not be imposed on renewable energy sources, but solely on fossil fuels and nuclear power. Hazel O'Leary, Energy Secretary, has stated that, combined with a $2.5 thousand million investment programme in promoting conservation and renewables, the tax should 'reduce greenhouse gas emissions by about 25 million tonnes in the year 2000'.[3] The tax should also be important in removing an obstacle for the introduction of the EC's proposed carbon/energy tax (see below).

By the end of April 1993, these developments made Clinton feel able to make his first formal presidential commitment on the CO_2 issue by pledging that the US would now set specific targets for reducing greenhouse gas emissions to their 1990 levels by 2000. This brought the US into line with other industrialised countries [*Miller, 1993*].

While acknowledging these early achievements, it should not be forgotten that the US remains a polity deeply constrained by interest group politics [*Cigler and Loomis, 1991*]. The ability of the new president to effect significant policy change is likely to be restricted. Clinton and (especially) Gore will find themselves frustrated in their ability to live up to their expectations of office, although they have the advantage of a Democratic Presidency with a Democratic Congress, which has not occurred since Carter. The ability of the coal and oil lobby to slow down legislation or the implementation of programmes designed to limit emissions is significant. Alan Miller reports that the last time a president sympathetic to the EPA was in office (Carter), the Department of Energy and lobby interests were still able to block EPA initiatives (quoted in *Tiempo*, No.6, Sept. 1992, p.14). And already, as Clinton unveiled his economic plan, US lobbyists started to work to get the energy tax modified or scrapped in Congress. Charles DiBona of the American Petroleum Institute claimed that it would 'seriously harm economic recovery and be a job killer on a massive scale' (quoted in *Financial Times* 19 Feb. 1993, p.10). He suggested that it would reduce GDP by $170 thousand million over five years and destroy 600,000 jobs. Even some Democrats, such as Senator David Boren, stated they would be seeking to amend it in Congress (*The Guardian*, 19 Feb. 1993, p.22). Thus the optimism expressed here about Clinton is only really clearly relevant when put into the context of the preceding Bush Administration.

It is possible that not much more can be expected in the short term than a formal commitment to CO_2 stabilisation by 2000, which is in effect what will be achieved by existing policy. However, the US is likely to become keen to retake the initiative at the international level, to regain its reputation as an international environmental leader. Given the previous apathy of the Bush Administration and the stagnation in Europe (see below), this may not be difficult to achieve. This is likely to provide fresh impetus to negotiations in the near future.

The EC: The Interdependency of Climate Politics

In the EC, the Community's climate change strategy has run into several problems. The cumulative effect of these is that, while the Community is likely to live up to its commitment to stabilise its CO_2 emissions at 1990 levels by 2000, it is unlikely in the short term to be driving negotiations forward in the international arena. Beyond 2000, whether the Community will commit itself to actual reductions in emissions remains an open question.

The EC's policy on global warming was initiated in October 1990, when the Council of Energy and Environment Ministers adopted and announced the Community's intention to stabilise its CO_2 emissions at 1990 levels by 2000. This decision was taken without a strategy designed to meet the target, and was intended primarily to influence the outcome of the Second World Climate Conference then meeting in Geneva, and to precipitate international negotiations on global warming. The next step was to devise a strategy to meet the target. This would be threefold, with a package of directives on energy saving and renewables, a carbon tax, and sets of complementary national-level measures. Some programmes on energy saving and renewables were already planned, and these programmes, THERMIE (on new energy technologies), ALTENER (on renewable energy), and SAVE (on energy efficiency), were strengthened to become part of the climate strategy. In addition, on 25 September 1991, the Commission announced a proposal to introduce a Community-

wide CO_2-energy tax. It would be based half on the carbon content of a
fuel and half simply on the energy use. It would initially be set at $3 a
barrel of oil equivalent, and would rise to $10 a barrel by 2000. The
Council of Energy and Environment Ministers approved this proposal in
principle at a meeting on 13 December 1991, and asked the Commission
to come up with a detailed draft directive (*ECO*, 16 Dec. 1991, p.1). The
aim was to have a draft directive ready for March which the Council could
approve in time for UNCED. In the end, after much internal wrangling,
the Commission came back with such a draft on 13 May 1992, which was
approved by the Energy Council on May 27.

   However, by this time, the Community's strategy had run into several
problems. The biggest was the general crisis into which the Community
was thrown during 1992 over the Danish referendum on Maastricht. This
threw many areas of Community policy into confusion. In particular, it
added urgency and ideological potency to the subsidiarity principle
written into the Maastricht Treaty. Consequently, development of a
Community-wide climate strategy, such as the CO_2-energy tax or the
three programmes developed by the Commission to implement the
Community's stabilisation target, has been significantly impaired.

   In addition, large sectors of European industry had campaigned
heavily against the tax proposal in particular, claiming it would seriously
affect their competitiveness. *The Economist* suggests that the lobby was
'probably their most powerful offensive against an EC proposal' [*The
Economist, 1992: 91*]. Those objecting claimed that the tax would destroy
900,000 jobs in the EC. The lobby included a consortium of seven of the
largest power-generating companies [*Beavis, 1992*], the European Coal
and Steel Community [*ECSC, 1992*], the oil companies, and many other
energy intensive industries. In addition, the oil-producing states, through
OPEC and the Gulf Co-operation Council, lobbied hard against the tax,
and threatened to retaliate by radically restricting oil production and
thereby pushing up prices rapidly, evoking fears of 1973–type crises
(*Financial Times*, 4 March 1992); [*European Environment, 1992:1*].

   The effects of these problems were twofold. Firstly, they simply slowed
the whole process down. Secondly, they meant that the wording of the
draft directive on the carbon tax was significantly weakened. It contained
exemptions for most energy-intensive industries 'whose energy consumption, expressed as a percentage of value added, exceeds 8 per cent [*CEC,
1992a*], purportedly in the name of international competitiveness [*Grubb
and Hope, 1992: 1111*]. And in particular it included a sentence which
made it clear that the introduction of the tax would be 'conditional on the
introduction by other member countries of the OECD of a similar tax or
of measures having a financial impact equivalent to those provided for in

this Directive' [*CEC, 1992b*]; (*Europe*, Thursday, 28 May 1992, p.10). Thus the EC tied itself to what looked (then) like a very bleak chance of action in the US. It is also worth noting how the equivalence of action was to be measured *financially* rather than in terms of the effect of emissions. Arguably this makes the conditions for the application of the tax even more restrictive, since it limits its conditions to fiscal measures.

Of course Clinton's election may make a great deal of difference here. The energy tax proposed in the US, while not being technically a financially equivalent measure, will possibly undercut arguments within the EC that stress the competitiveness problems associated with the EC's tax. However, in 1993 the tax proposal in the EC still has significant blocks to it. A UK Treasury Minister stated on January 15 that the UK was 'not yet convinced that a Europe-wide tax was a necessary or appropriate response to global warming' (quoted in *Financial Times*, 19 Feb. 1993, p.5). The EC Environment Commissioner, Ioannis Paleokras-sas, has suggested that internal debates will mean that the tax is unlikely to make much headway in 1993 (ibid.).

The other effect was on the other three other programmes – SAVE, ALTENER, and THERMIE – which made up the Community's climate strategy. These were being cut back heavily. In a rush to have an agreed strategy before UNCED, key areas of the programmes were cut back to secure the agreement of particular states. The SAVE programme was reduced to the one existing directive on boilers (from seven proposed directives), and the rest were left to national discretion. The budget for ALTENER was reduced to ECU40 million, insufficient to build even one power station [*Grubb and Hope, 1992: 1111: Warren, 1992*].

In recognition of some of these problems, in particular the subsidiarity one, but more practically the fact that the EC strategy, as it now stood, no longer looked likely to meet the EC's target [*Grubb and Hope, 1992: 1112*], the Council turned to a new approach. It decided to lay more emphasis on the national programmes to be submitted to the Commission by December 1993. The Commission would then review these to see if they added up to the Community's collective target. In May 1992 it created a monitoring mechanism to cover this process. Unfortunately, it remained undecided what would happen if they do not add up. Further-more, by April 1992, only four of the 12 member states had submitted their programmes (*Financial Times*, 16 April 1992, p.6).

Japan: Plus ça Change?

A short note on Japan is in order. During the negotiations before UNCED, Japan took a line somewhere between the US and the Europeans. On the one hand Japan was not particularly keen to sign up to hard and fast targets on emissions. On the other hand, Japan's opportunism, technological confidence, and lack of indigenous energy sources has meant that in practice it has been relatively progressive. It has been keen to develop further its already formidable achievements in energy efficiency, and to export its technology to other countries, especially the East and Southeast Asian NICs. Since Rio, little has changed formally in Japan, but there has been a fierce internal debate over a carbon tax between the Ministry of International Trade and Industry (MITI) on the one hand, arguing that no tax can be introduced at least until the recession is over,[4] and the Ministries of Environment and Foreign Affairs, which argue that such a tax should be introduced. Should the latter win this battle, the likelihood of increased coherence within the bloc of Northern countries looks highly plausible.

Implications for North and South

Despite these setbacks, the likelihood in the near term is that the industrialised countries will live up to their unilateral commitments to stabilise CO_2 by 2000, and that, given the US election result, the US will join this commitment.[5] Some CO_2 protocol, or amendments to the control articles of the Convention, may therefore be likely in the next two to three years.[6] However, it remains debatable whether industrialised countries will commit themselves as a whole to anything more than this.

The implications of this for most industrialised countries are not necessarily greatly damaging in the short to medium term. They are likely to be committing themselves to greater adaptation costs due to the greater level of warming, but it would be difficult to assess this with any degree of accuracy. Compared to what they might have had to contemplate had they taken no action, the change is probably insignificant, but compared to the costs they could avoid if they embarked on a considerably more stringent abatement programme, it is probably a big difference.

The implications of this for many countries in the South could be severe. In particular, small island states, and others highly vulnerable to the impacts of climate change, look set to be hit by a 'double whammy'. On the one hand, commitments so far made by industrialised countries to limit their own emissions are by no means adequate to slow global warming significantly, as shown above. On the other hand, it is unlikely that the Clinton-Gore presidency will have enough domestic political clout to sanction the large amounts of financial and technology transfers estimated to be necessary to enable developing countries (especially large and semi-industrialised ones such as India and China) to 'tunnel through' to efficient energy technologies, especially given the US's persistent budget deficit. It is also unclear that they have the political will to try to enact such a strategy, and despite rhetorical claims and small amounts of money flowing through the GEF, most European states seem similarly to be only committed to such transfers in a decidedly ambiguous fashion. At a meeting of the World Bank's International Development Association (IDA, the 'soft loan' agency), which had been promised an 'Earth increment' at UNCED, the issue failed even to get on the agenda [Pearce, 1992]. Thus the effort to abate world emissions will be restricted further. This latter problem arguably has even more important consequences in the long term, since those countries will then be sinking capital into inefficient technology which will be used over the next 40–50 years.

The IPCC Report, as a consensus document, was fairly cautious especially in its assessment of potential impacts. Yet it was able to state for example that 'relatively small changes in drought risk represent potentially the most serious impact of climate change on agriculture' [IPCC, 1990: 4]. While they could not say for certain whether global agricultural production would decline (largely because of uncertainty as to whether increased CO_2 fertilisation will offset other losses), they did state that some areas would experience significant agricultural losses; these areas would include 'Brazil, Peru, the Sahel Region of Africa, Southeast Asia, the Asian Region of the USSR, and China' [ibid.: 2]. They also suggested that 'significant movements of people' were entirely possible as a consequence of sea level rise, changes in disease patterns, and agricultural migrations [ibid.: 5]. What Working Group II did emphasise was that the severity of the impacts depends crucially on the rate of climate change; in Michael Grubb's words, 'irrespective of whether a stable warmer world might be better or worse, rapid changes could disrupt both human societies and natural ecosystems' [Grubb, 1990: 7]. Other studies have been less circumspect in giving potential figures. For example, it has been suggested that in Bangladesh alone, approximately 30 million people may become environmental refugees as

Thus it seems that the worst fears of many may be realised with regard to global warming. Current commitments by industrialised states will not make any significant impact on the rate of warming, and the rate of growth in the emissions of developing countries seems to be likely to go unabated. Thus it seems entirely plausible that many of the projections made of the likely impacts of global warming may still occur, assuming assessments such as that of the IPCC were reasonable in the first place. While the potential impacts are well documented, a brief résumé is worthwhile here, to stress how little has yet changed.

a result of relatively small sea level rises (ones within IPCC ranges) [*Thomas, 1992: 130;* also *Wirth, 1989*].

Explanations

Behind these setbacks are two basic problems for climate politics. The first is that global warming has simply declined as a political issue in industrialised countries since 1990. The pressure on politicians to act has therefore eased. We may be facing a repeat of the issue attention cycle problem [*Downs, 1972*], or of 'interest fatigue', so that the electoral and domestic pressure on governments to act has declined significantly. Ungar [*1992*] observed this issue cycle systematically through media coverage of global warming between 1988 and 1992, and found coverage to decline significantly and become less radical in its predictions and prescriptions.[7]

Alongside this decline in political attention, and to a large extent underlying it, is the world recession which has extended throughout this period, in particular since 1990. This has slowed policy developments on global warming, both by diverting attention away from it, and by reinforcing arguments about the costs of action. Policy-makers are less likely to undertake potentially costly actions while under pressure from falling government revenue, increased welfare spending, and falling profitability for many companies.

Thus an assessment of likely developments on global warming in the near future depends on an assessment of what may happen to the world economy. Should the economies in the industrialised world pick up out of recession, it appears plausible both that environmental pressure groups will regain space to affect public opinion and governments, and that governments themselves will have more room for manoeuvre in introducing regulations and fiscal measures to combat global warming.

This assessment depends however on an acceptance of the conventional view of the economic crisis of the early 1990s – that it is simply another cyclical recession into which capitalist market economies periodically plunge themselves, and out of which they autonomously climb. Tanzer [*1992*], gives compelling reasons for remaining sceptical of this viewpoint, and for believing that the causes of the current crisis are not cyclical, but structurally located in the evolution of the world economy since the Second World War, which he characterises as a steady slowdown in average growth rates, saturation of many consumer durable markets, the relative decline of the US, and the growth of financial speculation [*ibid: 5–6*]. Tanzer is thus pessimistic about the ability of industrialised countries to respond effectively to environmental problems in the near future, both because of capital shortages, and because persistent economic problems will undermine the cooperative ventures that states may seek to undertake to resolve environmental problems. Given worries about the growth of protectionism in the recent GATT negotiations, fuelled as well by Clinton's election, these fears appear plausible.

Conclusions

This study has reviewed some of the political developments since Rio which will have an influence on the course of international climate politics over the next few years. These developments appear to have basic ambiguities, and there remain two plausible scenarios that can be constructed.

The first is a relatively optimistic one. It involves the combinations of a modest recovery in the economies of the West, institutional flexibility in the INC, leadership from the US, and the EC's position holding together at least enough for it not to be obstructive. This could lead to a reasonably rapid improvement in the way in which the international community responds to global warming, compared to the stagnation of the last two years.

The second is the pessimistic scenario. It involves persistent stagnation in the world economy, stagnation in the INC because of restrictions on its remit, the inability of Clinton and Gore to generate sufficient political support to provide leadership at the international level, and persistent problems in the EC over the CO_2–energy tax. This could lead to a stalling of climate politics at the present level, where industrialised countries only commit themselves to stabilisation of emissions, and where the achievement of that objective remains problematic.

Which of these is more likely remains an open question. It may be possible for NGOs to generate political pressure to tip the scales towards the former. But they will be constrained by the current recession, and more general 'interest fatigue'. My belief, based on other research, is that direct pressure on governments is only likely to be effective under fairly unusual conditions where governments feel the need to appease environmental concerns. A strategy more likely to be effective in the medium term is to concentrate on building the cognitive base on which states make decisions, a strategy which necessarily involves engaging with the international organisations working in such areas. Such a strategy also builds on the influence that those institutions can have over states' decisions.

To conclude on a more critical note, it may be that even if the former of these two scenarios is realised in the short term, it will undercut its own success in the longer term, by being based on current notions of economic success. While it may be that economic recovery will generate capital and political support for more action on global warming, it will also itself generate more emissions, unless strong abatement action is introduced early on. And in the longer term, the success of political strategies which assume it is only possible to act while economies are growing will be flawed if growth, or at the least the form in which growth occurs, is itself part of the problem.

NOTES

1. For a fuller account of the history of this, see Bodansky [*1993*], or Paterson [*1992a*]. I assume that readers are familiar with the basic scientific and political characteristics of global warming. For a good introduction, see Grubb [*1990*], or Leggett [*1990*]. It should also be noted that I am not particularly concerned here with the political impacts of likely climatic changes (for example, through desertification, environmental refugees, and so on). I am also not largely engaging in some of the arguments as to why states should take ameliorative action, although it is clear that I believe they should. Although these arguments are clearly important, I focus more here on the political pressures that will affect how states may improve their abatement efforts with regard to CO_2 in particular.
2. See, for example, Berreen and Meyer [*1992*]; Bodansky [*1993*]; Grubb [*1992*]; Pachauri [*1992*]; and Paterson [*1992b*].
3. Quoted in Charles [*1993*]. The US emitted 5020 Mtons of CO_2 in 1990 [*IEA, 1992*]. This is then only half a per cent of current emissions, but would presumably be added to the effect of existing programmes. At the time of writing I have not seen any critiques of the programme by US environmental groups. Apparently there is some sort of truce operating between them and the Administration.
4. MITI does not seem to be doing nothing, however. They did seek a five per cent increase in funding for energy conservation for the fiscal year 1993 (*Japan Times Weekly*, 7–13 Sept. 1992, p.8).
5. I make this claim simply because I believe its achievement to be significantly easier than we would be led to believe by states' announcements about the 'pain' which will be inflicted by policies to achieve it.
6. This of course depends on whether the INC decides to press on with these negotiations or whether it has no authority to do this and must wait until the Convention enters into force.
7. Although media coverage is not necessarily a good indicator of the level of genuine public concern – which, as Rüdig shows, has not declined since 1990 [*Rüdig, 1993*] – it does show how that concern has been politicised, in the sense that the media (literally) mediates public opinion. The fact that the media's coverage has declined quantitatively, and has become more conservative qualitatively, is a reasonable indicator of declining political pressure on decision-makers.

REFERENCES

Beavis, Simon (1992), 'Electricity Generators Launch Campaign Against Proposed European Carbon Tax', *The Guardian*, 21 May, p.14.

Berreen, Jim and Aubrey Meyer (1992), 'A Package Marked "Return to Sender": Some Problems with the Climate Convention', *Network '92*, No.19, June–July, pp.6–7.

Bodansky, Dan (1993), 'The United Nations Framework Convention on Climate Change: A Commentary', *Yale Journal of International Law*, forthcoming.

CEC (1992a), *A Community Strategy to Limit Carbon Dioxide and to Improve Energy Efficiency*, Commission of the European Communities, Brussels, 1 June, COM (92) 246 final.

CEC (1992b), *Proposal for a Council Directive introducing a Tax on Carbon Dioxide Emissions and Energy*, Commission of the European Communities, Brussels, 30 June, COM (92) 226 final.

Charles, Dan (1992), 'Deep Rumblings at Little Rock', *New Scientist*, 12 Dec., pp.12–13.

Charles, Dan (1993), 'Clinton Opts for a Greener Economy', *New Scientist*, Feb. 27, p.4.

Cigler, Allan J. and Burdett A. Loomis (1991), *Interest Group Politics*, Washington, DC: Congressional Quarterly Press.

Downs, Anthony (1972), 'Up and Down with Ecology – The Issue Attention Cycle', *Public Interest*, Vol.28, pp.38–50.

The Economist (1992), 'Europe's Industries Play Dirty', 9 May, pp.91–2.

ECSC (1992), 'Resolution of the Consultative Committee of the European Coal and Steel Community', *Official Journal of the European Communities*, 19 May 1992.

European Environment (1992), Vol.2, No.4 (editorial).

Grubb, Michael (1990), *Energy Policies and the Greenhouse Effect: Volume One*, Aldershot: Dartmouth.

Grubb, Michael (1992), 'The Heat is on', *The Higher*, 5 June.

Grubb, Michael and Chris Hope (1992), 'EC Climate Policy: Where There's a Will ...', *Energy Policy*, Nov. 1992, pp.1110–14.

Gwynne, S.C. and Elizabeth Taylor (1992), 'We're not measuring the Drapes', *Time*, 19 Oct., p.70.

Hare, K. (1992), *ECO*, UNCED Issue, June, p.2.

IEA (1992), *Climate Change Policy Initiatives*, Paris: International Energy Agency.

INC (1992a), 'Report of the Intergovernmental Negotiating Committee for a Framework Convention on Climate Change, held at New York from 30 April to 9 May 1992', Document A/AC.237/18 (Part II)/Add.1/Corr.1, May.

INC (1992b), 'Draft Report of the Intergovernmental Negotiating Committee for a Framework Convention on Climate Change on its 6th Session, held at Geneva 7–10 December 1992', Geneva, 10 Dec.

IPCC (1990), Policymakers Summary of the Working Group II Report, Geneva: Intergovernmental Panel on Climate Change.

Leggett, Jeremy (ed.) (1990), *Global Warming: The Greenpeace Report*, Oxford: Oxford University Press.

Linden, Eugene (1992), 'The Green Factor', *Time*, 12 Oct., pp.28–32.

Miller, Susan Katz (1993), 'Clinton Vows to Take the Lead over Conservation', *New Scientist*, 1 May, p.7.

Pachauri, R.K. (1992), 'The Climate Change Convention ... What It May Mean for the Poor', *Network '92*, No.19, Aug.–Sept.

Paterson, Matthew (1992a), 'Global Warming', in C. Thomas, *The Environment in International Relations*, London: Royal Institute of International Affairs.

Paterson, Matthew (1992b), 'The Convention on Climate Change Agreed at the Rio Conference', *Environmental Politics*, Vol.1, No.4, pp.267–73.

Pearce, Fred (1992), 'Doubts Grow over Earth Summit Promises', *New Scientist*, 3 Oct., p.6.

Rüdig, Wolfgang (1993), *Dimensions of Public Concern over Global Warming: A Comparative Analysis of West European Public Opinion*, Paper for the 4th Global Warming International Conference, 5–8 April, Chicago USA.

Tanzer, Michael (1992), 'After Rio', *Monthly Review*, Nov. pp.1–11.

Thomas, Caroline (1992), *The Environment in International Relations*, London: Royal Institute of International Affairs.

Ungar, Sheldon (1992), 'The Rise and (Relative) Fall of Global Warming as a Social Problem', *Sociological Quarterly*, Vol.33, No.4, pp.483–501.

UN General Assembly (1992a), 'Framework Convention on Climate Change: Implementation of Resolution 46/169 and Possible Requirements for Future Work' Report of the Secretary-General, Document A/47/466, New York 5 Oct.

UN General Assembly (1992b), 'Draft Resolution', Document A/C.2/47/L.58 25 Nov.

United Nations (1992), *United Nations Framework Convention on Climate Change*, New York: United Nations.

Warren, Andrew (1992), 'Brussels Spout', *Evening Standard* (London), 28 Sept., pp.55–56.

Wirth, David (1989), 'Climate Chaos', *Foreign Policy*, Spring, pp.3–22.

Population Dynamics and Environmental Degradation in Nepal: An Interpretation

YAGYA BAHADUR KARKI

When the relationship between population and environment is examined, and the central role in global consumption of natural resources played by the 15 percent of global population living in the developed world is acknowledged, the relationship between population growth in developing countries and the natural resource base on which the majority of the global population currently depends for daily survival emerges in sharp perspective. Global population growth prospects are examined briefly. The case of Nepal illustrates the difficulties confronting developing countries which attempt practical implemention of the population policy guidelines set out in Agenda 21. Past and current population programmes in that country have failed to see the population problem as multidimensional, and have failed also to encourage grassroots participation. Rapid population growth in Nepal has had a significant impact on natural resource depletion and consequent environmental degradation. Economic stagnation and poverty encourage a large family size, and are delaying declines in fertility, where land encroachment is high and where natural resources like forests and water are depleting fast. A multidimensional approach with greater investment is to be advocated.

The population – environment debate has been politicised in a simplistic way, with advocates from the North blaming the growing millions of the South for environmental degradation, and advocates from the South blaming the consumerism of the wealthy states for global environmental destruction. A more balanced approach is to acknowledge the roles played by each in the depletion of the world's resources, and the requirement for action by both parts of the world if the global environ-

Yagya Bahadur Karki is affiliated to the Central Department of Population Studies, Tribhuban University, Kathmandu.

ment, on which we all ultimately depend, is to be saved. The purpose of this study is to examine the special problems faced by developing countries, which have to sustain increasing populations from a depleting natural resource base.

Since people in developing countries have a simple and rustic lifestyle, the larger the human population the faster the destruction of natural resources. Rapid population growth has been a major impediment to development and a major cause of environmental degradation in the developing countries [*World Bank, 1992*]. The strong inter-relationships between population, development and the environment require that any development programme should be designed to account for population and environmental stresses.

The June 1992 Earth Summit agenda did not include the population issue, despite its importance in the environment – development debate. The issue was politically too hot to handle. First, the UNCED was attended by the religious leader Pope Paul, who would have been offended by a population debate which raised details such as contraception, sterilisation and abortion. Second, inclusion of the population issue could well have further exacerbated existing political tensions between the heads of states or governments from the developed and developing countries. Heated debate was nevertheless clear in the press: the North blamed the South for not controlling population growth, while the South accused the North of overproduction and overconsumption. The importance of population was often implicit.

On 13 June 1992, the Rio Declaration on Environment and Development proclaimed 27 Principles. Principle 5 stresses sustainable development and a higher quality of life for all, asking states to reduce and eliminate unsustainable patterns of production and consumption, and to promote appropriate demographic policies.

The following day the UNCED adopted Agenda 21. Chapter 5 of Agenda 21 is devoted to 'Demographic Dynamics and Sustainability', and has three programme areas. The first addresses the links between demographic trends and sustainable development, calling for more research on population, environment and development interactions. The second calls on governments and other actors to formulate integrated national policies for environment and development, taking into account demographic trends and factors. The third calls on governments and local communities to implement integrated development and environment programmes that take demographic trends and factors into account. This section especially urges governments to ensure that women as well as men have the right to decide the number and spacing of their children, and have access to the information, education and means to exercise this right in keeping with their freedom, dignity and personally held values, taking into account ethical and cultural considerations. Fulfilment of these three programme areas will not be without difficulty in developing counties.

The Demographic Position

Until the middle of the twentieth century the growth of world population was not a serious cause of concern. In the year A.D. 1 the world population was about 300 million, and it took more than 1,500 years to double. Growth was unsteady as crises such as war or plague periodically reduced populations. By the eighteenth century, population was rising steadily. From 1750, world population doubled again in about 150 years to around 1,650 million in 1900, an unprecedented rate of about 0.5 per cent a year. Growth was faster (0.7 per cent) in today's developed countries than elsewhere (0.4 per cent) [*Durand, 1967*].

The twentieth century has witnessed still higher population growth rates. During the first 50 years world population grew at about 0.8 per cent a year – the developing countries growing faster (0.9 per cent) than the developed countries (0.8 per cent). The annual growth rate of the world population reached its peak of 2.06 per cent during the 1965–70 period – a landmark in demographic history – and now stands at about 1.7 per cent [*El-Badry, 1992*]. Population growth has also decelerated in the developing countries since the 1970s, and now stands at 2.0 per cent and above.

Today's world population (around 5,600 million) is increasing by about 93 million a year – equivalent to the combined population of Mexico and Switzerland. World population may reach 10,000 million by the middle of the next century, rising to 11,200 million by 2100. These projections are optimistic in assuming that fertility rates will continue to fall. With less rapid falls, population may grow to some 18,000 million, with about 90 per cent of people living in today's developing countries [*UN, 1991*]. The distribution of the world projected population by major regions by 2100 is likely to be as follows: four per cent in Europe, three per cent in North America, 0.4 per cent in Oceania, four per cent in the former USSR, 26 per cent in Africa, 9.4 per cent in Latin America, 12 per cent in China, 16.2 per cent in India and 25 per cent in other Asian countries [*UN, 1991*].

Population Growth in Nepal

Nepal exemplifies a developing country where fertility is high and mortality is declining fast, resulting in a high rate of population growth. It took 60 years for the 1911 census population of 5.6 million to double to

11.6 million in 1971. The 1991 census yielded a preliminary population of 18.46 million, an average annual growth rate of 2.33 per cent for the 1971–91 period. If this trend continues, Nepal's population will again double in 30 years' time. Nepal's population may not stabilise below 39 million even if Net Reproduction Rate of 1 is reached in the next 50 years. With a much slower fall in fertility the total population could grow to 108 million by 2141. Given Nepal's pace of socio-economic development and the limited impact of population programme efforts, Nepal's population will probably grow well into the twenty-second century and stabilise at about 70 million [*Karki, 1993*].

Population Programmes and Policies

His Majesty's Government of Nepal's (HMG) first two economic development plans (1956–61 and 1962–65), while recognising the link between population growth and consumption of national physical resources, emphasised reclaiming the Terai (the southern plains) forests to absorb the increasing population. It was not until the third plan (1965–70) that family planning policies were incorporated, setting a series of birth reduction targets. In order to give greater attention to population, HMG instituted the National Commission on Population in 1978 under the chairmanship of the Prime Minister. This body came to be seen as a hindrance to the implementation of population programmes, and in late 1990 it was dissolved. Following political change on 8 April 1990, the new democratically elected government formed the National Population Committee under the chairmanship of the Prime Minister. While a welcome development, the Committee would be strengthened by inclusion of population experts and more frequent meetings.

Programme Impact

Since the early 1960s a host of governmental and non-governmental family planning service delivery agencies have sprung up. Despite reasonable investment, until 1990 Nepal's population programme efforts were not very effective [*Ross et al., 1992*].

Only the overall impact of population policies and programmes can be assessed, through data from several surveys and censuses. Various family planning survey data show the increasing spread of contraceptive knowledge and use. Among currently married women aged 15–49, the proportion who have heard of a family planning method has risen steadily from about 21 per cent in 1976 to 93 per cent in 1991. The proportion ever using a method has gone up from about three per cent to 24 per cent. In 1991, female sterilisation comprised nearly half of the contraceptive usage compared to about five per cent in 1976. This strongly reflects male dominance in Nepal. Virtually no couples practise contraception before having at least one living son [*Karki, 1988*].

Despite some achievements, the Total Fertility Rate (TFR) has remained high by world standards although it has recently been reducing (TFR is the number of live births a woman would expect to give were she to live through her childbearing years and to bear children at each age in accordance with the prevailing age-specific fertility rates). In 1976 the TFR was estimated at 6.3 [*MOH, 1977*], where it remained until 1981 [*Karki, 1984*]. By 1986 it was lower – 5.75 [*MOH, 1987*] and the last survey shows it to be 5.08 [*NIV, 1992*]. By comparison the developed countries in 1990 had their TFRs below replacement level (considered to be 2.1 for developed countries) [*World Bank, 1992*].

The high growth rate of population is in part attributable to the success of health policies. The infant mortality rate has fallen from about 200 per 1,000 live births during the early 1950s to about 100 in the late 1980s, while life expectancy has risen from about 28 years to about 55 years now.

Nepal's Demographic Dynamics

In Nepal the balance of births and deaths largely determines the growth of population, although population movement between Nepal and India is said to be enormous because of the open borders. Unfortunately no data are available on international migration to make any estimates or adjustments.

Within a country some regions are more densely populated than others, contingent upon the socio-economic and physical environments which attract or deter people. Areas which are more propitious for living tend to have high density and grow fast. The Nepal Terai, comprising only 23.1 per cent of the total land area but about 49 per cent of total cultivated land, has witnessed highest population growth (3.48 per cent per annum) during the last 20 years, compared to the mid hill (1.64 per cent) and the high mountain (1.20 per cent) regions [*CBS, 1992; 1987*].

Demographically, Nepal's population is very young, as the proportion of 0–14 age group in total population has remained at 40 per cent or more since 1961 (the proportions of 0–14 population were, in percentages, 40.01, 40.45, 41.35, and 42.28 in 1961, 1971, 1981 and 1991 respectively). Given this age structure, Nepal's population cannot stabilise before reaching 45 million if mortality decline is moderate, even if the currently estimated TFR of about 5.27 for mid-1991 [*Karki, 1992*] is reduced to 2.5 by as early as 2000. Even with a drastic reduction in Nepal's TFR, the total population would increase until 2100 before stabilising [*Karki,*

1993]. Unless large scale emigration or Malthusian checks like war, famine or disease take their toll, Nepal must be prepared to cater for at least 45 million people in the next century.

Mortality reduction programmes can be expected to enjoy greater success than fertility control programmes because people try their best to stay alive and healthy. Mortality is declining fast in the developing world, but infant mortality is more difficult to reduce. The factors that contribute to the reduction of infant and child mortality are related to the general pace of social and economic development, which is usually slow. Successful bearing and rearing of children correlates with education, health, social status, housing and economic well being of mothers. Since these indicators are all low for most Nepalese women, it is no wonder that infant mortality is still above 100 per 1 000 live births. Female education is perhaps the most important indicator, as it has been linked to substantially reduced infant mortality [*Caldwell, 1986*].

Reduction of mortality, particularly infant and child mortality, is very much related to fertility fall. Parents will not avoid pregnancy unless they are sure that their existing babies will survive to adulthood. Therefore in a high mortality region like Nepal parents opt for a large number of births in order to allow for mortality risks. Thus fertility reduction programmes can hardly succeed.

Fertility Transition

In Europe and Japan fertility transition took place under varied conditions. The major factor responsible in Europe was the European marriage pattern characterised by late age at marriage and high proportion of people remaining single. Other factors were country-specific – industrialisation and urbanisation in England and Wales, and education, urbanisation and strong will-power among the people in Japan. In France fertility declined without the benefits of industrialisation, urbanisation or other modern amenities.

The European nations which underwent fertility transition around the turn of the century or earlier had relatively low preindustrial birth rates (generally in the mid-1930s) and took a comparatively long time to make the shift – over 100 years for England and Wales and France, and about 80 years for Germany, Sweden and Italy. Their rates of decline in their birth rates were not more than about three points a decade. The developing countries of today may complete fertility transition more rapidly. China's birth rate commenced decline from just over 40 in the early 1950s, and by 1977 it was 27 – the rate of decline was 5 points/decade since 1950s and more like six points/decade since 1970. Other LDCs started their fertility transition from still higher – around 44 in 1960 – and their rate of decline has been more rapid (about seven points/decade for the 1970s thus far, with an annual rate for 1977 of over ten points/decade [*Eberstadt, 1980*]. Fertility decline has already occurred in a number of countries – Sri Lanka, India (Kerala), Thailand, China and Indonesia – each with only limited developmental changes and with populations that are overwhelmingly poor and rural. Just how much change, and in what combinations of conditions, is sufficient to motivate fertility decline is unclear. Sri Lanka, Kerala and China have substantive changes in common like better health, high education, welfare institutes and good communication and transportation facilities. In addition, the LDCs can probably enjoy the models, ideas and products developed and tested by the North. The combined effects of these factors are probably affecting parental perceived costs and benefits of children.

In addition to socio-economic developments there are cultural factors, of which the political context is perhaps the most important. This is the case in China, where due to the strong revolutionary political system the generally high fertility characterising Chinese culture was transformed to low fertility in a matter of less than two decades. Thailand, Sri Lanka and Kerala in India [*Nag, 1989*] have shown that even with development at a moderate level, fertility has dropped fast. In these societies the position of women is unusually good. They are active in the labour force, involved in social and economic affairs and not disadvantaged by the parental preference for sons.

In Nepal fertility in terms of crude birth rate remained constant at 45 per 1,000 population for three decades until 1981. Thereafter it has apparently begun its downward trend – for 1991 the CBR is estimated at 38 [*NIV, 1992*]. Fertility reduction programmes face a number of challenges. Recently, there has been much emphasis on the village as the place where development and population change must be rooted and motivated. This emphasis is often related to the idea that equity in the distribution of goods and services makes for low fertility. It is difficult to say whether it is equity or the improvement in the standard of living that is relevant. Either way, however, such changes at the grassroots are improbable unless local communities are effectively linked to larger systems of resources and interchange. Without that, rhetoric and grandiose plans in a capital city are irrelevant.

In Nepal and other LDCs of South Asia and Africa little change in fertility has occurred. An important common factor is that the governments have been unable to set up administrative, communication and transport systems capable of reaching the village masses, either with the ideas of the outside world or with the minimal services and goods that make the new ideas and aspirations credible.

Contraception

Both government and non-governmental agencies involved in contraceptive distribution have to overcome many hurdles to meet their targets effectively. It is a familiar story in Nepal that contraceptives which are recorded as delivered are often in storage in a district or local health post. Thus service statistics, although collected regularly, are never believed nor much used. The distribution system lacks an effective strategy that can reach the target population. In mountain and hill terrains, where now slightly over 50 per cent of the total population resides with very little transportation and communication infrastructures, the task becomes even more formidable. Perhaps to make programmes cost-effective it may be wise to concentrate more in urban and densely populated areas.

Programmes currently operating in Nepal are showing little success in limiting family size. Birth control follow-up service is virtually non-existent. Most contraceptive acceptors have adopted sterilisation, performed speedily in mobile camps by a group of medical workers mostly from the capital city. Once the job is done the clients cannot be monitored for possible complications. This approach makes the programme unpopular. Women weakened by several pregnancies and inadequate nutrition are quite likely to suffer from side-effects. Moreover, for women successful bearing and rearing of a large number of children makes the marriage bond strong and raises social status within the family and in society. The impact of sterilisation can easily lead to post-sterilisation trauma, for which they are unprepared, and this mental stress can lead to physical disorders.

Sterilisation is popular because it is convenient and simple. Other birth spacing methods like the pill, condom, rhythm, and IUD are all too complicated and place additional responsibilities on poorly educated women. Success of these methods depends on correct usage. The pill and IUD need regular counselling with family planning and health workers who are often unavailable, particularly in rural areas. Even if they are present, the villagers find it difficult to communicate with them; a big gap exists between the government officials and the people. Government officials whose presence in their office is enough to earn their salary see no extra benefit from being very helpful and involved in the field. Upward mobility is based on whom you know and whether you are related to high officials [*Bista, 1992*].

Housing poses severe constraints on contraceptive choice and use in Nepal. Few couples sleep in a separate room, and the waste disposal systems of the developed world are absent. Several generations often live together, and the use of birth spacing methods by younger generations would be frowned upon by the older family members.

Recently, injectable contraception has gained popularity; its use has quadrupled between 1986 and 1991 to two per cent [*NIV, 1992*]. This is probably due to its comparative convenience in application and administration.

Future Prospects

The fertility level in Nepal has started its downward trend but still is high by world standards. There is no room for complacency. Given their duration and the amount of resources expended, Nepal's family planning programmes have largely failed. The tiny success in fertility control is more likely due to non-programme efforts like education and development activities contributing to low fertility attitudes.

If Nepal's fertility level is to be reduced fast the population programmes need to be drastically overhauled. The approach must attack many problems simultaneously. Pushing and distributing contraceptive methods alone will clearly not work. The conventional media methods alone will not work either. Because the momentum of population growth is high it is imperative to initiate programmes as soon as possible. The insight of local people who understand the complexity of local problems is invaluable.

The implementation of population programmes must be improved, along with the provision of a range of contraceptive types. The government must be committed and prepared to pay for the costs of programmes if it is to translate its rhetoric into concrete actions.

In order to improve the quality of service, the government has to provide a thorough training to its workers at all levels in the dynamics of contraceptive methods. Selection of workers must be based primarily on competence and commitment to public service. Government civil servants must drastically change their outlook and behave as facilitators. Given the poor performance of the government sector so far, further expansion of the government's population programmes and infrastructures may be marginally productive. Encouragement and support of the non-government sector might be a step in the right direction. Perhaps the government in its own initiative should help establish NGOs dealing with population dynamics, as they have been found more effective in mobilising community leaders and involving the grassroots in programme implementation.

Since the political change in 1990 Nepal has witnessed a mushroom growth of NGOs but only a handful of them have made a breakthrough. Open policies alone are not the solution. The new NGOs have had to operate under unchanged resource constraints and a bureaucratic structure. It is also said that a good number of NGOs were opened just because it was easy to register them. Perhaps it is now time to examine the problems and potential of NGOs in Nepal.

Fertility-related social programmes are the other important area which the government, donor agencies and NGOs could consider. Women are at the centre of fertility-related issues. Thus programmes would be needed that can make women knowledgeable, raise their standing in society, increase their decision making power and enhance their independence from social, cultural and economic deprivations.

Population and Environmental Degradation

Nepal, a landlocked country surrounded by India and China, is located on the slopes and in the foothills of the Himalayan mountain chain. Because of the steepness of the terrain combined with torrential rains during the monsoon, Nepal is subject to powerful natural erosion. The Himalayas are the world's youngest, highest and steepest mountains, composed of fragile sedimentary rock. Nepal is one of the world's most delicate ecosystems, easily damaged by human factors.

The rapid rise in population contributes to degradation in the form of soil erosion, deforestation, air and water pollution, desertification and depletion of water supplies. About 53 per cent of landslides are estimated to be due to human causes [*NPC, 1985*]. Water supply decline is leading to agricultural problems and a growing incapacity of natural environments to support present human numbers. Yet the country's natural resource base is central to the national economy with agriculture the largest single development sector. In 1990, the agricultural sector accounted for 60 per cent of Nepal's GDP [*World Bank, 1992*] and employed 80 per cent of the labour force [*CBS, 1992*].

Population growth controls the man-land ratio because the amount of total land area is fixed. Nepal's total land area is estimated at 147,181 square kilometres and the 1911 census reported a population density of 38 persons per sq. km. This ratio more than tripled by 1991 (see Table 1).

Remarkable differences are found in population density analysed by ecological zones. Nepal's three ecological zones run parallel from east to west: the mountain zone ranges in altitude from 16,000 feet to 29,000 feet; the hill zone lies between 2,000 feet to 16,000 feet; and the area below 2,000 feet is known as the Terai or the plains. In 1971 the Terai had the highest density – that is, 128 persons per sq. km. compared to 22 for the high mountains (Table 1). Until 1991 the pattern remained the same but the rise in density was the highest in the Terai – it nearly doubled.

The high mountain zone has lowest population density because nearly half of its area is difficult for human habitation due to steep rocks and

TABLE 1

DISTRIBUTION OF POPULATION, LAND AREA AND CULTIVATED LAND
AREA AND DENSITY PER SQ. KM. BY ECOLOGICAL ZONES, NEPL 1971-91

| | | Land in sq. km. | | | Population density in sq. km. | | | | | |
| | | | Cultivated | | | Total land | | | Cultivated Land | |
Ecological Zone	Total[a]	1971[b]	1981[a]	1991[c]	'71	'81	'91	'71	'81	'91
Mountain	51,817	970	1,223	1,600	22	25	28	1,174	1,065	903
Hill	61,345	6,060	9,490	13,990	99	117	137	1,002	755	601
Terai	34,019	12,930	13,934	14,930	128	193	253	336	471	576
Nepal	147,181	19,960	24,637	30,520	79	102	125	579	610	605

Sources: (a) [CBS, 1987]; (b) [Dhital, 1975]; (c) [HMG/ADB/FINNIDA].

harsh climatic conditions. The hill region is the best for human habitation because of its temperate climate, but here too most of the area is covered by mountains and rocks. Still until about the late 1960s people preferred to live there as the Terai was malarious. The eradication of malaria in the lowlands led to large-scale migration – particularly from the highlands – and as a result in some 10 of the Terai's 20 districts the average annual population growth rates ranged from 4 to 6.5 per cent during the 1970–80 period [Gurung, 1989].

The cultivated man–land ratio best explains population pressure on agriculture. The total cultivated land area increased by about 53 per cent from 1971 to 1991. The hill zone had the highest increase (about 131 per cent), followed by the mountain zone (about 65 per cent) and the Terai (about 15 per cent) (Table 1). Because a relatively larger area was brought into cultivation in the mountains and hills during these two decades, population density in cultivated land there has slightly decreased. In the Terai it increased enormously from 336 to 576 people per sq. km. It is noteworthy, however, that the 1991 population census has been questioned for its reliability and coverage. If this author's estimate of the 1991 census population of 18.9 million is used, the cultivated man-land ratios become 618 for the country as a whole, 922, 615 and 589 for the mountain, hill and Terai regions respectively [Karki, 1992]. But if Natrajan's estimates are used the corresponding ratios become 672 for the country as a whole, with 1,002, 668, and 683 for the three ecological zones [Natrajan, 1993].

Although mountain and hill areas show a declining cultivated man–land ratio they still have high population pressure today, with the highlands facing the greatest pressure (Table 1). Given Nepal's demographic potential it is likely that this will be worse in the years to come. The increasing incapacity of highland agriculture pushes people out to look for livelihoods elsewhere. Massive movements of people from the highlands to the lowlands suggest that by the year 2000 the cultivated manland ratio in the Terai will be as high as in the highlands.

Cereals like rice, maize and wheat occupy nearly 97 per cent of the total cropland. The Terai accounts for about 62 per cent of the total land under cereals, the hills 32 per cent and the mountains six per cent. Although the total cultivated land area has increased steadily, average yields of three major crops have actually declined: paddy yields in Mt/ha have declined from 1.92 in 1961–62 to 1.83 in 1984–85; and the corresponding figures for maize and wheat were 1.89 and 1.45 to 1.20 and 1.09. Nepal presents a picture of a declining economy. The food balance was negative as early as 1974–75 in the highlands although the national average was positive because the Terai compensated for the deficit. Nepal continued to show surplus of food-grains but the size of the surplus was declining fast [NCP, 1988]. However, since 1979–80 the food balance has been erratic; it was negative in 1979–80, 1982–83, 1986–87 and 1989–90 [CBS, 1988; 1992]. The Terai which is known to be Nepal's 'bread basket' is no longer able to produce enough to support its growing population, let alone the highland slopes and the valleys.

The gloomy picture of Nepal's population size, land and food balance has to be understood in the context of how agriculture is practised. The economy, which has evolved over two centuries requires a unique pattern of land use system to enable man to live in harmony with nature. A study of a farm unit by Sharma and Bhadra [1987] represents this. Their study is of a family consisting of 5.5 persons (similar to the national average of 5.52 persons in 1991 [CBS, 1992] with about 1.5 hectares of cultivated land (this is about 65 per cent higher than the national average of 0.91 hectares [ibid.]) and about five livestock. A resource in the rural area has multiple uses:

> The supply of foodgrains depends on cultivated land. The farmers also grow fodder trees on the cultivated land and after the harvest they have a crop residue which has multiple uses. It is either used as a substitute for fuelwood, for livestock consumption or as compost. Since the size of the crop residue is limited relatively more use in one area will leave little for other uses.

> The livestock, on the other hand, supply meat, butter and milk for domestic consumption and bullock power for cultivation. It, how-

ever, needs pasture land for fodder. The higher the number of livestock, the lower will be the availability of grazing land. This, in turn, will increase the demand for fodder from farm, leaving less crop residue for energy and compost. It will effect the yield from farm due partly to less availability of compost and due partly to depletion of forested land.

The energy demand of the household is met from three sources: (a) agricultural waste (b) fuelwood and (c) animal dung. Since the supply is limited, the use of input in various activities is determined in a unique pattern for which detailed information is not available.

Human contribution in such a system is in terms of labour supply for crop production, livestock rearing, fuel collection and post harvest processing. The family uses a significant part of time for household activities (36 per cent) followed by agriculture (28 per cent) and livestock raising (26 per cent): only a marginal amount of time is allocated for off-farm activities [*Acaharya and Bennet, 1981*].

Until the early 1950s the natural resource base for human activities was relatively abundant; forest and shrub lands could be reclaimed for cultivation, more cattle could be raised, the farm, man, forest, cattle cycle could be expanded like a spiral. Since the early 1960s the situation has changed, primarily due to the rapid growth of population. Development projects ignored the natural resources – soils, forests (plants), water, atmosphere and climate – that support the economy. Attempts to develop the non-agricultural sector to release population pressure on farm land has not been very successful. Spontaneous population redistribution through internal migration from the hills to the Terai is now perhaps saturated as indicated by cultivated man–land ratio. Emigration abroad as a safety valve for employment is also dwindling because of the gradual shrinkage of employment opportunities in India and abroad. An increase in farm size will require more land for cultivation, which in turn calls for more livestock and more grazing land at the cost of virgin lands and forests. This generates further pressure on the deteriorating environmental resource base.

Rural folks and the majority of urban dwellers are dependent on forest resources like fuelwood, materials for construction and handicrafts and fodder for livestock. About 87 per cent of the country's energy consumption for all purposes comes from firewood, with the major part of energy consumption in the domestic sector, cooking, lighting and heating purposes accounting for 93 per cent [*Upreti, 1989*]. It is estimated that the felling of trees for energy and construction purposes consumes nearly 18 million cubic metres of forests each year. Current estimates show that

Nepal's forests are being destroyed at the rate of three per cent per annum [*Bhattarai, 1983*].

Once a heavily forested country, today over half of Nepal's forestable land is denuded. Time trend data on land use are not available. Reliable data on land use were only recently made available [*HMG/ADB/FIN-NIDA, 1988*], according to which land under forest stood at 38.1 per cent; shrub land, 4.7 per cent; and grassland, 11.9 per cent. Together, these constitute 55 per cent of the total Nepalese land area. Several studies show an increase of forest encroachment for human settlement and cultivation, particularly in the Terai plains. According to Gurung [*1989*] during the 1964–74 period nearly 315,300 hectares of forest land were cleared in the plains alone for hill migrant resettlement activities. There are data difficulties due to how 'forest land' and 'forested land' are defined. In Nepal the former, in strict legal terms, includes all land that is not private.

Depletion of forest resources is attributed to a number of reasons. In the first place, a change in government policy is believed to have led to accelerated forest depletion. HMG, wishing to maximise revenue from forests, nationalised all forest in 1957. This had a very negative effect on forests that were collectively supervised and managed by the village communities. Since the forest ceased to be community wealth it was exploited to its extreme. When government administrative machinery was not adequate for management, felling of trees continued unabated so that the area could be claimed as private farmland later. This was the beginning of the deforestation trend which was to bring severe environmental deterioration 25 to 30 years later. With the ever-increasing population the process was perhaps even more reinforced.

Forest and shrub lands are also destroyed because of livestock which depend heavily on fodder and grass. Because livestock are essential to farming their number is very large (about 15 million in 1985/86). These animals are grazed in forests, shrubs and grassland, inadvertently causing overgrazing and depletion of forests. About 50 million tons of green leaves are lopped from forest trees to feed the animals [*Upreti, 1989*].

Forests are also destroyed because of the increasing demand for lumber for housing in both private and public sectors. Nepalese artisans heavily use forest products for handicrafts and cottage industries, as raw material as well as fuel.

The continual depletion of forests, shrubs and grassland exacerbates soil erosion. The agricultural sector continues to remain the major source of livelihood for the bulk of the population. The agricultural practices are primitive and use too much natural resources, causing soil erosion and degradation of soil quality. Although about 47 per cent of soil erosion in

Nepal is believed to be due to young geology the rest is assumed to be man made. Some five per cent of the accelerated erosion is attributed to road construction [*Joshi, 1988*].

Nepal's other major natural resource is water which has a potential of generating 83,000 MW of electricity. Four major rivers (the Sapta Kosi, the Narayani, the Karnali and the Mahakali) and their 6,000 tributaries run north to south. These perennial major rivers originate from the Himalayas. The smaller rivers contain very low volume of water from mid-November to mid-June but swell in the Monsoon (July, August and September), when they are useful and essential for the farmers, but also destructive. Every year about 240 million cubic metres of soil are carried away by these rivers to the Bay of Bengal. Nepal is losing 17 mm. of top soil every year which nature takes 35 to 70 years to make. Bed levels of these rivers in the Terai are rising at the rate of 15 cm. to 30 cm. annually; soil loss per hectare per year has been estimated between 20 to 50 tons. About seven per cent of total land area (10,000 sq. km.) is devoid of vegetation and is in the process of desertification.

Environmental degradation most severely affects the poorest sections of society, and especially a rural society in a predominantly agricultural economy. It is most often women and children who are hit the hardest. Because of the increasing trend of forest degradation, deforestation, over grazing, cultivation of marginal land and other improper use of land, water springs and wells are drying up. This directly affects women's allocation of time for water, fodder and firewood collection. Every year they have to travel further or queue longer for water. This is true of rural and urban areas. At present, it is estimated that the total work burden for rural woman amounts to 10.81 hours a day. When male adults migrate in the slack season the woman's work burden is increased. Some 80 per cent of wood collection for domestic use is done by women and girls; up to 20 per cent of the daily available time is spent on this task.

Discussion and Conclusion

Nepal's mountains are prone to environmental degradation, but this process has been accelerated by the rapid growth of population. The natural resource base which is essential for the survival of the vast majority of the Nepalese population is depleting rapidly. Cultivated man–land ratio has increased dramatically, agricultural farming has become decreasingly productive, and forests and common lands have been encroached upon beyond their limits for human habitation and cultivation.

Economic and social development has taken place during the last four decades. Indicators such as literacy, education, life expectancy, contraceptive prevalence rate, population coverage by mass media and transportation facilities have all increased. However, the pace of development was not fast enough to raise living standards for the bulk of the population. Nepal remains one of the poorest of the poor countries, and has declined in economic growth. In the 12 years before 1992 Nepal's rank in per capita GNP output slipped from 119th to 121st of 125 countries listed [*World Bank, 1980; 1992*]. The fast growth of population was largely responsible for reducing returns from development investments. Development activities themselves contribute to population growth initially. Improvement of general health can lead to reduction of mortality and enhance fertility, leading to high population growth. Apparently Nepal is now passing through this stage.

Population has become a liability on the natural resources, which are scarce and badly managed. Because resources are constrained the opportunities for self improvement are rare. This, combined with the traditional outlook favouring a large number of children, leads a family to economic hardships. They now try to eke out their living by cultivating marginal lands and very steep slopes, accelerating erosion. The government's resettlement programme settled thousands of families in the Terai at the cost of largely forest areas. Many public work programmes like dams, roads, canals and industrial establishments were undertaken without foreseeing environmental consequences. Had the remaining forests and shrub lands been properly managed, the loss due to public works could perhaps be compensated. There has been some forest conservation; 7.4 per cent of the total land area is protected as national parks. Several donor agencies (Australian Forestry Project, the British Forestry Project in east Nepal, and so on) have also been involved in promoting community forestry in Nepal for nearly 15 years. But these are not enough to stop encroachment on forests and shrub lands. The people have no alternative to the daily firewood, grass and animal fodder without which they cannot survive.

Recently urbanisation has added another dimension to the environmental problems of Nepal. There are now 36 urban centres located in mid hills and the Terai. These towns lack the infrastructures to cater for the growing needs of the urbanites. Recently shanty towns have been cropping up. Even the capital city of Kathmandu is incapable of providing basic services such as transport, communication, water, electricity, drainage, sewerage, health and education to its dwellers. The city is growing unmanageable even for the most democratic municipality to run. The Bagmati river which flows through the middle of the valley has now turned virtually into an open sewer of the valley, a breeding ground for bacteria. Tourists who dream of visiting Kathmandu to breath fresh air are now very much disappointed to find it filled with vehicle exhaust smog.

The people of Nepal are caught up in economic hardships due to the depletion of the natural resource base. This was realised in the early 1970s [*Blaikie et al., 1980*] and in 1979 when this author was conducting field work in Nepal. Then the author observed respondents singling out the deteriorating hill environment and the economic cost of raising children as responsible for their hardships; they spoke in support of a shift towards smaller family size if they could. Those families who had good land are now only moderately well off. Inheritance customs continually divide large estates between several sons; thus more sons means less land for each. Many villagers, therefore, linked the poverty of the people to large family size [*Karki, 1982*].

The Nepalese government has been officially sponsoring a Family Planning Programme since 1968. The problem is that while to the government it may be beneficial to limit family size, parents may desire a large family for prestige or economic reasons. About 90 per cent of the population are Hindus and value sons much more highly than daughters. Girls are economically useful until they marry and leave home while sons also provide old age security.

These great obstacles to the government's aim of reducing the birth rate can possibly be overcome by carefully designed population policies, correctly implemented. These should take into account the experience of other countries with similar problems. Two and a half decades of family planning programmes have failed because of wrong emphasis and wrong approach. The government at least in policy documents propagated integrated population programmes, but in practice it utilised the scarce resources of donor agencies by holding seminars and other programmes at national, regional and district levels. Programmes never reached the community level. What is now needed is an integrated, multidimensional approach which emphasises literacy, education (particularly for women) lowering infant mortality and providing contraceptives along with follow-ups. Information, education and communication programmes must be reinforced by health or community workers at the village level who can teach the villagers – the involvement of women must be encouraged here. Perhaps at this stage local NGOs can be effective as they can mobilise the community better than the government officials. Even appropriate government policies fail, however, because of administrative inefficiency.

Birth rate is the main component of population growth. In order to reduce this as early as possible the government must not only concentrate on direct birth control. The greatest action must consist of fostering a higher rate of planned economic and social development than has occurred so far. Without an improvement in the standard of living, birth control programmes may well be empty frameworks. Nepal's population will increase sharply for some time to come, and so development must be at a pace sufficient to ensure higher standards of living, while meeting the demands of population growth. The scale of national investment must take account of this double requirement. It must also recognise that desirable social change (defined here as encouraging economic development and the emergence of new reproductive patterns) may involve expenditure beyond that justified by pure economics. Economic and social development must be shown to have meaning for, and impact on, the population in general. Social programmes are needed that might help to convince ordinary people that to aim at a small family size is beneficial, and a positive contribution to the present and future welfare of their children.

REFERENCES

Acaharya, Meena and Lynn Bennet (1981), *The Status of Women in Nepal*, Vol.II, Kathmandu: Centre for Economic Development and Administration, Tribhuban University.

Bhattarai, Shusil (1983), *State of Environment in Nepal*, Kathmandu: Environmental Impact Study Project, His Majesty's Government of Nepal.

Bista, Dor Bahadur (1992), *Fatalism and Development, Nepal's Struggle for Modernization*, Calcutta: Orient Longman.

Blaikie, Piers, Cameron, John, and David Seddon (1980), *Nepal in Crisis, Growth and Stagnation at the Periphery*, Oxford: Clarendon Press.

Caldwell, John C. (1986), 'Routes to Low Mortality in Poor Countries', *Population and Development Review*, Vol.12, No.2, June.

Central Bureau of Statistics (CBS) (1987), *Population Monograph of Nepal*, Kathmandu: National Planning Commission Secretariat (NPCS).

Central Bureau of Statistics (CBS) (1988) *Statistical Pocket Book*, Kathmandu: NPCS, June.

Central Bureau of Statistics (CBS) (1992), *Population Census – 1991* (Advance Tables), Vol.I, Kathmandu: NPCS.

Dhital, B.P. (1975), 'Population Growth and Agriculture', in D.C. Upadhyaya and Jose V. Abueva (eds.), *Population and Development in Nepal*, Kathmandu: Tribhuban University Press.

Durand, J.D. (1967), 'The Modern Expansion of World Population', *Proc American Philosophical Society*, Vol.3, No.137.

Eberstadt, Nick (1980), 'Recent Declines in Fertility in Less-Developed Countries: What the Population Planners may Learn from Them', *World Development*, Vol.8. No.1.

El-Badry, M.A. (1992), 'World Population Change', *AMBIO*, Vol.21, No.1, Feb.

Gurung, Harka (1989), *Nepal: Dimensions of Development*, Kathmandu.

His Majesty's Government of Nepal (HMG), Asian Development Bank (ADB)/FINNIDA (1988), *Master Plan for the Forestry Sector, Nepal*, Country Background, Kathmandu: HMG, Dec.

Joshi, M.D. (1988), *Environment of Nepal*, Kathmandu: Watershed Management and Conservation Education Project, Department of Soil Conservation and Watershed Management.

Karki, Y.B. (1982), *Fertility and the Value of Children: A Study of Rural and Urban Populations in Nepal*, Ph.D. Thesis, London School of Economics.

Karki, Y.B. (1984), *Estimates of TFRs for Nepal and its Geographical Sub-divisions and Administrative Zones, 1971 and 1981*, Kathmandu: National Commission on Population 1984.

Karki, Y.B. (1988), 'Sex Preference and the Value of Sons and Daughters in Nepal', *Studies in Family Planning*, Vol.19, No.3, May/June.

Karki, Y.B. (1992), *Estimates and Projections of Population, Nepal: 1981–2031*, Kathmandu: Centre Department of Population Studies (CDPS), Tribhuban University (TU).

Karki, Y.B. (1993), 'Nepal's Population Problem: A Time Bomb', Paper presented at National Seminar on Population and Sustainable Development in Nepal, CDPS, TU, March.

Ministry of Health (MOH) (1977), *Nepal Fertility Survey, 1976. First Report*, Kathmandu: Nepal Family Planning and Maternity Health Project (FP/MCH), World Fertility Survey, Nepal Project.

Ministry of Health (MOH) (1987), *Nepal Fertility and Family Planning Survey Report, 1986*, Kathmandu: Nepal FP/MCH Project.

Nag, M. (1989), 'Alternative Routes to Fertility and Mortality Decline – A Study of Kerala and Punjab', in *Population Transition in India*. Vol.I.

Natrajan, K.S. (1993), *Report on the Evaluation of the Coverage of 1991 Census of Nepal*, Nepal: United Nations Population Fund (UNFPA), Country Office, March.

National Planning Commission (NPC) (1985), *The Seventh Plan, 1985–90*, Kathmandu: NPCS.

National Commission on Population (NCP) (1988), *Population and Development in Nepal*, Kathmandu: Singha Durbar.

New Era, IIDS and VaRG (NIV) (1992), *Nepal Fertilit, Family Planning and Health Status Survey, 1991*, Kathmandu: NFHS.

Ross, John, Mauldin, A., Parker, W., Green, Steven R. and E. Roman Cooke (1992), *Family Planning and Child Survival Programs* (as assessed in 1991), New York: The Population Council.

Sharma K.S. and B. Bhadra (1987), *Food Energy Relations in Nepal*, mimeographed, Kathmandu: NCP.

Third World Resurgence (1992), 'Earth Summit, Third World Views', No.24/25.

United Nations (UN) (1991), *Long Range World Population Projections*, ST/ESA/Ser. A/125.

Upreti, B.N. (1989), 'Impact of Population on Environment in Nepal', Paper presented at Population and Environment Seminar, Kathmandu: NCP, July.

World Bank (1980), *World Development Report, 1980*, New York: Oxford University Press.

World Bank (1991), *World Development Report, 1991*, New York: Oxford University Press.

World Bank (1992), *World Development Report, 1992*, New York: Oxford University Press.

Freshwater and the Post-UNCED Agenda

DARRYL HOWLETT

Freshwater is a finite and vulnerable resource. The fragility of the world's water resources is likely to become more acute unless future strategies recognise the crucial links between water, the environment, development and international security. Environmental change could have resounding effects on water, leading to extreme scenarios of drought or flooding. Developmental practices that treat water as a plentiful and robust resource are likely to result in severe depletion of its quality and thereby diminish its capacity for human consumption and other uses. Water is already scarce in certain regions of the world. Uncertainty about future supplies may exacerbate political tensions within states and lead to conflict between them, especially over international watercourses.

Some of the problems affecting water are not new. Conserving and managing water has been a necessary feature of many societies throughout history [Clarke, 1991]. What is new is the heightened demands currently being placed on water.

Water problems affect all regions of the world, developed and developing. However, it is in the developing world that the effects of water stress are likely to be hardest felt and the most difficult to alleviate. The developed world will also not be immune. Demographic factors, industrial and agricultural development, coupled with uncertainties over environmental change, could place further stress on water resources unless measures are taken to minimise potentially detrimental effects. A holistic approach to water represents the only viable strategy for meeting the challenges to the world's water resources.

Dr Darryl Howlett is a Senior Research Fellow in the Mountbatten Centre for International Studies, Department of Politics, University of Southampton, United Kingdom.

The International Water Debate and Agenda 21

The 1992 UNCED and Agenda 21 are part of an ongoing international debate concerning water-related issues. This debate has yielded considerable knowledge about the problems confronting water resources and enhanced our understanding of the global hydrological cycle [*Thomas and Howlett, 1993; Falkenmark, 1986; Postel, 1984*].

There have been several previous milestones in the international debate over water. In the 1960s there was the Arid Zone Programme established by the United Nations Educational, Scientific, and Cultural Organisation (UNESCO). This was followed by the International Hydrological Decade. The 1972 UN Conference on the Human Environment held in Stockholm also marked a major step in placing the environment and water on the international agenda. In 1977 the UN-sponsored Mar del Plata Water Conference focused specifically on water and yielded the Mar del Plata Action Plan. At the turn of the 1980s, the UN initiated the International Drinking Water Supply and Sanitation Decade (IDWSSD, 1981–90), which is continuing as a result of the Global Consultation on Safe Water and Sanitation for the 1990s held in New Delhi in 1990. The United Nations Environment Programme (UNEP) has also launched its Environmentally Sound Management of Inland Waters (EMINWA) strategy. Finally, in 1992, the International Conference on Water and the Environment (ICWE) was held in Dublin just prior to UNCED.

Water resources did not receive much attention during UNCED. Rather, it was the Dublin ICWE which attempted to raise the profile by calling for a 'water shock' to alert the international community to the crisis currently affecting the world's water resources.

The primary focus of the ICWE was on 'the development, management and utilisation of water resources in harmony with environmental conservation and the concept of sustainability'. The Dublin Statement, issued as a result of the ICWE, identified four guiding principles for future action on water and sustainable development:

Principle No. 1 – Fresh water is a finite and vulnerable resource, essential to sustain life, development and the environment;

Principle No. 2 – Water development and management should be based on a participatory approach, involving users, planners and policy-makers at all levels;

Principle No.3 – Women play a central part in the provision, management and safeguarding of water; and,

Principle No.4 – Water has an economic value in all its competing uses and should be recognised as an economic good.

Gaining widespread acceptance for these principles represents a major challenge to the international community. It will demand radical changes in attitude to water and the role this critical resource plays in economic development, environmental change, international security and ultimately, human sustainability.

Significantly, Chapter 18 of Agenda 21 marks an important step in forging an international consensus for adopting a holistic strategy for water. It embraces the principles enunciated at the Dublin Water Conference by focusing on key aspects of water protection, management, conservation and use.

Several ideas related to water resources emerged in the lead up to the Dublin and Rio Conferences and were reflected in the agendas of both. It was recognised that future strategies could fail if adequate financial resources were not forthcoming and mechanisms for implementation identified. Stress was placed during the preparatory stages on the need for education about water conservation and use, and on the role of the human agent in these activities, referred to as 'capacity building'.[1]

Although the importance of making links between water management at all levels was also identified, it was the emphasis on participation at the local level, especially by women and indigenous peoples, that represented a major innovation. Although women play a crucial role in water use in many societies, they are rarely represented in water planning and management strategies. Similarly, the involvement of indigenous peoples has often not been sufficient to ensure that water projects achieve their own 'sustainability' once outside advisers have left.

Agreement on the language of Chapter 18 was largely settled before the Rio Conference. This notwithstanding, there is one important area where the wording is remarkably limited. Because international rivers and groundwaters which traverse more than one state are regarded as important resources, there is an urgent need to develop strategies aimed at their equitable apportionment and for conflict avoidance. Yet Chapter 18 devotes only a few lines to this problem. It does, however, acknowledge the need to pursue co-operative strategies:

> Transboundary water resources and their use are of great importance to riparian States. In this connection, co-operation among those states may be desirable in conformity with existing agreements and/or other relevant arrangements, taking into account the interests of all riparian states concerned.[2]

The main emphasis in Chapter 18 is to set specific targets in seven programme areas which individual states are expected to pursue. There are no legally-binding or firm commitments. Rather, the wording throughout the chapter reflects a more fluid approach, based on the following general statement of intent: 'All States, according to their capacity and available resources, and through bilateral or multilateral co-operation, including the United Nations and other relevant organizations as appropriate, could set the following targets . . .'. The seven programme areas for action are: integrated water resources development and management; water resources assessment; protection of water resources, water quality and aquatic ecosystems; drinking-water supply and sanitation; water and sustainable urban development; water for sustainable food production and rural development; and impacts of climate change on water resources.

Integrated Water Resources Development and Management

The recognition of water as a finite and vulnerable resource has important implications for sustainable development. Without a holistic approach to the management of water within the context of national development plans, further degradation of the resource is likely to occur. Ultimately, this would place a severe constraint on socio-economic development.

There are several impediments to achieving the goal of holistic water management. One of the most important relates to the disparate way the resource is currently managed within the national context. Because several sectoral agencies may have responsibility for differing aspects of water, any lack of coordination between them could have a detrimental effect on the strategic direction of policy and the resource itself. Chapter 18 consequently directs future action towards multi-sectoral coordination between all agencies with a view to harmonising water management. This would also entail integrating land and water uses within the water catchment basin or sub-basin.

For the strategy to have any chance of success, states will need to coordinate all levels of water management with expected plans for economic development. Implementing such a strategy could prove difficult. It implies a high degree of administrative oversight. It also means that effective controls would need to be introduced and enforced. This may not be easily attainable in the developed world, although some states have started to move in this direction. In the developing world, the task is multiplied. Here the administrative structures may not be sufficiently mature to enable administrative coordination and controls are likely to be difficult to enforce.

This strategy also requires the establishment of new institutional structures for managing the entire river catchment area. And within local communities, changes to existing practices and institutions may be necessary. Provision must be made to educate people to think of water as an economic and social good, with an intrinsic value. Similarly, the role of women as prime agents in the use and conservation of water demands that they be included in all stages of water management.

Beyond the local and national levels, harmonising water management and economic planning within the context of a transnational river basin will not prove easy. This could become a major impediment to economic growth if water use by one riparian state diminishes the resource for others sharing the river.

Water Resources Assessment

A prerequisite for sustainable development is the need for accurate information to achieve a comprehensive assessment of the hydrological resources of the planet. More data than currently available will be required for this goal to be realised.

Further information is needed in two particular areas: one is to determine the quantity and quality of water resources and their use in industry, agriculture and for domestic purposes; the other is an accurate assessment of how the land–ocean–atmosphere relationship affects the hydrological cycle. Neither is likely to prove easily obtainable, but such knowledge would aid the task of planning water strategies so they are consistent with sustainable development. Similarly, the effects of pollution, floods, droughts, deforestation and desertification might be reduced if reliable data were at hand to formulate policy.

Much of the hydrological information available on the world's water resources has been achieved on a piecemeal and largely small-scale basis. Within the context of the river basin, research has tended to focus on relatively small catchment areas. The knowledge required for the future will need to be on a grander scale. The task is therefore to conduct hydrological studies at the level of macro-scale modelling encompassing the entire river basins. These models can then be used to assess changes to water flows and other factors which may affect the river basin. Gridded climatic data can then be applied to gauge possible effects from climate change. Information from other disciplines, such as geography, geology, oceanography and international relations can also add to this data gathering process.

Constructing a comprehensive global freshwater assessment will inevitably require a spirit of co-operation between states to share and compare relevant information. This might be aided by establishing national and international data resource centres to collate and assess information and implement monitoring procedures. Such centres would need to be staffed by personnel with the relevant technical skills. This might involve the training of a new cadre of multi-disciplinary specialists who are aware of the scientific and engineering issues confronting water, and the economic, social, political and environmental ones.

Protection of Water Resources, Water Quality and Aquatic Ecosystems

The vulnerability of both surface and groundwaters to development practices which treat freshwater as an abundant and cheap resource is only now being recognised. Altering perceptions and changing practices to reduce and, if possible, eliminate, the problems of pollution caused by ill-conceived irrigation schemes, untreated sewage and industrial waste discharges require education, and prevention and control strategies. An effective long-term policy therefore requires a careful balancing between the needs of economic development, human health, and the environment.

Protection and conservation strategies have been identified in Chapter 18 as important elements for the long-term sustainability of water resources and aquatic ecosystems. Coupled with the need to obtain more complete data of the world's water is the need to ensure that the quality of these supplies is not changed irrevocably by pollutants.

Several international water-quality monitoring and conservation programmes already exist for this purpose. The Global Environmental Monitoring System (GEMS)/WATER, established as a result of the Mar del Plata Conference, has achieved some success in providing information and the monitoring of freshwater quality [*Meybeck et al., 1989*]. UNEP has introduced the Environmentally Sound Management of Inland Waters (EMINWA) strategy and there is the Convention on Wetlands of International Importance Especially as Waterfowl Habitat (The Ransar Convention).

These agreements, conventions, and monitoring strategies will need to be strengthened if the goals of water quality protection and conservation are to be met. As with the collation of data concerning the quantity of global resources, a major task is to ascertain data about water quality at all levels, from the local to the international. This is especially required at the level of transboundary water resources where pollutants and water-associated diseases could easily traverse between states.

An overall strategy for improving water quality will probably mean that many current practices and institutions will need to be changed or modified. In the developed world, policies for improving water quality are already a feature of environmental strategy. Germany has begun introducing stringent controls to limit the effects of industrial effluent in watercourses. Within the European Community as a whole, a legislative framework has been devised aimed at improving the quality of water for all member states [*Gregory, 1993*]. In 1978 the United States and Canada negotiated the Great Lakes Water Quality Agreement, which adopted a comprehensive approach involving air, land, water and the organic world and the entirety of the Great Lakes drainage basin. This Agreement was expanded in 1987 when a protocol was signed to account for groundwater and lake sediment rehabilitation [*Jackson, 1993*].

Similar efforts to improve water quality will also be needed in Russia. As the old Soviet system gives way to a search for development through the nexus of the market economy, the fear is that resources and technology will not be made available to curb industrial pollution and replace outdated sewage systems. Lake Baikal and the Aral Sea are already heavily polluted. Without remedial action, the effects on human health will be considerable. Intestinal illnesses have been reported, even cases of cholera [*Hyde-Price, 1993; Boulton, 1993*].

For many states, particularly in the developing world, their capacity for improving water quality will be limited without the provision of means for implementing environmentally sound and developmentally sustainable policies. Many states in developing regions lack the basic infrastructure for remedial action, and for monitoring and enforcing controls. The consequence of inaction to introduce water-quality management structures will undoubtedly be further degradation of resources together with an increase in attendant health problems.

Drinking Water Supply and Sanitation

The provision of safe drinking water in sufficient quantities to sustain human life, and adequate sanitation facilities to ensure a healthy environment, remains one of the major challenges confronting many governments.

Population growth in many states is already stretching supplies of water available for human consumption. For the demand to be met, traditional solutions to increasing drinking water supply, such as the de-salination plants used throughout the Middle East, will need to be supplemented by techniques for re-cycling urban water. The continuing search for new and accessible water supplies also remains a priority, as does the task of ensuring that existing sources remain unpolluted.

International efforts to improve water quality are crucially linked to attempts to address the problems caused by contaminated drinking water supplies and poor sanitation. The associated health problems are considerable. Children are particularly susceptible. But water-related diseases affect all sectors of the population in many developing states. One estimate is that 90 per cent of all diseases in the developing world are caused by the consumption of contaminated water. More disturbingly, without effective action, the stresses on drinking water and sanitation are set to increase with the rapid population growth in the developing world and the migration trend from rural to urban environments.

Previous attempts to introduce safe drinking water and hygienic sanitation systems have met with qualified success. During the IDWSSD, experience indicated that a strategy of introducing low-cost technologies at the community level represents the most scope for alleviating sanitation problems. Rather than large-scale programmes, headway could more easily be made by providing low-cost sanitation technologies such as the pour-flush latrine and ventilated improved pit (VIP) [*Wright, 1987*].

Even with a policy, adopted at the 1990 New Delhi meeting, of 'some for all rather than more for some' approach, the scale of the problem is considerable. An estimated 2 billion people are still without adequate sanitation. Therefore a selective strategy, aimed at under-served rural and poor urban areas, may be the most appropriate way of implementing the 'some for all' approach.

Water and Sustainable Urban Development

Rapid urbanisation and industrialisation represent two of the greatest challenges to water management. Existing resources are already stretched to meet the demands of domestic and industrial consumers. Degradation of resources is occurring in many large cities of the world due to poor water treatment practices and technologies, unsustainable consumption patterns and the sheer scale of urban population growth.

In Latin America, for example, the growth of huge shanty towns on the outskirts of the region's large cities has created a new dimension to already strained municipal water supply and treatment services. The absence of piped water and inadequate or non-existent drainage and sewage systems, make such places vulnerable to disease and high mortality. The outbreak of cholera in Peru and its spread to neighbouring regions, even to cities such as Buenos Aires where tap water has generally been considered safe to drink, served as a sharp reminder that this situation may not endure [*Calvert, 1993*].

The task of alleviating the stresses caused by urbanisation is immense. Chapter 18 calls for all states to have attained, by the year 2000, a target which ensures that 'all urban residents have access to at least 40 litres per capita per day of safe water and that 75 per cent of the urban population are provided with on-site or community facilities for sanitation . . .'.[3] This is a mammoth undertaking. Yet not to provide such basic standards of drinking water and waste disposal services will condemn vast sections of the world's population to a life of severe discomfort and ill-health.

Much of the challenge for implementing such services will fall on local authorities. While national governments have a responsibility for overall drinking water and sanitation policy, it is incumbent on municipal authorities to see that the treatment of sewage is adequate and that drinking water is of sufficient quality for human consumption. In many states, however, much of the technology for sewage treatment is old and inefficient. Replacing this with modern waste disposal plants will commonly require assistance beyond the levels that municipal authorities can hope to attain. Support from external agencies will therefore be necessary if problems are not to be exacerbated in coming years. Where municipal authorities probably could implement policy without the need for great resources is in the area of overall effluent discharge controls, particularly resulting from industrial uses.

Water for Sustainable Food Production and Rural Development

Within the developing world, food security has become one of the major driving forces of national policy. This has direct implications for future water strategies. Sustainability of food supplies and water are inextricably linked. Deterioration or depletion of the latter inevitably diminishes the capacities for developing states to replenish vital foodstocks. Policies are therefore required that acknowledge the vital links between food security and water management.

More than two-thirds of all water used is in agriculture, primarily for irrigation and the production of food crops. Some states, such as Egypt, are virtually dependent on irrigation for crop production. In many others, rain-fed crop production needs to be supplemented during dry seasons with water supplied by irrigation.

A major stumbling block in implementing effective responses is that many existing irrigation techniques are inefficient, due to ageing or ineffective technology, or are simply over-exploited. This can lead to such problems as waterlogging, soil erosion, salinisation, and eventually to major losses of land for cultivation.

Pollution of water can also occur as a result of agricultural practices. The run-off of pesticides and fertilisers, used as a means of improving food production, can have the negative effect of diminishing the quality of water, which in turn limits its future use. This has significance because of the need for water of sufficient quality to meet livestock requirements and the world's freshwater fisheries, on which large numbers of humans depend for an immediate and accessible source of food. But care must also be taken to ensure that livestock do not become a major source of pollution in their own right, which can happen if animal waste is allowed to enter water supplies.

Increasing population means that the demand on water for agriculture will increase in the future. For some states, especially those that are dependent on irrigation for food production or that are near the limit of rain-fed agriculture, ensuring access to supplies of water has become a primary goal of national policy. Some may have already reached their maximum sustainable upper limit of water resource use.

The Food and Agriculture Organisation (FAO) has established an International Action Programme on Water and Sustainable Agricultural Development (IAP–WASAD) to assist developing states with water and food management. Improvements in existing irrigation systems have been undertaken and, where necessary, new techniques introduced. Drainage schemes are also being used for land reclamation. However, as acknowledged in Chapter 18, introducing new, more efficient technologies for irrigation may be a double-edged sword if this is done without an overall environmental impact assessment. Such techniques can reduce water loss, but they also run the risk of increasing water pollution and sedimentation problems.

Impacts of Climate Change on Water Resources

Global climate change could have a major affect on water. Its precise impact on global resources is as yet indeterminate, although scientific knowledge does reveal that certain linkages may exist. Studies of a cross-section of the world's regions from India, the Panama Canal area, Malaysia and the Côte d'Ivoire indicate a significant relationship between forests and climate, particularly rainfall [*Myers, 1988*]. Research at Manaus in the Amazon basin reveals a similar pattern of rainfall being crucially linked to level of forest cover. This research does suggest that it would require major forest clearing to reduce total rainfall drastically. If small-scale clearing occurs, especially in areas not far from the sea where atmospheric moisture can compensate for forest loss, then rainfall reduction may not be experienced [*Douglas, 1993*]. Extensive deforestation may therefore be an important determinant of climate change and consequently of rainfall distribution. Our understanding of localised forest clearing should also not preclude the possibility that if it is practised persistently and over a widespread area reduced rainfall could occur.

Other climatic-induced changes to rainfall distribution might result from global phenomena such as the warming effect induced by radiatively active greenhouse gases (GHGs) [*Frederick and Gleik, 1989*]. In 1990, the Intergovernmental Panel on Climate Change (IPCC) considered that unless greenhouse gas emissions were reduced, the earth's surface temperature would rise by one degree Celsius by 2030 and three degrees by 2100. If this were to occur, then a further uncertainty would be added to water availability.

General circulation models (GCMs) are not yet available to provide conclusive evidence of climate change and its effects on water resources. Trends in the Sahel region of north Africa indicate that since the early 1960s a sustained period of rainfall depletion has been experienced. Although rainfall regimes in Africa are traditionally variable, the drought in the Sahel is disturbing because of its persistence. Over the last 30 years there has been a marked decline in the surface waters of Lake Chad. If this trend were to continue there would be further desertification of the region, soil erosion, more frequent and intense dust storms and, ultimately, loss of land for agriculture and a shortening of growing seasons for crops [Hulme, 1993].

These changes to the rainfall pattern in the Sahel, and Africa generally, may result from other causes, such as land use change and the oceanic-atmospheric phenomenon of the El Nino-Southern Oscillation (ENSO). Prudence therefore dictates that further research seek to determine the causes of such rainfall changes and, where possible, execute measures to reduce their effects.

The Need for International Water Co-operation

The consequences of scarce water resources are already being felt in many regions of the world. The security implications are considerable. Competition for water might induce or exacerbate internal instability or conflict between states. In this connection, much has been made of the water-related problems in the Middle East, where development efforts, agricultural demands and demographic trends (especially population growth and urbanisation) are already placing stress on existing water supplies [Lonergan and Kavanagh, 1991; Beschorner, 1992; Joffe, 1993]. Yet other regions of the world are not immune to these kinds of stresses and threats to security.

Water may be used in various ways by states as an instrument of foreign policy or even as a weapon of war. The ability to withhold or release water, divert river flows, pollute waters, and construct dams affects the power relationship between states [Mandel, 1991]. Dams can also become a prime target during conflict. The recent ethnic conflict in former Yugoslavia provides ample testimony. Retreating Serbian forces detonated three mines across the Peruca hydro-electric dam in southern Croatia which threatened to release millions of gallons of water onto nearby towns and villages. The structure of the dam was repaired without major water release, but the threat of impending devastation from flood nevertheless induced considerable fear among the local population.

It should be noted that this focus on the conflictual elements of water security may obscure converse instances where states have cooperated over water resources. These instances are numerous. Even in the Middle East, formal agreement and tacit cooperation among states over shared rivers and groundwaters does exist [*Dellapenna, 1992*]. In South Asia, India and Pakistan have fought three wars since 1948 but have cooperated over their shared waters of the Indus river system. Yet there always remains an underlying tension that this state of affairs may not endure, especially if water resources become more uncertain in the future [*Concannon, 1989; Khan, 1990; Biswas, 1992*].

There is consequently a need to develop more formal institutions and mechanisms for water management and conflict resolution at the level of the entire river basin, including both surface and groundwaters. Chapter 18 was remarkably silent on the ways this might be accomplished. Assessing the experience of how existing transboundary river authorities have managed shared water resources would be one obvious starting point. The Mekong, Nile, Senegal and Indus rivers, for example, all have authorities with this kind of historical experience.

These assessments might be coupled with further consideration of the ways in which international water law might be improved. The current basis of this embryonic legal system rests on four competing concepts: unlimited territorial integrity; unlimited or absolute sovereignty; community in the waters; and limited territorial sovereignty [*Menon, 1975; Caponera, 1983*].

Upstream and downstream riparians often differ over which concept should be upheld. Upstream states have tended to assert absolute sovereignty, claiming a right to full use of the waters flowing within their territory irrespective of the effects beyond its borders. Downstream states, seeking to limit potential damage to the watercourse from outside their boundaries, have argued for unlimited territorial integrity, which prohibits any state from damaging the river or altering its flow in any way.

One compromise, although not always accepted, has been for both sets of riparian state to agree on a limited territorial sovereignty concept. This grants all riparians rights to use the waters providing it does not affect other users. The concept underpins the 'Helsinki Rules on the Uses of the Waters of International Rivers' adopted by the International Law Association (ILA) in 1966. The Rules are concerned with pollution, navigation, and the prevention and settlement of disputes. The critical feature of the Rules is that they incorporate the idea of the equitable sharing of water resources and identify the 'international drainage basin' as the principal unit for river management.[4]

Some states have rejected the concept because it has been interpreted as including the land areas as well as the water resources within the drainage basin. This is unfortunate because the concept does incorporate mechanisms for conflict avoidance and resolution over such issues as the siting of dams and transboundary pollution [*McCaffrey, 1991*].

Since 1966, further rules have been drafted by the ILA covering flood control, pollution, navigability, protection of water installations during armed conflict, joint administration, flowage regulation, joint administration, general environmental concerns, and groundwater. Consideration has also been given to incorporating the idea of 'substantial damage', whether to the environment or to extra-territorial waters, into legal form. Similarly, the concept of 'community in the waters' is beginning to feature in discussions over international rivers as a more appropriate idea for river basin management and conflict avoidance.[5]

The Way Forward: Implementing a Holistic Strategy for Water

Chapter 18 of Agenda 21 is a major achievement in the on-going international debate over water. Agreement on its wording indicates that both developed and developing states are beginning to grant water issues the prominent position on the international agenda they deserve. Yet the challenges confronting the world's water resources do not end with the negotiation of this Chapter. They are, instead, just beginning. For as our knowledge of the fragility of water resources increases, it has become imperative that this knowledge be translated into policy action. But herein lies the crux of the problem. Political will and financial resources will be required to implement a holistic strategy for water at local, national and international levels.

Experience from previous water conferences suggests a need for follow-up mechanisms to ensure action is taken on specific targets, of which Chapter 18 has many. It has been agreed that the work of UNCED will continue through the UN Commission on Sustainable Development (CSD). One task of this body is to assess national action plans. Those for water will be addressed under cluster H, which also includes the oceans and the atmosphere.

The resources needed to implement the specific action plans identified in Chapter 18 are vast. The UNCED Secretariat has estimated that the total annual cost (1993–2000) for reaching the targets outlined in the seven programme areas is in excess of 55 thousand million. It is unlikely that anything approaching this figure will be made available. However, the risk of not devoting the kinds of resources demanded is that the fragility and uncertainty surrounding the world's water will simply increase. The consequences could be considerable.

NOTES

1. This issue was addressed at a Symposium on a Strategy for Water Resources Capacity Building, held in Delft, June 1991. Capacity building comprises the following elements:

   - creating an enabling environment with appropriate policy and legal framework;
   - institutional strengthening and development, including local community participation;
   - human resources development, including the strengthening of managerial systems and water users interests;
   - awareness building and education at all levels of society (Preparatory Committee for the United Nations Conference on Environment and Development Third Session, Geneva, 12 Aug.–4 Sept. 1991, Working Group II, Agenda Item 3, A/Conf.151./PC/WG.II/L.17, United Nations General Assembly, p.4).

2. Agenda 21, Ch. 18, para. 4.
3. Para. 58 (a).
4. Article II states that 'An international drainage basin is a geographical area extending over two or more States determined by the watershed limits of the system of waters, including surface and underground waters, flowing into a common terminus'.
5. Ibid.

REFERENCES

Beschorner, N. (1992), 'Water and Instability in the Middle East', *Adelphi Paper 273*, London: International Institute for Strategic Studies.

Biswas, A.K. (1992), 'Indus Water Treaty: the Negotiating Process', *Water International*, Vol.17, pp.201–9.

Boulton, L. (1993), *Financial Times*, 7 April.

Calvert, P. (1993), 'Water Politics in Latin America', in Thomas and Howlett [*1993: 55–57*].

Caponera, D.A. (1983), 'International River Law', in M. Zaman, *River Basin Development*, Dublin: Tycooly International.

Clarke, A. (1991), 'Water: The International Crisis', London: Earthscan.

Communique from the International Conference on Water and Environment (1992), Dublin, 26–31 Jan.

Concannon, B. (1989), 'The Indus Water Treaty: Three Decades of Success, Yet, Will It Endure?', *International Environmental Law Review*, Vol.55.

Dellapenna, J. (1992), 'Building International Water Management Institutions: The Role of Treaties and Other Legal Arrangements', in *Water in the Middle East: Legal, Political and Commercial Implications*, Conference Papers, London: SOAS, Nov.

Douglas, I. (1993), 'Logging, Deforestation, Rivers and Sedimentation', Conference on Hydrology and Sustainable Development, London: Royal Geographical Society.

Falkenmark, M. (1986), 'Fresh Waters as a Factors in Strategic Policy and Action', in A.H. Westing (ed.), *Global Resources and International Conflict*, London and New York: Oxford University Press for SIPRI, pp.85–113.

Frederick, K.D. and P.H. Gleik (1989), 'Water Resources and Climate Change', in N. Rosenberg *et al.*, *Greenhouse Warming: Abatement and Adaptation*, Washington, DC: Resources for the Future.

Gregory, F. (1993), 'The EC and Freshwater', in Thomas and Howlett [*1993: 171–84*].

Hulme, M. (1993), 'Rainfall Trends in Africa: Resource Implications, Conference on Hydrology and Sustainable Development, London: Royal Geographic Society.

Hyde-Price, A. (1993), 'Eurasia', in Thomas and Howlett, [*1993: 149–70*].

The Independent (1993), 29 and 30 Jan.

The Independent on Sunday (1993), 31 Jan.

Jackson, I.C. (1993), 'The Great Lakes: Exploring the Ecosystem', in Thomas and Howlett [*1993: 23–45*].

Joffe, G. (1993), 'The Issue of Water in the Middle East and North Africa', in Thomas and Howlett [*1993*: 65–85].

Khan, M.Y. (1990), 'Boundary Water Conflict Between India and Pakistan', *Water International*, Vol.15, pp.195–9.

Lonergan, S. and B. Kavanagh (1991), 'Climate Change, Water Resources and Security in the Middle East', *Global Environmental Change*, Sept., pp.272–90.

Mandel, R. (1991), 'Sources of International River Basin Disputes', *Annual Meeting of the International Studies Association*, Vancouver, BC, Canada, March.

McCaffrey, S. (1991), 'International Organizations and the Holistic Approach to Water Problems', *Natural Resources Journal*, Vol.31, pp.139–65.

Menon, P.K. (1975), 'Water Resources Development of International Rivers with Special Reference to the Developing World', *International Lawyer (Chicago)*, Vol.9, pp.441–64.

Meybeck *et al.* (eds.), (1989), *Global Freshwater Quality: A First Assessment*, GEMS/ WATER, WHO and UNEP.

Myers, N. (1988), *Tropical Deforestation and Climate Change*, Conference on Climate and the Geosciences, Louvain-le-Neuve, Belgium.

Postel, S. (1984), *Water: Rethinking Management in an Age of Scarcity*, Paper 62, Washington, DC: Worldwatch Institute. *Report of the United Nations Conference on Environment and Development* (1993), Rio de Janeiro, 3–14 June 1992, A/CONF. 151/ 26 (Vol.II), 13 Aug. 1992.

The Times (1993), 1 Feb..

Thomas, C. and D. Howlett (eds.) (1993), *Resource Politics: Freshwater and Regional Relations*, Buckingham and Philadelphia, PA: Open University Press.

UNDP (1991), *Human Development Report*, Oxford: Oxford University Press.

Water International (1993), Special Issue on Water in the Middle East, Vol.18, No.1, March.

Water Quality: Progress in Implementing the Mar del Plata Action Plan and a Strategy for the 1990s (A Report sponsored by UN/GAPD/DIESA, UNDP, UNEP, and WHO).

Wright, A. (1987), 'Low-Cost Sanitation Options', *IDWSSD Decade Watch*, Dec.

Environment, Development and Security

PAIKIASOTHY SARAVANAMUTTU

The link between environment, development and security is not readily acknowledged because it is fundamentally subversive of the conventional wisdom and paradigm of *international* relations. Encompassing contentious questions about thorny issues such as national sovereignty, intervention, development, security and human rights, it redefines the imperative of survival in international politics within a context of global politics. In so doing, this linkage underpins an alternative awareness of the emerging international society from the established structures of the interstate system. Accordingly, it meets resistance from the North which sees itself as the chief executive of the 'New World Order' in which its ideas have apparently triumphed, and also from the South, where national sovereignty and state-centric realism exercise a compelling hold against all odds. What the environment–development–security nexus militates towards is a new culture of world politics which transforms attitudes consonant with meaningful interdependence. This also entails the recognition of the importance of non-state actors as determined by their functions in world politics and the progressive democratisation of the activity itself.

Security: Interstate System or International Society?

The distinction between *system* and *society* is of primary relevance to the idea of a new culture of world politics, particularly in the aftermath of the cold war. In investigating the environment–development–security nexus and its requirements, it is important to identify whether existing structures are conducive to it and in what way. It may well be the case that with the ostensible ideological hegemony of the post-cold-war world and the

Pakiasothy Saravanamuttu is Visiting Lecturer in International Politics, University of Colombo, and the Bandaranaike Centre for International Studies, Sri Lanka.

explicit international concern with the domestic sources of insecurity at present, the domestic analogy of *society* better approximates international political activity with all the normative connotations this entails. The question nevertheless remains as to what kind of society it is and what kind of society it should be.

Accordingly, another distinction may be pertinent. The environment–development–security nexus may only be fully comprehended within a world society context, but initially it will have to gain recognition within one that is better described as *international* society.

System, the favoured characterisation of international politics by state-centric realists, depicts an interaction between cohesive units called states which mechanically replicates habitual behaviour according to unchanging rules. These rules are expressions of an overarching and axiomatic self-interest which in turn is defined by the ambiguous concept of power. The principal rule is, of course, sovereignty of the individual units and their mutual respect thereof. Consequently, overall system maintenance becomes synonymous with the balance of power, best described by Vattel as 'a state of affairs such that no one power is in a position where it is preponderant and can lay down the law to others' (cited in Bull [*1977: 101*]). From this essentially anti-hegemonic ethos springs the notion of an 'anarchical society' – anarchical in the sense of an absence of government rather than chaos.

The realists' presumption is to claim monopoly over objectivity and to proclaim their value-free credentials through the elevation of power to the status of a self-evident truth. No vulgar moralising for them. Competition, conflict, self-interest – these are the driving forces regardless of how asymmetrical they may be. For four decades we had two superpowers, and governments always invited them to intervene in their affairs. Neither in the spirit nor in the letter was the system impugned in this formulation and in any event if there was any doubt, the system was so constructed as to turn intervention itself into an essentially contestable concept. There was one coin and it had two sides.

Of course the practice was different. Simultaneously with the deadly minuet of the East–West relationship proceeded the grossly asymmetrical North–South tug of war. Different aspects of security were emphasised – the balance of military power on the one hand and economic dependence on the other. In the assertion that each side stressed the dimension of security that served its interest, realism was vindicated in the theory and practice of international relations.

The point to stress at this juncture is that according to realism this is natural and would always be. No account of change is necessary because even if the players change, the ground rules cannot. Realism presents itself as natural and intrinsic to the activity of politics itself. Competing ideas and moral arguments are dismissed as dangerous irrelevances to the business of politics and by extension to development and security.

International society has different assumptions and emphases. The individualism of the component units is tempered by notions of collective responsibility and a more positive acknowledgement of the merits of interdependence. Instead of the exclusive reliance upon the balance of power, the strategem for security is collective security. A community of states is defined according to shared values and, through international organisation and law, acquires the resources to deter and punish threats to itself. The policeman to enforce law and order from the domestic analogy is pertinent here. The community is indivisible and therefore the notion of security holistic. A threat to anyone is a potential threat to everyone and as such requires collective action.

The interventionary opportunities are manifold in international society and in practice the solid realist virtue of prudence operates to remind people that the path to hell is paved with good intentions. Sovereignty is not so much superseded by a higher value, but rather there is the expectation that its exercise would incorporate the other shared values that distinguish the community – which today can be identified as good governance and economic liberalisation.

A clearly identifiable collective legitimacy is central to the *raison d'être* and operation of international society where intervention is not taboo but a constant option. Collective legitimacy may in practice be labelled collective acquiesence in the prevailing power configuration but that, too, is indicative of the ties that bind. The ties that bind any society are at no time entirely voluntary or involuntary. Alternatively, the costs and benefits of being a part of, outweigh those of being apart from.

It is the contention of this study that with some qualifications international political activity better approximates society than system in the post-cold-war world. From the Gulf to Bosnia, Somalia and Cambodia, not to mention Mozambique, the Middle East, Angola and the structural adjustment conditionality that affects the South, international intervention has become part and parcel of the contemporary political architecture.

Through international financial institutions and multilateral security organisations, good governance and trade liberalisation criteria are the order of the day. Cultural relativism is fighting a rearguard action along with purist notions of national sovereignty, in the face of a seemingly unstoppable wave of interdependent linkages. Both the UNCED in Rio and the Human Rights Congress in Vienna were parallelled by simultaneous discussions between relevant non-governmental organisations.

The debate now is not about the linkages *per se* or the actors but about their respective content and functions.

Setting and Implementing the Environment–Security–Development Agenda

The security agenda is widening in the era since the cold war. It is not that the non-military aspects of security are a recent discovery or indeed even the linkage between environment, development and security. What is new is the disposition to consider them legitimate items on the inter-state security agenda.

Success nevertheless in agenda-setting is quite a different matter from success in agenda implementation, as the North–South balance of power has shown. A consensus on agenda implementation requires a change in attitudes, the self-conscious construction of a new paradigm – in short a cultural change. As will be discussed below, the thread of continuity that links the original Group of 77 demands (1963) to the New International Economic Order Charter of Economic Rights and Duties (1974), the United Nations Conference on the Environment and Development (UNCED) Rio Declaration and Agenda 21 (1992), attests to this inability to move beyond agenda-setting.

This is indeed what is old about the New World Order – the demonstrable limitations of the South, the enduring and compounded asymmetry of the North–South relationship which allows for the assumption of international society and the sanctioning of hegemony as universal consensus. However, as the costs of the cold war percolate and the preoccupation with domestic concerns are expressed through introspection in place of the earlier insularity in the North, there is the possibility that the growing awareness of the scale of the environmental problem will blossom into political pressure for a more enlightened understanding of its implications.

In a recession-hit North this would seem unlikely. Protectionism in trade and cutbacks in aid would be given greater prominence than arguments about the responsibilities and sacrifices associated with the future of the planet and sustainable development.

At the same time there are signs that the obsession with the standard of living is now being challenged by arguments about the quality of life. They grow out of the concerns of persons, for the world they inhabit and their children would inherit, for the consequences of the expenditure of their tax dollars and the cost of living. Once galvanised into the groups of civil society they could become more politically effective and, like the popular pressure for good governance and human rights criteria in developmental assistance, environmental consciousness could be expressed as a domestic source of foreign policy.

Indeed, it is this journey on the part of the South as well – of moving away from the allure of conspicuous consumption to the qualitative concerns of sustainable development – that lies at the heart of the environmental–development–security nexus. Yet it is a long journey and one that requires assistance along the way. Therein lies the dilemma.

The internal–external divide is crucial to the political psychology of Southern states and central to their pretensions. Having inherited the baggage of statecentric realism as part of their colonial legacy they are trapped in the obsessive assertion of sovereignty and at the same time by the compelling need for external assistance to buttress it in military security and economic development terms. In the domestic arena, governments bred in the belief that their function is that of provider of welfare and well-being and protector against external attack often plead circumstances beyond their control to explain poor performance. The circumstances beyond their control explanation has a variation – the external threat – that is invoked to justify the state in its role as predator on the rights of its citizens.

In Africa, Asia and Latin America there are environmental issues of desertification and river water management that have important repercussions for security and development, and alternatively domestic conflicts which result in environmental degradation and large-scale refugee movements. The environment–development–security component of these issues goes unheeded because of the zero-sum realist preoccupation of Southern states and the imposition of this upon the evolving nation and state-building process. Given the realist bias of states, environmental issues are often used as levers of influence and coercion in pursuit of narrow self-interest rather than explored as profitable avenues of co-operation for mutual benefit. Consequently, environmental factors are manipulated to the detriment of national development and security, though ostensibly for their enhancement.

These are not issues that necessarily require external intervention or assistance for their resolution. External involvement in the context of the cold war often compounded rather than cured and in its aftermath, would sap the legitimacy of the interventionary agent and local state. Bilateral or regional action or a combination of both is required at one level, and the conscious provision of democratic space to various groups to defuse nation-building tensions at another, to resolve these problems. Water in the Middle East is wrapped up in the Israeli–Palestinian antagonism amongst others; and in the Tigres-Euphrates basin, with Iraqi–Syrian rivalry and Kurdish nationalism. In South Asia Indian insistence on bilateralism over sharing the Ganges waters with Bangladesh stands in the way of constructive exploitation of the subcontinent's water resources.

Whether future wars in the Middle East are to be fought over water, or economic prosperity in South Asia held hostage to Indian military security fears, empowerment of groups that are alienated from over-centralised and coercive states and a more enlightened grasp of the potential of interdependence is necessary on the part of Southern states to solve the more localised disputes encompassing environmental, development and security concerns. It is worth quoting from the conclusion of a study [*Hassan, 1991: 65*] on the host of environmental issues in South Asia which have security implications:

> The study indicates that in South Asia environmental deterioration has a very direct and immediate impact on the economy of the state, which in turn affects social relations in ways detrimental to political stability. Environmental degradation has clearly undermined the political order in South Asia, and is continuing to do so, thereby prolonging and generating national and international tensions.

Another study, published in winter 1992–93 on water resources and instability in the Middle East, concludes that the unresolved water-related economic and strategic issues do not necessarily constitute a major threat to regional security but are a source of tension. Aware of the realist bias of states, Beschorner [*1992/93: 71*] emphasises that

> the long-term co-operative development of international water resources in the Middle East thus presents the greatest challenge to policy-makers within and outside the region ... These are objectives which are widely considered desirable, but they are only practicable so long as the water issue is not separated from its wider political context.

The Not So New NIEO

Whilst localised environmental issues lie within the competence of the South and provide opportunities for a change in perspective, the overarching global issues necessitate Northern co-operation and the paradigm shift in attitudes demanded since the 1980s.

The arguments about interdependence and life-boat ethics, of one planet, islands of prosperity in a sea of poverty, are well known. That they are still valid is also known. What is now being suggested is that environmental degradation constitutes a security threat and developmental concern that is not bound within territorial limits. It affects all and, most importantly, in political terms it challenges the well-entrenched orthodoxy that all the South has to do is develop according to the Northern model. Prescribed and manufactured by the North, swallowed by the South, it is now a pill for the North to digest. To pursue the analogy, the remedy threatens to be worse than the malady. Can the remedy be interrupted and the malady arrested?

Southern governments would only undermine their legitimacy if they were even to attempt to redirect their development strategies and the rising socio-economic demands for mass consumption on the part of their burgeoning populations. Structural adjustment programmes that are to effect the change from tradition and socialist stagnation to dynamic capitalist modernity have taken their toll in losses of legitimacy. Poverty alleviation programmes have partly ameliorated this through some democratisation of the development process, but populist rhetoric and revivals of ethnic chauvinism designed for the same purpose have aroused unreal expectations without reinforcing legitimacy.

There is a widespread perception fed by the North's advocacy of modernisation and proclamation of victory in the cold war, that the pressures for mass consumerism are so great that any attempt to slow the pace of liberalisation or dampen socio-economic demands is fraught with immediate political risk, regardless of long-term wisdom. Political self-interest and short-term regime survival are paramount. One must also add that in the global village of mass communication, also known as the world market, the South is bombarded with images of conspiciuous consumption that are meant to, and do, make up their life expectations. Such advertising and such imitation have a powerful momentum of their own which is good for international business but bad for the planet!

Taking these considerations into account, the South Centre (the follow-up office of the South Commission) produced a paper in preparation for the Rio Summit entitled 'Environment and Development: Towards a Common Strategy of the South in the UNCED Negotiations and Beyond' [*The South Centre, 1991*]. The concerns it outlined and the emphases it placed reflect the persisting and intractable nature of the North–South relationship, mentioned above.

As a representative sample of Southern views, it is worth quoting at length. It testifies to the scope of Southern aspirations and to the extent of their fears and shortcomings. Although written before Rio, it is valid as an enduring political position paper that links past, present and future concerns into a negotiating strategy.

Under the heading 'Strategic Considerations for the South', the Centre stresses that in the UNCED and negotiations concerning the conventions on climate and biodiversity, the South should ensure that it has adequate 'environmental space for its future development' and that global economic relations are restructured so that 'the South obtains the required resources, technology, and access to markets enabling it to pursue a development process that is not only environmentally sound but also *rapid enough to meet the needs and aspirations of its growing population*' (emphasis added).

A comprehensive negotiating strategy for the South which included the pooling of technical resources and the establishment of mechanisms to maximise collective advantage, a firm pledge to avoid agreements that were not attached to international action, definite commitments on North–South development and, perceptively, a public information campaign to publicise and canvass support for Southern positions in Northern public opinion were also proposed.

The South Centre argues that the 'essential question, in the context of the North–South dialogue, is how the burden of adjustment is to be shared in an equitable manner' [*1991: 3*]. Crucial to this, in its view, is a steadfast Southern insistence upon the principle 'that the development of the South can in no way be compromised by the North's pre-emption of the global environment space' [*1991: 4*]. The North must assume the burden of global environmental adjustment as the principal culprit in environmental degradation and its beneficiary. The Centre stresses that

> ... the concept of sustainable development does not mean only that the needs of the present have to be met without prejudice to the satisfaction of future needs. It means also that the needs of the North should be met in ways that do not compromise the satisfaction of the present and future needs of the South [*1991: 7*].

The report points out that the introduction of the environmental dimension into the development process further widens the resource gap in the South. Consequently, the crux of the environment–development issue is the increased volume of resources needed by the South for development that is 'adequate in terms of tempo and at the same time is environmentally sound' [*1991: 8*]. In this connection, the report argues that the concept of 'additionality' which had featured in preparatory meetings – essentially the additional costs of incorporating environmental concerns into specific projects – must be broadened if it is to be of practical utility. Without resources for overall development, the gains of environmentally sensitive projects would be mitigated.

Turning to the negotiating strategy, the Centre warns, in a reflection of power realities and the prevailing pattern of interaction, against Southern acceptance of legally-binding agreements and even non-binding declarations in one area without corresponding Northern commitments to meet Southern aspirations. The fear is of cross-conditionality which, given the balance of power in the North's favour, could be built into the conditionality of multilateral financial institutions [1991: 6–7].

The central thrust of the Centre's recommendations and the distinguishing feature of the South's position at Rio and beyond, is to emphasise that the developmental concerns of the North–South dialogue are inextricably bound up in environmental concerns, and that any attempt to delink the two would be disastrous.

Nothing that Agenda 21 would address perennial items on the North–South agenda such as

- poverty, economic growth and the environment,
- commodities and the environment,
- international trade and the environment
- structural adjustment and the environment
- external indebtedness, resource outflows and the environment and
- big industrial enterprises, including transnational companies, and the environment,

the Centre recommends that this opportunity be seized to 'restart the North–South dialogue and negotiations on development' [1991: 10].

With regard to the negotiating process, the recommendations recognise that the Rio summit would be the beginning of a process and that both parallel and follow-on consultations would be necessary. On the question of institutional arrangements, the traditional Southern position is reiterated; 'democratic governance and transparency within the UN system and an integrated vision of a problem that has hitherto been approached in a piecemeal fashion' [1991: 14]. What is sought is a move away from the World Bank/IMF stranglehold on international development assistance through a not so veiled reference to the democratic pretensions of the 'New World Order'.

UNCED

The South Centre's recommendations notwithstanding, the Rio UNCED produced mixed results. Whilst the evidence for international society was to be found in the convening of the conference itself and in the recognition accorded to the Brundtland Report on Environment and Development (1987) which served as an intellectual antecedent to it, the claims of a more realist international system were upheld in the enduring polarisation of views along the North–South axis.

This will not go away. Those who argued in vain that this, and not the East–West antagonism, was the central power configuration in international relations will always be vindicated as long as the culture of state-centric realism holds sway. The move away from system to society, as discussed above, does not entail the wholesale jettisoning of statecentric realism but the attempt to accommodate it within the format of interdependence. As such, as in any society, distributive justice and burden-sharing will be salient issues along with the apportioning of responsibility and mechanisms for accountability, but they will also be essentially contested concepts.

UNCED produced a 27–page Declaration of general principles for environmentally friendly development-binding agreements on climate change and biodiversity (the latter was not signed by the US at Rio) and the 720–page Agenda 21 document (see Keesings [*June 1992: 38947*]).

The Rio declaration posited the goal of establishing a 'new and equitable global partnership' and confirmed the environment–development link as well as the particular responsibility of the richer states in this regard, given the pressures they place upon the global environment. It also acknowledged the sovereign right of states to exploit their natural resources, thereby ruling out any suggestion of external intervention on environmental grounds. This concern was covered in the provision that states should not exploit their resources in a manner that would be injurious to the environment of other states. In this respect the declaration is a compromise that is open to interpretation, should the need arise.

The declaration also posited general principles regarding the rights of women, free trade and poverty eradication. It incorporated the 'precautionary principle' that the absence of conclusive scientific data should not be used against the enactment of measures to halt environmental depreciation.

The essential elements of Agenda 21, presented as a 'blue print for action', dealt with the implementation of UNCED resolutions. To this end a Sustainable Development Commission has been established under the auspices of the UN General Assembly to oversee progress towards the realisation of UNCED objectives. The Global Environment Facility (GEF), jointly administered by the World Bank, the UN Development Programme (UNDP) and the UN Environment Programme (UNEP) is to co-ordinate the essential additional funding to the South for sustainable development.

The binding Biodiversity Convention which the US refused to sign at Rio (an action reminiscent of its attitude towards the UN Law of the Sea treaty), outlined steps to preserve ecologically important areas and species and envisaged a listing of globally important areas in the future. Significantly, the convention provided access for Southern states to technology and financial resources for this purpose and for compensatory payments to the South for the extraction of genetic resources. This provision is an extension of the New International Economic Order (NIEO) arguments about sovereign control over natural resources and raw materials which are used in Northern manufactures and sold to the South at commercial rates. It is especially relevant to the activities of biotechnology companies and it was US concern for the latter that determined Washington's refusal to sign the Convention at Rio. Finally, the Convention recognises the role of indigenous people and rural communities in preserving biodiversity and identifies them as primary beneficiairies of conservation efforts.

The Convention on Climate Change called for limitations on the emission of 'greenhouse gases' such as carbon dioxide (CO_2). In the face of US opposition, no binding date was set for reductions but it was recommended that the North should aim to stabilise such emissions at 1990 levels by the target date already agreed by the European Community – the year 2000.

UNCED had also intended to produce a binding Convention on tropical forest use, but succumbed to resistance mounted by timber-exporting states led by Malaysia. Instead, a non-binding Statement of Forest Principles consonant with sustainable development principles was agreed upon. Opposition to a binding convention was based largely on the grounds of national sovereignty and illustrates the Southern attitude and dilemma with regard to the environment–development–security nexus. The South is not unilaterally going to take the initiative in foregoing the export-oriented and mass consumption development strategies imposed upon it without corresponding and proportionate sacrifices by the North.

Conclusion

At the outset it was stated that the environment–development–security nexus was fundamentally subversive of the established paradigm. It demands that in a world of burgeoning populations, mass consumption and nation- and state-building conflicts, development and security have to be redefined and the environment cannot be ignored. Existing structures and institutions will find this difficult. They are mobilisations of bias and values from a different ethos and are therefore bound to project these concerns into their consideration of this linkage. This is the practical policy-making reality of global security management.

What prospects, then, are there for a mature appreciation of the argument that the environment–development–security nexus does not have to be a zero-sum one?

We have to deal with states but states have to deal with people. Citizens or persons are relegated to the periphery in the traditional paradigm of international relations but have a habit of asserting themselves as instruments of change. They are indeed the catalysts for the new culture of world politics mentioned above. However, the manner in which they will assert themselves with regard to this important linkage is not necessarily going to be harmonious or non-conflictual. The establishment of a holistic view of security as the conventional wisdom of the day will come on the heels of exhausted conflict and competition of the old paradigm, if it is to come at all.

In the South – and it is my suspicion that it is here that this drama will be principally enacted – the challenge is not sustainable development, if Doomsday scenarios are to be averted. This term is now being laden with pejorative connotations of 'environmental imperialism' and the whole gamut of neo-colonialist fears. It is not the way to initiate a constructive dialogue about global survival. Benign intent needs to be demonstrated on both sides about mutual benefit.

Instead of sustainable development, 'replicable development' would be more appropriate.[1] It captures the developmental aspirations of the South and the environmental fears of the North in a manner that is not prejudicial to security.

The 'replicable development' issue will be with us and at the heart of international security concerns, if not at the forefront, in the future. The promise of the good life has an eternal allure and relative deprivation is a powerful force.

NOTE

1. I am indebted for this term to Dr Gamani Corea, former Secretary General of UNCTAD and member of Sri Lanka's delegation to UNCED.

REFERENCES

Beschorner, N. (1992/93) 'Water and Instability in the Middle East', *Adelphi Paper*, No.273, London: Brassey's, for the International Institute for Strategic Studies.
Bull, H. (1977), *The Anarchical Society*, London: Macmillan.

Hassan, S. (1991), 'Environmental Issues and Security in South Asia', *Adelphi Paper*, No. 262, London: Brassey's, for the International Institute for Strategic Studies.

Keesings (1992), *Keesings Record of World Events*, Bristol.

South Centre (1991), 'Environment and Development: Towards a Common Strategy of the South in the UNCED Negotiations and Beyond', Geneva: South Centre.

Index